Next Generation
Computing

SIGS Reference Library

Donald G. Firesmith
Editor-in-Chief

Additional Volumes in Preparation

Next Generation Computing

Distributed Objects for Business

Edited by Peter Fingar, Dennis Read, and Jim Stikeleather

The Technical Resource Connection, Inc.
Tampa, Florida

SIGS
BOOKS & MULTIMEDIA

New York • London • Paris • Munich • Cologne

Library of Congress Cataloging-in-Publication Data

Next generation computing : distributed objects for business / edited by Peter Fingar, Dennis Read, and Jim Stikeleather.
 p. cm. - - (SIGS reference library series)
 Includes bibliographical references and index.
 ISBN 1-884842-29-1 (pbk. : alk. paper)
 1. Object-oriented programming (Computer science) 2. Electronic data processing - - Distributed processing.
3. Information technology.
I. Fingar, Peter, 1946–   . II. Read, Dennis, 1960–   . III. Stikeleather, Jim, 1953–   . IV. Series.
QA76.64N47 1996
658.4'038'0285511 - -dc20   96-4308
                                                                                            CIP

PUBLISHED BY
SIGS Books & Multimedia
71 West 23rd Street, Third Floor
New York, New York 10010

Copyright © 1996 by The Technical Resource Connection, Inc.

Any product mentioned in this book may be a trademark of its company.

SIGS Books ISBN 1-884842-29-1
Prentice Hall ISBN 0-13-261892-3

Printed in the United States of America

"Objects should not touch because they are not alive. You use them, put them back in place, you live among them: They are useful, nothing more. But they touch me, it is unbearable. I am afraid of being in contact with them as though they were living beasts."

Jean-Paul Sarte — *Nausea*

Foreword

The existentialist quoted above was recoiling from objects as the manifestation of the sheer horror of existence. Consequently, there are perfectly normal people who recoil in the same way when considering a move from one technology to another. These are the same people who will end up looking for work in three to five years.

Every ten years or so, the computer industry gets all excited about the commercial applicability of a new technology. We are four to five years into the current one. It's called Distributed Objects. It's a technology that gives us the infrastructure to build truly distributed applications using the old stuff — while building the applications that are more specific to the appropriate line of business.

So why will this one work better than the rest? The free market, believe those with a capitalist bent, is a powerful catalyst for ingenuity, imagination and jobs. Since the beginning of the computer era in the late 1940s, giant leaps have been made by enterprising thinkers and builders from Watson to Jobs, Kapor and Gates. The freedom to discern a business problem that could be solved with some form of automation — and the freedom to do something about it — created the hardware and software giants of today's computer industry.

On the other hand, for at least a hundred years, national and international organizations have sought to agree proactively on standard interfaces and descriptions for everything from screw threads and fabric weights to electrical power transmission and data communications. Some governments and corporations have then used these standards to set procurement guidelines, hoping to save countless dollars, yen or pesos on training, redundant purchasing and other by-products of incompatible materials and systems.

The challenge then is to cooperate. With technology changes coming as rapidly as changes in the weather, we must agree on infrastructure technology that will carry us through the next computing era. To begin with, the world has changed significantly in the past ten or thirty years. Definitions of interoperability from ten years ago — even three years ago — aren't sufficient to create the plug-and-play freedom that interoperability implies. We can't even assume that everyone uses the term in the same way.

Additionally, the IT industry — like our political system — has a life of its own. It operates and thrives according to some basic business propositions that aren't always in perfect harmony with the ideals expressed in the original charter. "Government of, by and for the people" is the ideal. But what we tend to get is just "government." Hence, we still have the feeling that the IT politicians are just reissuing new campaign slogans.

All of these vendors and others have learned (or should have learned) that change is inevitable, and that the simplest concept must be reevaluated in the context of an increasingly complex real world. The original ideas are still important, I hasten to add. Price/performance still sells a lot of hardware (but now we want it based on industry-standard microprocessors). Spreadsheets are still an essential tool (but did I forget to mention word processing, databases and graphics, too?). And yes, we still file and print our documents (but we also want to do other things with our servers). How do I make these things integrate and interoperate?

In addition, distributed systems have gained a tremendous research and development following over the last ten years. This is primarily a result of trying to satisfy the need for (or the mess of) integrating widely disbursed, multi-vendor applications; it is also a result of the growth of local-area and worldwide networking capabilities. Converging with the communication technology is a software technology uniquely suited to designing and building distributed systems — object technology. The challenge we face as an industry is to integrate and to interoperate using object technology as the basis for this new infrastructure. It's a new revolution and revolutions always go forward.

And so it is with integration and interoperability, simple concepts that remain all too elusive — but become all the more important — in an increasingly more complex world of distributed, heterogeneous networks. Large complex systems have always been the bane of software engineers.

Object technology restores order to this chaos and increases the belief that software construction really is an engineering field. And so it shall be written that object technology is the fundamental underpinning of software standardization that can be summarized in one sentence: "Applications that already exist need to exist and work with applications I want to build. Please make this work."

The time for deploying this technology is now. The enclosed set of white papers produced by The Technical Resource Connection will provide you with a top view, big picture perspective necessary for planning your competitive advantage. The papers cover everything from a glossary of terms to understanding the architectures of today and tomorrow, as well as a blueprint for what you need to get started. Enjoy them. I did.

Chris Stone
CEO
The Object Management Group, Inc.

Preface

No one sat down and decided to write this book. It was born of necessity. *Next Generation Computing* was conceived in response to the chaos companies find around them as they position themselves for 21st century business.

"Reinvent your company or die" is the mandate of the 1990s' business world. Modern businesses are under assault. Driven by rapidly advancing technology and the globalization of markets and competition, companies are using information technology to make radical changes in the fundamental ways they organize work and conduct business. The new way of competing demands a sharper focus on customers, cost-cutting, quality and constant adaptability. At stake is survival in the business world during the coming millennium. Emerging technologies such as object-oriented and advanced client/server computing are essential enablers of business reinvention. However, these next generation technologies pose steep learning curves to the business and information systems professionals who run our companies.

An unlikely book producer, The Technical Resource Connection, Inc., is a firm dedicated to the technical implementation of next generation computing for progressive corporations. The firm is not staffed by academics and theorists. It is staffed by *doers*, technical implementors. We don't just talk about the next generation, we are already working in that environment. The experience gained from *doing* is what gave birth to this book. Our clients demanded we share the lessons learned from our hands-on experience.

The Technical Resource Connection's core competencies are earned through live projects carried out for industry leaders who recognize the business impact of next generation computing systems. In February 1994, the firm's senior partners met to discuss how the firm could help close the knowledge gap faced by our business clients. In response to the widespread need for information about the merging technologies, the white papers were developed to inform, to educate and to foster understanding of next generation computing in business.

In mid-March 1995, five first-cut drafts of the papers were the subject of a planning and consolidation effort. It was then that we made a major commitment to move the project fast-forward. A series editor was hired, incredibly short deadlines were established, and a relentless drive to the goal line began. Before the first milestone could be achieved — four complete papers by the end of April — approximately 30 individuals had contributed. Writing well is a very difficult task, and to achieve quality, the efforts of many people were required: writers, subject matter experts, copy editors and artists.

The first four of the papers were unveiled at the Patricia Seybold Conference in Boston in May. The following week, they were introduced at a conference for Wall Street executives sponsored by Object Design, Inc. The papers hit the mark.

Why so many papers in the series? First, the papers had to cover the most pressing topics on the minds of business and technology professionals. Next generation computing is not one topic, but many interrelated topics. Second, each paper had to bring value to the busy professional who has very little time to read. Each paper was designed to provide substantive information within a reading time limit of approximately 30 minutes. Respecting the reader's time was a key criteria used in writing the papers. Other guidelines adopted included:

- Always make a strong business case as well as a strong technology case.
- Do not trivialize or oversell the content.
- Do not draw unsupported conclusions.
- Make content relevant to both IS managers and technicians.
- Take the reader from current IS practice to where they can be with next generation computing.
- Describe how to get there.

The white paper team did not work alone. The Technical Resource Connection's core competencies are centered on technical implementation, but companies wanting to migrate to next generation computing are keenly interested in business engineering and transitioning technical staff through training. We explained our goals to Open Engineering, Inc., a firm specializing in object-oriented business engineering, and Knowledge Systems Corporation, the firm recognized for formalizing the apprenticeship approach to object-oriented technology transfer. Both firms recognized the needs and benefits of providing information and education to the marketplace and immediately decided to contribute.

Momentum also came from technology firms that share our vision. Sun Microsystems, Expersoft, Forté, Iona, the Patricia Seybold Group, IBM and Object Design recognized the need to supply their existing and future customers with the information needed to be effective with emerging technology. These firms have supplied the white papers to their customers. Sun distributed copies of the first four papers at the Sun World Conference '95 in San Francisco. GTE Service Corporation has included news releases about the papers in its technology newsletter for 5,000 readers throughout the GTE family of companies.

The white papers flow from "first reads" to in-depth coverage of more technical topics. For example, *Getting Started With Object Technology* and *Client/Server Architectures* are "first reads" that lead the reader *to Distributed Object Computing for Business.* However, basic ideas are restated or summarized so each paper can be read as a standalone document — another way of saving time for the busy professional.

As learning instruments, the white papers belong to you, the reader. To enhance their usefulness, we invite you to join in our conversations and continuing analysis of the impact of emerging technology in business. We invite your comments, questions and feedback. We look forward to your thoughts and comments as we pursue the future.

Please read, enjoy and learn ...

Peter Fingar
Dennis Read
Jim Stikeleather

The Technical Resource Connection
nextGeneration@trcinc.com

Table of Contents

asynchronous messaging. It illustrates the needs of an effective transparent communications framework for concurrent computing objects in conformance with the event service specifications — a part of the common object services specifications approved by the Object Management Group.

Getting Started
With Object Technology

By Peter Fingar and Jim Stikeleather
In collaboration with the Object Technology Staff of The Technical Resource Connection

Contents

Abstract

This white paper explores object-oriented technology from the perspective of business and information technology professionals responsible for planning, designing, constructing and maintaining corporate information systems. This paper presents the essential concepts of a very complex subject and relates these concepts to the practicing professional who requires clear and practical information, rather than the theoretical underpinnings of the technology.

The paper answers fundamental questions such as: What is object orientation? Is object-oriented technology only for programmers? Why is it so important to business in the 1990s? What systems development methods are required to design and deploy object-oriented information systems? How do companies make the transition to object orientation?

21st Century Business Technology

The seed for object-oriented technology was planted in the 1960s in Norway. Kristen Nygaard and Ole-Johan Dhal of the Norwegian Computer Center developed a programming language, Simula-67, to support the modeling of discrete event simulations of scientific and industrial processes with *direct representation of real world objects*. Why, a quarter of a century later, has the business world begun to express great interest in object-oriented technology?

Today's business is under assault from multiple, simultaneous revolutions from both business and technological arenas. Author Rob Mattison[1] explains that most large corporations are coping with concurrent:

Business Revolutions, characterized by:

- increased competitiveness and pressure to reduce costs, increase productivity, and increase responsiveness

- increased global competition

- a breakdown in the centralized hierarchical management concepts

- pressure to achieve continuous improvements in core business processes

and Technological Revolutions:

- the distributed systems revolution (LANS and WANS)

- the PC revolution

- the client/server revolution

- the graphical user interface (GUI) revolution

- the Open Systems revolution.

Businesses that will thrive in the next millennium will have overcome the chaos introduced by these concurrent revolutions. Significant business reengineering efforts are under way in corporations that have recognized the need for major change. Some companies have undertaken radical change efforts while others have sought a gentler approach through continuous process improvement.

As with most major endeavors, the task of business redesign is not as easy as it may first seem. Both business processes and computer information systems are extremely complex. The increasing complexity of applications is compounded by the fact that corporations are automating mission and life critical applications. Our approach to taming complexity and bringing order to chaos requires new approaches to problem-solving and new ways of thinking about business processes and information systems.

The critical challenge facing today's IS organizations is to provide leadership in business process improvement. The information systems that are needed for tomorrow's business must be far more robust, intelligent and user-centered than the data processing systems of today. Unfortunately, the increased sophistication of tomorrow's information systems involves the introduction of complexity that overwhelms the current approaches to systems development.

Lessons learned from initial efforts with business process redesign are many. A 70 percent failure rate of initial reengineering efforts indicates the degree of difficulty. Lessons of note for this discussion include:

- Redesigned business processes are not "final products." Business processes must be designed for constant change.

- Constant change in both the worlds of business and technology requires that *change* must be a first class business concept and process.

- As business processes change, the underlying information systems must also change, and in competitive industries, the lead time for such change approaches zero.

- Rapid change requires that both business processes and their underlying information systems be modeled and evolved together.

Object-oriented technology is based on simulation and modeling. Although this may be interesting in and of itself, the use of models represents a *breakthrough* in the way business information systems are developed. Instead of deploying the traditional application development life cycle, models of a business or business area are constructed. These models are shared by individual computer applications. Essentially a "computer application" becomes a unique use of the model, not a separate development activity resulting in stand-alone software constructed for "this application only."

The quality of the model is a key determinant of "reuse" and adaptability. The model itself must be designed for change. Business processes change and

> *Object technology holds great promise as a means of designing and constructing the adaptive information systems needed for 21st century business.*

their change is based on using the business model to simulate proposed processes. Modelers can play "what if," run simulations of various process alternatives, and learn from the simulations.

The focus of IS shifts from applications development to the enhancement and maintenance of common business models. *Business models and software models become one and the same.* Applications become derivatives, alternate views and refinements of the business models.

The modeling approach to business innovation is not possible without a software approach suited to the task. For these business reasons, object-oriented technology has become of vital interest to both commerce and industry. Business and technology must be fused if corporations are to maintain the competitive advantage. Object-oriented technology can be the foundation for that fusion. With object-oriented technology, change and the management of complexity are first-class concepts. Object technology holds great promise as a means of designing and constructing the adaptive information systems needed for 21st century business.

An Object-Oriented Technology Primer

Object orientation, as a way of thinking and problem-solving, applies to a broad spectrum of technology disciplines and tools including:

- analysis and design methods
- programming languages
- development tools
- databases
- code-libraries/frameworks
- and operating systems.

However, object orientation is not limited to technology, it also provides a way of thinking about business and business processes. Leading thinkers such as Ivar Jacobson[2], David Taylor[3], Robert Shelton[4] and James Martin[5] have developed the foundation for applying object orientation to business modeling and problem-solving.

In the interest of providing a practical guide to object-oriented technology, we will begin our discovery of the essential concepts by limiting our initial definitions to the key ideas behind the technology. We will focus on object concepts "in-the-small" and later scale up our discussions to broaden our understanding of object orientation at the enterprise level.

What are the fundamental concepts of object orientation? *Object orientation is a way of modeling real systems in the real world.* Within object orientation, there are several fundamental concepts that contribute to the modeling process. Since people regard the world around them in terms of objects, business and software models based on real world objects will reflect reality more naturally. Thus business object models can be easier to understand and communicate than traditional computer-centered models. Business people think in terms of people, places, things and events. Examples of business objects include: people and the roles they play (stock clerk, head cashier), places (store, warehouse, shelf), things (cash drawer, check out lane, delivery van), and events (sale, delivery, payment).

What is an object? *An object is a self-contained software package consisting of its own private information (data), its own private procedures (private methods) that manipulate the object's private data, and a public interface (public methods) for communicating with other objects.* An object contains both data and logic in a single software entity or package. Objects provide properties representing a coherent concept and a set of operations to manage these properties. The fusion of process logic with data is the distinguishing characteristic of objects.

Each object is capable of acting in much the same way as the real object behaves in the real world. Objects are assigned roles and responsibilities, and they contain all of the information they need to carry out their actions. The only way to use an object is to send it a *message* that requests a service be performed. The receiving object acts on the message and sends the results back as a message to the requesting object.

The object-oriented developer surrounds him or herself with objects relevant to the tasks to be automated. If an office-related application is being developed, objects in the mind's eye of the developer may include pencils, file folders, word processors, spelling checkers, in-baskets and documents. The developer's task is to create new objects that use messaging to communicate dynamically with the other objects in the application setting.

When a service is requested of an object, the object is sent a message, much like a traditional function call. However, the difference is that the rest of the system does not see how the object is implemented and cannot suffer any integration problems if the object's internal implementation (code) is changed. This means programming without assumptions, where functionality is well-defined and programmers do not make assumptions about how the shared routines or systems work on an internal level.

Additionally, object orientation inherently supports and extends the concepts of modularity. "Chunking"[6] is a mechanism used to build larger components from smaller components so that any view of a problem under study typically is limited to seven (nine at the very most) components at one time. These are the maximum number of concepts that the human mind can maintain at one time. This approach to modularity results in object-based systems being very *granular* or being formed by simple components that can be reused in other systems. Such reuse is the key to many of the benefits of object technology: productivity, quality and consistency. Another important benefit is that modifications tend to be local to a single object. Thus, maintenance is simplified and less costly. Changes are automatically propagated throughout all the systems of the enterprise.

From a technical perspective, an object may be more precisely defined. The first principles include: *encapsulation, inheritance* and *polymorphism.* These concepts were originally applied "in-the-small" as a means of programming, but today carry over into other object technologies, such as analysis and design methods. Our next step is to explore these concepts to deepen our understanding of objects.

Encapsulation

All, or at least most, of the descriptions of operations (behavior) and data (attributes) within an object-oriented model or system reside within objects. The only way to use or manipulate an object is to send it a *message.* The hiding of internal information within objects is called *encapsulation.* To use an object, the developer needs only to be aware of what services or operations it offers (to which messages the object responds).

A system comprised of objects is constructed in a modular fashion, in which each module (object) is engaged only through its defined interface (its messages). Objects do not become interdependent on their internal code or structure. The advantage of encapsulation is that the implementation of objects can change (being improved or extended) without having to change the way the object is used by the rest of the system. The result is that changes tend to be local to an object and maintenance is simplified.

Furthermore, as object-oriented information systems are implemented, additional reusable components (objects) become available so that programming becomes more a matter of "assembly" rather than coding. As an object-oriented infrastructure matures, programming is reduced to "exception" programming based upon modifications of existing objects. Such assembly and exception concepts are demonstrated by the new graphical programming environments where objects are simply "wired" together to create applications.

Classes and Inheritance

In any given information system, many of the objects will have similar characteristics such as information structure and behavior (procedures or methods). Further, large scale commercial systems may be composed of hundreds of thousands, perhaps millions of objects. Organizing principles must be adopted to avoid a chaotic environment.

The concept of "classes" brings order to the world of objects. *Classes* are templates used to define the data and methods of similar types of objects. An object created from a class is referred to as an *instance* to distinguish the object from the mold from which it was created (the class). Object-oriented programming languages and analysis and design methods both use classes to provide a means to share common characteristics among objects.

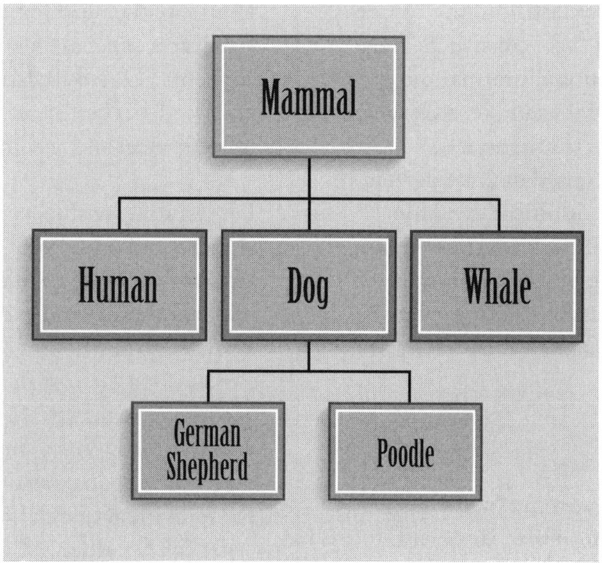

Some objects of the same general type may have specialized characteristics. A mechanism is provided to address specialization. This mechanism is called *inheritance.* As the name implies, inheritance is a feature that allows one class of objects to acquire, or *inherit*, some or all of its information structure and behavior from another class, rather than force the developer to define or code the structure or behavior over again. Inheritance is a very useful mechanism for reuse.

Generalization and specialization are not unique to object-oriented technology. Many disciplines such as engineering and architecture use these concepts and techniques to manage complexity. And other information modeling methods provide support for sub-typing. Object-oriented methods and implementation languages support inheritance directly. They provide mechanisms to inherit *both* properties and operations.

Figure 1
Inheritance Hierarchy

In the example presented in Figure 1, *Human, Dog* and *Whale* inherit properties and behavior from *Mammal* (all mammals have lungs and hair), while *German Shepherd* and *Poodle* inherit properties from *Dog* and *Mammal* (a German shepherd inherits four legs and a tail from *Dog* and lungs and hair from *Mammal*).

Inheritance, as a core feature of object-oriented systems, will provide the developer with some important advantages. First, inheritance introduces support for code reuse at a language level. If a developer needs to change the way several classes of objects perform a certain task, the modified behavior is applied to each of the classes via inheritance. The developer needs to perform the change in only one place. Inheritance makes it very easy to modify information systems. Second, inheritance reduces redundancy. Duplicating code is discouraged by making it easy to reuse existing code.

Inheritance is a powerful concept for managing complexity. Most object-oriented languages do not provide support for re-classifying an object once it is instantiated. Over time, however, the meaning of an object to a business may change, requiring a re-classification of the object.

Emerging developments in object-oriented technology include new styles of inheritance called "prototype/

instance" and "multiple dynamic classification." While few languages currently support these constructs, they will become very important in future information systems. Referring to Figure 1, for example, a German shepherd can take on many roles throughout its lifetime such as pet, police dog, guard dog, herder, etc., sequentially and simultaneously. Multiple dynamic classification enables this capability at run time without predetermined programming. In business terms, this would allow the creation of a class like Person, whose instances can take on roles like *Employee, Customer* and *Stockholder* simultaneously.

Polymorphism

Polymorphism is a Greek term meaning "many forms." When applied to objects, polymorphism allows the developer to use one name for similar kinds of operations or functions. Rather than create unique names such as drawCircle, drawRectangle or drawSquare, a single method named "draw" may be used. The polymorphism mechanism of the receiving class, depending on the kind of object sending a message, will implement the appropriate method such as draw a square.

Classes represent real things in the business problem domain. Properties and operations are defined for these classes. The names of properties and operations are scoped to the class to which they belong. This allows different classes to declare the same name for a message that invokes a method or operation. It is up to the developer to ensure that the operations of multiple classes with the same method names are semantically equivalent.

The method to "pay" an employee may be defined in a general employee class, but when the message "pay" is sent to a sub-class of employee, say manager, the subclass will override the general method and apply operations unique to managers. Polymorphism can

eliminate the need for complex IF, ELSE and CASE structures and can enhance the use of inheritance concepts. Objects relate to other objects in the abstract and need not be concerned with the details of how other objects select and accomplish their operations.

For example, within a banking application with class *Account* and sub-classes *Checking Account* and *Savings Account*, a *Manager* object may send a calculate interest message to each and every account without regard to or knowledge of whether each account is a *Checking Account* or a *Savings Account* object. Likewise, each account type may perform a different calculation to arrive at the interest, and the system using the object does not have to consider every possible case. Over time, the individual calculations can change, or new account types can be added, all without modifying the using program.

Polymorphism also accommodates the temporal aspects of information. Allowing objects to be aware of their versions (changes in attributes and methods over time) and incorporating them in a persistence mechanism (the object-oriented equivalent to files and databases), results in systems that can be written to gracefully handle business change over time while maintaining historical integrity. In other words, the same message sent to exactly the same type or sub-type of object will apply the correct version of the method. This is something difficult or impossible to do with traditional techniques.

Again, what's an object?

In anthropomorphic terms, we can think of objects as individuals. Each individual has special knowledge (attributes) and special skills (methods), some of which it gains from its ancestors (inheritance). By communicating with each other (messaging), individuals are able to work together to accomplish very complex tasks — much like a society. Different individuals may react to the same request by performing different steps as long as

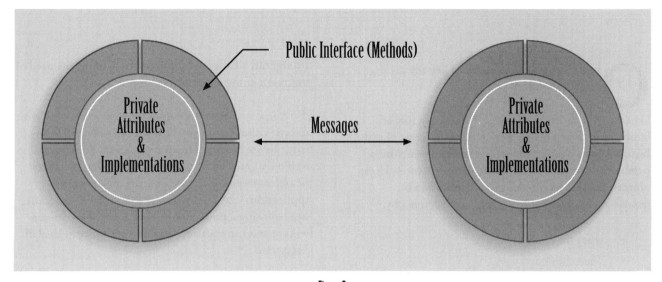

Figure 2
Object-Oriented Concepts
Including Messaging and Encapsulation of Functions and Data

the results are consistent with the intent of the request (polymorphism). It is neither necessary nor desirable for the individuals to disclose to the requesters exactly how they accomplish their tasks (encapsulation) and it is not acceptable for requesters to tell an individual *how* to accomplish something; only *what* to accomplish (micro-management is not allowed). Finally, individuals are free to determine the appropriate response when a request is received and are not tied to a prior determination of the best response (dynamic or run-time binding). Late binding means that programs are written to abstract classes. The *actual* types are determined at run-time, and so behavior is also determined at run-time.

Figure 2 helps summarize the essential concepts using the technical terminology of object orientation: *Objects encapsulate their knowledge and behavior, inherit*

common functionality, communicate entirely via messages, and respond appropriately based on their individual capabilities when messaged by other objects, often determining the exact response at run-time. Various object-oriented languages support these features to differing degrees, but the essentials of the technology are the same, regardless.

The Object Advantage

Object technology brings four key advantages to modern computing:

(1) *Objects reflect the real world.* When designing an application, it is more natural to think in terms of real business entities and concepts — customers, invoices, products — than procedures and data structures. Using objects, developers can design an application by describing familiar entities. Objects are defined by:

- what they know
- what they do
- with which other objects they collaborate.

While design is not easy, object orientation makes more sense than trying to design the application in terms of inputs, outputs and data flows, and then expecting the results to resemble the business. Modeling with objects that reflect real business entities and concepts means that changes in the business model can be directly implemented in the underlying software. In addition, the real world nature of objects enables business people to converse with corporate developers in the same language of recognizable business objects.

(2) *Objects are stable.* Objects don't change very much, while processes and procedures change all the time. As a result, objects are considerably more stable elements with which to build an application. For example, a customer will always have a name, address, phone number, other essential information and certain behaviors. Such information can be captured as an object, encapsulated and forgotten. Once the customer object has been created, it may be used in a wide number of applications for a variety of business process needs. As needs change, the modifications need only take place once, in one spot, and are propagated throughout all affected applications without the need of programmer involvement.

(3) *Objects reduce complexity.* Developers can work with objects without knowing how the objects work internally. To use an object in an application, developers need only know what an object is and what messages the object responds to, not *how* the object works. Applications may be divided into layers of abstraction, each exposing a particular level of detail. Developers looking at an application should see a uniform level of abstraction.

(4) *Objects are reusable.* The customer object, for instance, can be used in a billing application, a shipping application, a customer service application, and many others. A transaction object can be used in any application that uses transactions. Furthermore, through inheritance, new child-objects can be quickly created that inherit the functionality and attributes of the parent. The programmer need only define the new attributes that make the child-object different from the parent-object. This has the potential for delivering substantial increases in programmer productivity and dramatically reducing development time. For example, when the inheritance mechanism is used to add a new type of bank account, the new account automatically contains the inner workings of an account (i.e., deposit, withdrawal, balance). All that needs to be developed is how it differs from other accounts. With reuse and inheritance, object technology promises to usher in an era of application development by assembly.

The sum total of these benefits is that:

- The quantity of code needed to support a business is reduced.

- The time required to develop the code is reduced.

- All applications behave consistently (since they reuse the same objects).

- The quality of information systems is improved.

Object-Oriented Technologies

As discussed earlier, object orientation has been applied to a number of technology areas. These areas include object-oriented programming languages, analysis and design methods, databases, and operating systems. In the discussion that follows, we build on the fundamentals presented in the last section and progress from definitions to discovery of how object orientation applies to each technology area.

Object-Oriented Programming and (OOP) Class Libraries

In simple terms, object-oriented programming is the application of object-oriented principles and constructs to computer programming. However, these principles have been applied to differing degrees within programming languages that are labeled as "object-oriented." To be a true object-oriented programming language, a programming language must support the three pillars of object orientation: encapsulation, inheritance and polymorphism.

A programming language that supports encapsulation allows the programmer to define classes that contain both methods (behavior) and attributes (data). Some languages suggest that they support inheritance by stating that their tool includes a set of what the vendor calls "objects." But the questions that must be asked are "Can I define my own classes?" and "Do these classes encompass behavior as well as data?" The answer should be "yes" to both. Many of the popular development tools claiming to be object-oriented support only encapsulation. True object orientation requires support of encapsulation plus inheritance and polymorphism.

Support of inheritance varies among the object-oriented programming languages. In defining a class, a programming language should allow its user to designate that a class inherits behavior (methods) and data structure (attributes) from another class. A change to the super class should be automatically propagated to the inheriting sub-classes.

Some languages support the ability to inherit directly from two or more classes. This is called *multiple inheritance*. Multiple inheritance is a powerful construct, but is not required to consider a language as object-oriented. Systems designed using multiple inheritance can be redesigned using single inheritance.

Support for polymorphism also varies among languages. Yet, an object-oriented language should allow a segment of program code to send a message to an object knowing that the receiving object will respond correctly even if the precise class of the object is not known.

Programming languages that support only the concept of encapsulation are referred to as *object-based*. According to this classification, Ada and Visual Basic are considered to be object-based because they support the encapsulation concept. Smalltalk, C++, Objective-C, Simula and Eiffel are examples of object-oriented languages.

Within an object-oriented programming language, object templates are created by the programmer to define the characteristics of the system's objects. Such a template is called a *class*. A class defines an information (data) structure and the behaviors for an object. From these templates, objects are created by the system at run-time. Hence, within an object-oriented system, each object belongs to a class. An object that belongs to a certain class is said to be an *instance* of that class.

In written materials on object-oriented programming, the terms object and instance are frequently interchanged.

Class libraries are collections of classes that provide certain functionality and can be reused in application development. Class libraries are roughly the same as libraries in the traditional programming sense, but are in the form of classes and can be sub-classed as well as used directly. For example, an accounting class library could be purchased from a supplier of accounting software and modified to meet the user's specific needs without modifying the vendor-supplied code. Modification is accomplished by inheriting functionality from the vendor-supplied classes, then programming the exceptions. Several class libraries are available commercially that implement graphical user interfaces (GUIs), persistence, relational database encapsulation, inference processing, real time controls and communications.

The commercial viability of domain class libraries (for example, accounting) will increase over time. The Object Management Group (OMG) has established a special interest group dedicated to defining standards for business objects and processes (for more information on the OMG, see The Technical Resource Connection's white paper, *Distributed Object Computing for Business)*. These standards should aid in building momentum in the domain class library market.

Object-Oriented Analysis & Design (OOA/D)

The "structured" methods of the past decades contributed significantly to the development of reliable data processing applications. Yet, when applied to the application portfolios needed in the new competitive organization, the structured methods are strained, so object-oriented extensions are being added. For example, traditional structured methods apply techniques to normalize data, but not logic. However, these design techniques can be modified to normalize logic into object classes. Modified structured methods make it possible to develop object-oriented designs without throwing away existing skills. Unfortunately, modified structured methods tend to promote habits and ingrained ways of thinking that are not object-oriented. New, clean-slate, OOA/D methods have been introduced that foster object-oriented thinking throughout the entire analysis and design process.

We can summarize the nature of traditional and next generation methods:

- Structured methods are *function* centric.
- Information Engineering methods are *data* centric.
- Object-Oriented methods are *concept* centric.

Three major differences between Structured Analysis & Design (SA/D) and OOA/D are noteworthy. The first and most obvious difference is that OOA/D incorporates the use of classes with encapsulation of data and behavior into objects. SA/D encourages the separation of data and behavior early in the process. This change in thought processes can be difficult for developers well-versed and experienced in SA/D.

The second difference is more subtle. OOA/D encourages modeling the real world environment in terms of its entities and their interactions. The model of the system should look like the real-world even if there is no computer to perform the tasks. The focus is on stable, real-world concepts.

SA/D, on the other hand, encourages abstracting the real world in terms of functions, which are normally very fuzzy and subject to change in the early stages of development. Structured design separately identifies the data, its flow, its control and the processes that act upon data.

The third difference is in notations used during the stages of analysis and design. SA/D changes notations as each stage progresses. This makes tracing events and the overall repeatability of the process questionable. OOA/D uses uniform notations throughout the process, focusing on elaboration, rather than transformation.

One industry authority glibly described the difference between SA/D and OOA/D as the difference between processes pillaging and plundering across innocent and helpless data structures, and gentlemanly objects engaged in cooperative conversation to accomplish a goal. This description highlights the most valuable aspects of object-oriented models: stability and flexibility.

There are similarities between both methodologies. OOA/D incorporates some new ideas into existing SA/D techniques: *message-based communications between objects, encapsulation, classification* and *inheritance*. SA/D and OOA/D both contain the same basic parts: *process, terminology, diagrams, notations, constructs, verification techniques* and *metrics*.

Many of the current OOA/D methods do not contain all of these similarities, but OOA/D methods are currently in their infancy. SA/D methods have merged somewhat over the years to use, for the most part, common terminology, notations and diagrams; OOA/D methods have not yet evolved to this point. The basic process is fairly common: Identify the subjects and objects, and define the behavior and relationships. Also, the basic object-oriented terms remain fairly constant. However, notations are almost as numerous as the methods themselves. Most important, common techniques for verification and metrics are lacking in many current OOA/D methods. Great care must be taken in evaluating and selecting object-oriented methods.

Object Database Management Systems (ODBMS)

The seminal work of E. F. Codd, "A Relational Model of Data for Large Shared Data Banks," was published in 1970[7]. During the 1980s, corporations expended immense resources to exploit the capabilities of relational databases.

Relational database management systems (RDBMS) were the first systems to make it possible to decouple application issues from the design of a shared database. Before the era of the relational model, the imbedded pointers and links in hierarchical and CODASYL databases required that the developer focus on computer data storage models or data structures with cumbersome pointers and links. The new relational focus could shift to logical modeling of the application domain and away from the Direct Access Storage Device (DASD) physical data structure or other implementation issues with data being truly independent from process.

The relational data model represents the third stage in the evolution of database systems:

1.   early file systems

2.   hierarchical and network database management systems

3.   relational database management systems.

Data within a relational database is broken down and stored in two-dimensional tables in which each item exists as a *row* within a *table*. Complex (hierarchical) data items are arranged by *joining* rows from different tables and building artificial constructs such as *foreign keys* to facilitate reconstruction of the "real world" information. Languages such as Structured Query Language (SQL) provide a means for expressing how such data may be joined.

Objects in the real world often involve *hierarchical* arrangements of data. Object-oriented programming languages accommodate, and in fact simplify, the management and manipulation of such hierarchical data objects. Storing and retrieving those complex structures using a two-dimensional relational database forces the programmer to implement the *composition* and *decomposition* required for storing and retrieving data.

Object databases (ODB) have emerged as a means of providing a storage mechanism for hierarchical arrangements of data. In contrast, relational databases require programmers to translate data between their *in-memory* representation and their *storage* representation. An analogy would be the commuter who must take apart his car to park in his garage, then reassemble it when it is needed again. Object databases, on the other hand, store and manage data in the same way a program does — as objects.

The advantages of an object database are threefold. First, there is no semantic difference between data stored within a database and data in memory. Composition and decomposition programming is not required. ODBMSs are unique in their absence of a data manipulation language (DML). Second, because of the way data is stored (maintaining its hierarchical relations), retrieving complex arrangements of data is often much faster than in a relational system. A side benefit is that such an arrangement makes it possible to build information systems that span a network as though it were one large machine. Third, the encapsulated models produced during analysis and design are the same as the database models. In a traditional development life-cycle, the analysis model is different from the design model, which in turn is different from the programming model, which is also different from the database model.

The strategic reason to begin implementing an ODBMS is the ability to create true information management systems. Today, some object database management systems have (and eventually all will have) the capability to query processes (methods) of objects as well as the data (attributes). This means a user will be able to query for "past due customers" without knowing the business rules defining "past due" or having to structure those rules in the query language. By introducing access to object methods, even greater detail hiding is achieved. In such an environment, business process and rule changes do not disrupt existing applications or queries. Furthermore, the capability ensures the consistency and integrity of information presented by all applications, queries, ad-hoc programs, analysis and reports across the enterprise.

Although object databases represent the next generation, relational databases offer continuing advantages to corporations with heavy investments in relational technology. The two models will coexist for years to come. Relational data structures are used within object databases, and bridges to existing relational databases (wrappers) play an important role in preserving existing assets while incrementally migrating to objects.

Enterprise Migration to Objects

Object-oriented technology may be thought of as "in-the-small," where the perspective of the user is on the desktop (a single personal computer) or within a department. Concepts, methods and tools are relatively simple when object technology is adopted in-the-small. The real challenge begins when the technology is applied to the overall enterprise, when it is applied "in-the-large."

As Rob Mattison points out in his work, "New technologies and new approaches cannot simply be infused into an organization like a health serum. We need to restructure the very organization itself if we expect to take advantage of them. This change must occur both within the information systems support staff (changes in roles and responsibilities) and within the corporation itself, as business people determine new ways to take full advantage of the additional power and flexibility that is suddenly made available."[1]

Corporations must develop well thought-out strategies for transitioning to object-oriented information systems. These strategies must consider the current business culture, technology culture, and current knowledge and skill sets of both business and IS personnel. The transition to objects is not a transition in tools and techniques. It is an evolution into a new way of doing business and a new approach to business problem-solving.

The key to successful transitions is to take small, incremental steps. Each step requires three fundamental activities: education, training and experience. Once a step has been completed, the scope can be expanded, and the next iteration can proceed with additional education, training and experience. The transition requires heuristics as there are no cookbook or silver bullet solutions. Learn a little, apply a little; learn a little, apply a little. Each iteration increases the overall understanding of the object paradigm and the deepening understanding fosters better decision-making for the next iteration.

Since corporations are under assault from simultaneous forces, the adoption of object-oriented technology cannot be revolutionary. Transitions must be incremental and iterative. They must be evolutionary and steeped in today's existing business realities.

Transitioning to the object paradigm is not a computer system "conversion;" it is a process of *assimilation.* Furthermore, the process is a process of risk and asset management. The massive investments corporations have in existing information processing assets provide the life blood of current business operations. We are not "converting to a new system," we are designing new types of robust information systems that leverage existing corporate information assets.

Since the corporate goal is the insertion of object-oriented technologies into an already complex environment, successful transition strategies can deploy object-oriented notions to manage the complexities. We may speak of an "object-oriented adoption method" to convey notions of managing complexity throughout the assimilation process. Start small, build proof-of-concept prototypes, increment the scope of the problem domain, and iterate.

Although these beginnings are small, they can scale-up in an orderly fashion. The subject of developing a complete assimilation method is treated in detail in our white paper, *Object-Oriented Knowledge Transfer.* Beginning with proof-of-concept projects, a corporation can kick the tires, initiate low-risk demonstration projects, establish a corporate Object Technology

Center (OTC) to provide a focal point, and develop learning processes to expand the initial knowledge base. These are a few of the components of an overall enterprise assimilation strategy. Following are some previews of the issues and guidelines covered in the white paper on transitions:

- Recognize that object orientation is not only a technology, but also a framework for thinking about and solving problems. Mastering object technology in business requires a solid understanding of the concepts of object orientation, as well as the fundamentals of business process improvement. This will result in a synchronicity between the systems developed and the business that they model. As David Taylor points out in his book, *Business Engineering with Object Technology*, "Instead of managers posing problems for technologists to solve by creating new applications, the two groups must work together to create working software models of the organization."[3]

- By definition, "new ways of thinking and problem-solving" involve steep learning curves. Initial corporate pilot or proof-of-concept projects require hiring technology experts and teaming them with corporate domain experts. Given the assistance of an experienced object technology team, a few well-suited practice projects and the patience to follow a step-by-step process, the paradigm shift can be made and the technology mastered. Mentoring and team learning, centered on live pilot projects, are the keys to the paradigm shift.

- Above all, reasonable expectations must be set. The first few projects that are tackled should not attempt to demonstrate all the benefits of objects. The goals of the initial projects should be focused on exploration and discovery. A beginner is not expected to read a book on the techniques of chess and then successfully play in a tournament. No amount of book learning or classes will replace the need to get several projects under the belt and gain a level of experience comparable to the experience we have with more traditional technologies. Also, many of the benefits of object technology come from a well-developed approach for reusability; in the beginning, there is nothing to reuse.

- Pilot projects should be small and low risk. Although proof-of-concept projects must be based on live business applications to be meaningful, they must not be disruptive or mission-critical. A non-critical project that does not require a large team is best. The experts hired to assist in transitions may surprise you by letting you make mistakes. Making mistakes, adjusting, making more mistakes, and making more adjustments is how we learn to use new skills with proficiency. We do not want the expert to do our thinking for us, and true technology transfer experts view mistakes as learning-in-progress.

- Find a mentor. There is no substitute for experience. The best results have come from small teams working with an experienced, object-technology practitioner in a *craftsman-apprentice* relationship. This approach may be one of the best places to apply a consultant to an object project. Additionally, a good consultant, who truly knows object technology, can help develop the architecture and build the infrastructure that is necessary for success with object orientation on an enterprise level. The biggest mistakes early adopters have reported is that they did not build an infrastructure with strong configuration management capabilities, and did not have a guiding architecture. Both are necessary to ensure reuse and the associated benefits of productivity, quality and consistency.

- Choose the pilot project team members carefully. The team should consist of individuals that are fairly proactive and open to new ideas. These people will become mentors to the rest of the company on future object projects and should be chosen accordingly.

- Pick a technology. Do not try them simultaneously. A visual programming tool provides the most concrete and understandable implementation of the object-oriented concepts. By its nature, a visual programming tool prevents us from falling into established habits of procedural styles of programming.

- The technologies will work best when you apply object orientation throughout all stages and areas of the system life-cycle. However, as a word of caution, learn them *one at a time.* Be aware of object-oriented versus object-based tools. Object-based languages/4GLs are easy to learn, fast prototyping tools. However, to get the long-term benefits of objects, you will need the features of a true object-oriented tool supporting all three pillars of object orientation. Also remember to pay as much attention to your infrastructure as you do to the first application you build.

- Consider adopting an object-oriented analysis and design method whether you build the systems using object-oriented programming or not. This approach can be a gentler introduction to object-oriented concepts, while suppressing the details needed for consideration in implementations. Companies have reported success with this approach (highly granular, client/server-based systems are not terribly different than object-based systems). Remember, the biggest payback in reuse comes from the reuse of design. Accordingly, adopt a design technique that encourages reuse.

Conclusion

As corporations explore the shifts to business process improvement and emerging technologies, the overall goal is to realign technology with business. Much attention has been focused on client/server computing. However, as discussed in The Technical Resource Connection's white paper, *Client/Server Architectures*, the initial approaches to client/server computing have built-in limits due to coarse granularity in partitioning the business problem domain. Object-oriented technology can provide the organizing principles for fine-grained client/server architectures. Object-oriented client/server computing is referred to as Distributed Object Computing, and the fundamentals of this emerging technology are explained in our white paper on the subject.

The bottom line for the business world is that now is the time for corporations to begin to adopt object-oriented frameworks if they are to come to grips with client/server architectures, and if they are to construct the robust information systems needed to compete in the next millennium.

References

[1] Mattison, Rob, *The Object-Oriented Enterprise*, McGraw-Hill, New York (1994).

[2] Jacobson, Ivar, et al., *The Object Advantage: Business Process Reengineering with Object Technology*, Addison-Wesley, New York (1995).

[3] Taylor, David A., *Business Reengineering with Object Technology*, John Wiley & Sons, New York (1995).

[4] Shelton, Robert E., "Business Objects & BPR," *Data Management Review*, 4:11, pp. 6-20 (November 1994).

[5] Martin, James, *Enterprise Engineering*, Vol. 1-4, Savant Institute, London (1995).

[6] This term was introduced by Dr. David Taylor (see reference 3 above).

[7] Codd, E. F., "A Relational Model of Data for Large Shared Data Banks," *Communications of the ACM*, 13:6, pp. 377-387 (June 1970).

Suggested Readings

Tapscott, Don and Art Caston, *Paradigm Shift: The New Promise of Information Technology,* McGraw-Hill (1993). Tapscott and Caston provide an in-depth explanation of how a new era of information technology is enabling corporate rebirth. The book covers the impact of work-group computing, enterprise computing, interenterprise computing, open systems, network-based systems, and the shift from software craft to software manufacturing.

Mattison, Rob and Michael J. Sipolt, *The Object-Oriented Enterprise: Making Corporate Information Systems Work,* McGraw-Hill, 400 pp. (1994). This book is aimed directly at corporate information systems. Its in-depth coverage of large-scale business information systems makes the book indispensable for business and technology professionals. The book considers immediate and tactical applications of object technology and the use of design methods and CASE tools. More than two and a half years of research went into this book. The results are presented in a thorough discussion of the topic of objectification, the process of migrating to object-oriented corporate information systems. The book covers logical and physical architectures and the development of an object-oriented infrastructure.

Taylor, David, Ph.D., *Object-Oriented Technology: A Manager's Guide,* Addison-Wesley, 146 pp. (1991). This brief and award-winning primer is ideal for the busy manager. It explains the concepts, the business impact, and the advantages and disadvantages of object-oriented technology.

Taylor, David, Ph.D., *Business Engineering with Object Technology,* John Wiley & Sons, 188 pp. (1995). Taylor fuses business and software engineering into a new discipline: convergent engineering. The essence of his method is to express business concepts directly in executable software objects. This work promises to become one of the seminal works in object-oriented business process engineering (OOBPR).

Coad, Peter and J. Nicola, *Object-Oriented Programming,* Prentice Hall, 260 pp. (1993). Book and disk. This book represents a breakthrough in learning to "object think" and program. Coad and Nicola used accelerated learning methods to craft this book into a very effective learning resource. It provides an object-oriented programming primer, a graduated series of four examples, language summaries for both Smalltalk and C++, source code for the examples and patterns of program design.

Coad, Peter, *The Object Game,* Object International (1993). This is a board game that teaches "object think." Object International adopted the theories and methods of the Accounting Game to the world of objects.

Coad, Peter with David North and M. Mayfield, *Object Models: Strategies, Patterns & Applications,* Prentice Hall 450 pp. (1995). This book teaches totally by example and uses accelerated learning methods to amplify learning. The book makes a significant contribution to the world of business computing by providing familiar business application examples, and strategies and patterns that make it easy to extend the practitioner's current knowledge. The application examples include point-of-sale, warehousing, order-processing and data acquisition. The disk features an online version of the strategies and patterns in the form of a Windows help file.

Jacobson, Ivar, Maria Ericson and Agneta Jacobson, *The Object Advantage: Business Process Engineering with Object Technology,* Addison-Wesley (1994). This landmark work provides one method to integrate the work of reengineering a business, its processes and the underlying information systems. Going beyond the theory, the authors provide actual deliverables and a formal object-oriented method.

Client/Server Architectures

By Jim Clarke, Todd Bowman and Jim Stikeleather
In collaboration with the Object Technology Staff of The Technical Resource Connection

Contents

Abstract

As client/server technology evolves, organizations that are responsible for information management are beginning to see the benefits of performance economies, data integrity and code reuse. However, the client/server architectural models widely used in today's application development environments do not realize the full potential of client/server technology. This white paper overviews the two- and three-tier architectural models and introduces how an n-tier architectural model can further realize the potential of client/server technology for the business enterprise.

Introduction

Information systems have evolved through several generations or eras over the past 30 years. Each new generation of technology has been accompanied by a shift in how developers think about and design systems. Each new generation changes the computing paradigm.

Historically, applications were designed based on a centralized, terminal-to-host model. These systems, popularly termed *legacy systems*, placed the entire set of functionality of business applications in a host mainframe computer. Business processing logic, data maintenance and reporting functions were all processed on the central mainframe. Users gained access to their systems through dumb terminals that included character-based menus and data entry screens.

With the advent and widespread use of personal computers and local area networks in the 1980s, departments within an organization were empowered to automate many of the department's business functions without involvement of the central computing resources or staff. However, this approach often necessitated the maintenance of duplicate sets of information

that were not synchronized with the central information systems. The integrity of business information suffered as a result.

The next logical step was to solve the problem of providing data sharing and integrity. By incorporating the respective powers of both centralized and decentralized computing resources, client/server models of computing emerged and have continued to evolve. The first stage of client/server computing utilized the data storage and processing power of centralized database systems and decentralized presentation of information on desktop systems. Simply put, a client is an entity that requests that some service be performed. A server fulfills the requests. The terms, when used properly, have no implications for particular types of hardware or software components. Several means can be used to partition functionality (database processing, business application logic, and user presentation) between clients and servers. The common approaches to partitioning functionality are summarized in the sections that follow.

A Two-Tier Architectural Model

Early client/server systems were based on a two-tier model of partitioning functionality. The two-tier architecture consists of:

- a client, often referred to as the "front-end," responsible for application presentation and business application logic

The two-tier architectural model dictates that the client and server communicate directly with each other in a highly rigid and tightly coupled relationship. While the server may be capable of handling a wide-range of database requests, the client process expects results from the server to be presented in a well-defined, pre-ordained manner. Additionally, the communications

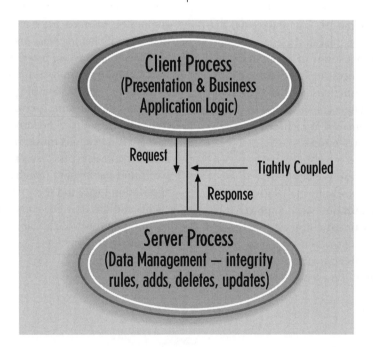

Figure 1
A Two-Tier Client/Server Model

- a server, often referred to as the "back-end," responsible for data management functions: data integrity, retrieving, adding, removing and updating.

A typical two-tier client/server application is shown in Figure 1.

mechanisms between client and server must be fully synchronized. Since the client and server are tightly coupled, when one process implements a change, the other process must be modified to accommodate the change. This applies whether the database scheme or functionality is changed. Extremely high maintenance efforts and costs are experienced with the two-tier model.

A Three-Tier Architectural Model

The three-tier architectural model advances the two-tier model by inserting a "middle tier." The middle tier is responsible for maintaining business logic, rules and access to data from the server. Therefore, the client process is responsible only for presentation and user interface logic. Figure 2 illustrates a typical three-tier client/server architecture.

front or back-end process, implemented as a Dynamic Link Library (DLL) or Application Program Interface (API), or accessed by Remote Procedure Calls (RPC) or messages. The major thrust here is that the middle tier provides a level of abstraction from both the client and server tiers. This abstraction creates a more loosely coupled interface between

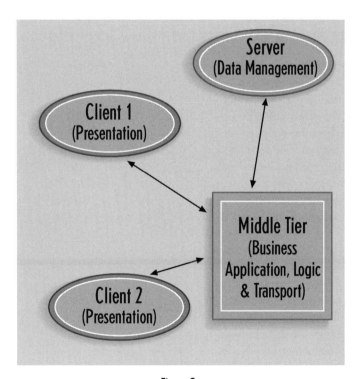

Figure 2
A Three-Tier Client/Server Model

The middle tier is a *logical*[1] tier and as such does not require a third level of hardware support. Instead, it is a process that could run on either the client or the server. The middle tier could be compiled into the

client and server while simultaneously providing a consistent interface to the server. This allows many unrelated clients to utilize the same server. If a server is constructed with all of the integrity rules for the domain it services, and all of the applications are clients that will defer to its rules, then all the applications will have consistent access to consistent information.[2]

The middle tier provides the added improvements of consistency, de-coupling and reuse. It provides a consistent interface between both the client and the server. The middle tier also de-couples the business application logic and the transport mechanism from the client's presentation layer. As a result of this de-coupling, the middle tier may then be reused across client project boundaries.

As client/server architectural models mature, higher levels of performance and greater cost savings can be realized. The two-tier model improves a completely centralized system by moving the presentation and logic functions to the client. This relieves the server of client presentation responsibilities. The server is free to specialize in data management and centralized resource services. However, the tight coupling between client and server perpetuates the high *maintenance* factor typical of host-based applications.

Similarly, the three-tier model provides improvements over the two-tier model by providing consistency, de-coupling and a higher degree of reuse. While this represents a marked improvement over the two-tier model, the overall system is still very coarse. As the system is further broken down into smaller chunks, the benefits of reuse and consistency increase. N-tier modeling allows the nature of the problem and the robustness of the infrastructure to determine how many tiers are used.

N-Tier Architectural Models

The n-tier architectural model describes a highly modular approach to creating client/server relationships. While this model is built upon traditional concepts of clients and servers, the "pieces" upon which it is built are smaller and functionally specialized components that can be reused across multiple projects. The functional pieces of the two and three-tier architectural models (presentation, business application logic, and data management) are broken down even further in an n-tier model.

With the exception of presentation, functional pieces are broken down into very small chunks. While these small pieces may be part of a larger functional piece, such as application logic, they may be referenced individually. With that in mind, the n-tier architectural model can be defined as a layered model, with each layer providing a specific function in the overall scope of the application. The number of layers comprising an application depends on the requirements of the application and systems resources available. Several services are needed to span the various layers and provide cohesion between them.

Figure 3 presents an example of how an n-tier client/ server model might be designed for a report generation

Presentation	Provides display services to specification and submission layers along with results verification.								
Specification	Who? Login ID	What? Request	Where? Destination	When? Schedule	Why? Purpose	How? Exec. Plan			
Submission	Joins Who, What, Where, When & Why (Complete Job Specs).						N A V I G A T I O N	S E C U R I T Y	M E T E R I N G & L O G
Re-Specification	Request is translated from a "what" to a command set.								
Triggering	Job awaits trigger (i.e., date/time, job completion, data available).								
Queuing	Provides load balancing and prioritizing of jobs.								
Accessing	Interfaces to services in the execution layer.								
Execution	Data Access	Column Ordering	Row Ordering	Formatting					
	Server executes any jobs that are submitted from the queuing layer.								

Figure 3
An N-Tier Client/Server Architectural Model

application. It is a combination of layers that are determined by both the functional requirements and the requirements determined by the common implications of an analysis and reporting process.

Each layer shown in Figure 3 provides either direct functional support to the overall application or a service to the functional processing layers. The services spanning the functional layers are represented by the vertical bars. The main exception is the "Re-Specification" layer, which is intended to provide the ability to adapt the front-end application without requiring significant changes to the lower layers. In this way, the application can adapt to changing user requirements more quickly, while the remaining portions of the architecture remain fixed.

The functional requirements of each layer are described briefly in the accompanying text. The individual services are straightforward. *Navigation* provides each functional layer with directions to the next layer. This results in processing that will flow from one layer to another without fixed connections that might require re-work at a later date. *Security* services control the ability of the user to access various layers and execution services. Security also verifies data access rights. *Metering and logon/logoff* services provide configurability and an audit trail that will assist in fine-tuning the system performance.

The number and type of functional support layers will vary across projects. The overall architectural model remains constant, however, and is capable of growing as an enterprise *grows into* a client/server environment. Additionally, this architectural model positions a business for adopting object-oriented technology.

An Object-Driven Client/Server Design

Some of the benefits of object orientation can be derived in fine-grained client/server applications without actually moving to objects. Figure 4, *A Customer Service Application*, illustrates how.

This application includes five viewers or human interface servers. First is an "action" viewer. When a user logs into the application, the action viewer is initiated along with any "applications" available to the user. When these applications start, they send a message to the action viewer with an icon(s) to display, and a message(s) to send when the icon is selected. In this case, the "new customer entry," "product viewer," and "new purchase order" applets "publish" themselves to the action viewer. Applets are single function applications or processes.

Also initiated at log-in, although not published to the action viewer, are an Automatic Number Identification (ANI) applet and a "Customer" domain server. When a phone call comes in, the ANI applet sends a customer inquiry message to the Customer server. It in turn accesses the customer database, packages up a customer message, and initiates and sends it to a customer viewer. The customer viewer parses the message for keywords (we have uncoupled the messages and applets from any data structure) to populate the screen, including an error message if the phone number was not found in the database. This Customer Viewer sends inquiry messages to the Account Server and Purchase Order (PO) Server, who in turn cause their viewers to display any information they have related to this customer.

All the information available about the customer is now on the screen ready for the customer service representative to field the call. The information comes from many sources (data content) and is brought together by the views (data context). The problem domain servers

— for example, the account, purchase order and customer servers — insulate the views from the technology. The Account Server is using a screen scraper via keyword messages to get to a mainframe system. If required, the mainframe system can be replaced with something else, and all applets using the Account Server will not need to be changed.

Let's say the customer needs information on a product they ordered. By double clicking the line item in the PO viewer, the Product server is launched and sends a message that, in turn, brings up the Product Viewer. This can show references and documentation, and access an expert system for help/questions, as well as show current inventory in case the product is being ordered. Notice the technology insulation (APPC) and the problem domain focus.

If the telephone interaction is for a new customer or a new order, selecting the appropriate icon brings up the appropriate viewer in new or blank mode. As the information is completed, a message is sent to the customer or PO server. This is the same message that is sent by the viewer if an existing customer or PO is changed. The server knows the message contains a modified "record" and passes it to an edit. The edit applet passes a "clean" message to the server, which then updates persistent storage. The servers have no idea what the viewers are displaying, or even how many views are outstanding. After sending the message successfully, the sender does not wait for the unit of work to be completed. Also, the PO view might broadcast a message for any customer. All such messages are asynchronous.

This application can evolve over time. A new accounting system does not change the system. Moving the shipping database from the mainframe to another

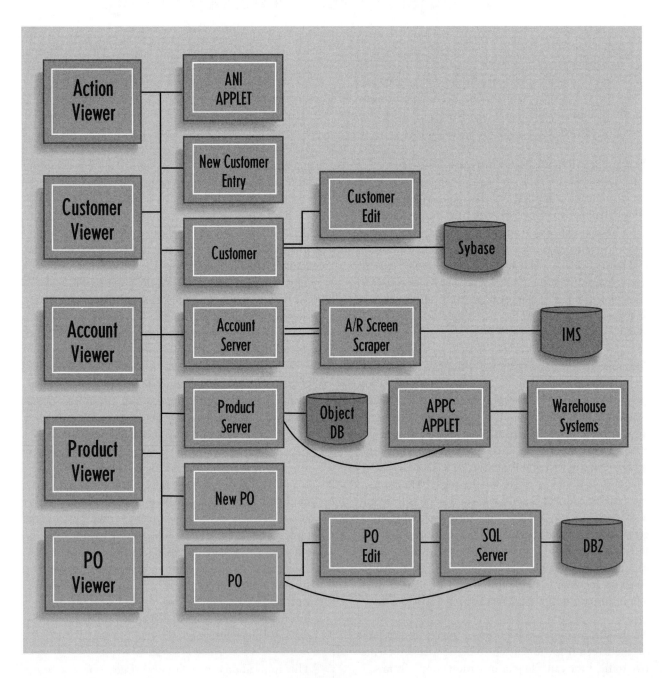

Figure 4
A Customer Service Application

machine does not change the system. Changing data formats of the messages — for example, EBCDIC to ASCII — does not change the system. The system could be expanded by adding a "Customer Credit" applet that checks balances for credit limits or accesses an on-line service for credit verification. Changing the business rules for granting credit does not change the system — it only changes one applet. Automatic mailing applets, such as order confirmations and product information, can be added. New systems, like an Internet-based, on-line ordering application, can reuse the same components. Whatever "application" is being used, the information is always displayed and interacted within the same consistent manner. In effect, we have gained most of the benefits of object technology, except inheritance, without totally going to object orientation.

Further, applications become very event — rather than transaction — driven. In a typical business, transactions and rules change rapidly, but events tend to stay constant. This makes the systems resilient to changes in the business and work flows. Code tends to be smaller and more easily grasped by a programmer unfamiliar with the applet, simplifying maintenance and reducing its costs. Applets can run on any system on the network. This type of architecture allows the business to take advantage of its hardware investment by dynamically reconfiguring applet execution on different machines for load balancing.

Some caveats are in order, since this application (see Figure 4) is a simplified example. We have not covered all the design issues and use-case scenarios, although the architecture is robust enough to handle them. And, we have not explained technically how to do things like addressing the messages. However, we can generalize some guidelines for object-driven client/server design:

- Client/server is a relationship, not a location.

- All executables can be both a client and a server.

- Messaging should be asynchronous and publish-and-subscribe-based if possible, to: a) promote information hiding; b) support parallel and pipeline processing to improve performance; and c) uncouple processes and encourage reuse.

- Separate functionality into separate servers: technology (communications), data content (files), data context (relationships), state maintenance (transactions), integrity (dependencies, security), interfaces (human, computer, EDI), business rules, processes (actual applications), and workflow (sequences of events).

- Create single-entity problem domains (e.g., Customer, Vendor, Product).

- Create applets: single functionality applications/processes in the problem domains (e.g., new customer entry, new purchase order, back order, etc.).

- Whenever possible, use the meta information (i.e., keyword-based messages) to uncouple clients and servers.

This section has led us through the evolving approaches to client/server architectures. An assessment of these architectures is presented next.

An Assessment of Client/Server Architectures

Most systems have several common requirements that any computing architecture must support. These requirements may vary in their relative weight and importance to the final solution. An n-tier architectural model supports each of these requirements and provides a framework for long-term solutions to enterprise information needs. Client/server architectures must meet the following requirements:

One of the strategic objectives of moving away from a monolithic implementation is to be responsive to business change.

server architectures, changes impact the system dramatically. In the case of two-tier architectures, changes in either clients or servers impact each other: A change in one requires a change in the other. In a well-designed three-tier architecture, the middle tier helps to insulate the impact of changes to some extent. However, maximum flexibility is achieved with the n-tier model if it is deployed in combination with better abstractions of the business.

Changeability

One of the strategic objectives of moving away from a monolithic implementation is to be responsive to business change. Unfortunately, client/server applications can be as difficult to change as the monolithic legacy applications they replace. For example, a legacy database application may be redesigned as a client/server solution, with clients that include both presentation and business logic, and a database server. Business rules and application logic are embedded in umpteen scripts and screens. Making changes as simple as lengthening the size of just one data element in this environment is tedious and prone to error.

The architecture and design paradigms used by the traditional client/server technology prevent them from resembling the business and adapting to changing business needs. In conventional client/

Object-oriented technology is the key to developing the needed business abstractions. Objects hide their data structures and implementation details from all other objects. Changes to objects have no effect on other objects as long as the interfaces (public methods) remain the same. The application of object orientation to client/server architectures holds much promise for developing information systems that can adapt to ever-changing business needs.

Fault Tolerance

The system must be able to handle the loss of a particular component. A two-tier architecture has three points of failure: the client, the network and the server. Strategies such as mirroring, replication and RAID are used to achieve server fault tolerance in two-tier architectures. A three-tier architecture adds another point of failure by introducing the middle tier. Techniques such as software routing can help protect middleware in a three-tier architecture.

Extending these lines of reasoning, n-tier architectures would appear to have many points of failure. While this may seem true, n-tier architectures allow the designer to create applications that can overcome component failures and run in a degraded mode of operation. To achieve a high degree of freedom and minimal interdependence between components, a fine-grained client/server architecture becomes necessary. Failure of a single component need not stop the entire application. For example, failure of the New Purchase Order server (see Figure 4) will not cause the system to collapse. Messages for this server can be queued for later processing when the server recovers. Unlike a two- or three-tier architecture that would simply stop, customer information, account information and the product information are still available for immediate processing with the n-tier architecture.

Scalability

Most off-the-shelf client/server development tools implement two-tier architectures, primarily as a means of data sharing. These environments may suit the need for very simple, low volume applications, which are fine for departmental solutions. However, when applied to enterprise scenarios, these data-sharing tools break down completely.

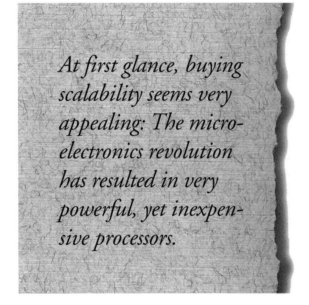

At first glance, buying scalability seems very appealing: The microelectronics revolution has resulted in very powerful, yet inexpensive processors.

Theoretically, scalability can be achieved either by hardware or by software upgrades. At first glance, *buying* scalability seems very appealing: The microelectronics revolution has resulted in very powerful, yet inexpensive processors. Prices continue to drop while power continues to increase. And operating systems have advanced significantly in recent years. OS/2, Windows/NT and various flavors of UNIX offer a wide choice of options in advanced operating systems. For example, OS/2, Solaris and Windows/NT provide for multi-threaded application support. If an application is designed to use the features of multi-threading and multi-tasking, scalability can be achieved by upgrading processors. Operating systems such as Windows/NT, Solaris and OSF/1 can exploit the power of multiprocessing to provide quantum improvements in performance.

However, the benefits of multiprocessing are attainable *only if* applications have been designed to use these advanced features of operating systems and hardware platforms. The failure to extract benefits from multi-processing is, by itself, enough to justify the move towards more scalable forms of computing.

Primitive Transaction Models

Let's consider the case of booking a business trip, where an airline reservation, a hotel room and a rental car are required. This transaction requires three actions to be successfully completed.

Using current transaction models, failure to obtain a rental car may make this entire transaction collapse. Transactions such as these are called *flat transactions*. A flat transaction can result in either of two outcomes: All actions within a transaction are committed, and the transaction is successfully completed; or failure of any action rolls back all actions within that transaction.

Let's review a different problem that flat transactions are unable to handle — an application requiring that a million updates be made to a database. The drawback to the flat transaction is that if the system fails with only one update incompleted, each of the preceding 999,999 updates are rolled back. And breaking this large transaction into a million individual transactions does not help. If the application treats each of these updates as an individual transaction and performs a million flat transactions, processing may take *at least* three times as long and lead to unacceptable response times.

Transaction models for the future will handle business events and the multitude of transactions they create dynamically. Event-driven systems, and the workflow applications they make possible, require a sophisticated and robust approach to handling complex, cascading transactions. The Object Management Group has developed standards for next generation transaction services.

Legacy Structure Re-implementation

Applications in today's client/server architectures are built around database schematics in much the same way they were developed on mainframes. The tendency is to transfer mainframe development concepts and thinking to client/server platforms. With this view, client/server computing is considered to be "hardware downsizing" from mainframes to database servers on workstations. Isolation of functionality and business

abstraction are not part of such thinking. This myopic approach transfers many of the problems found in monolithic solutions to the newer hardware platforms, including data management problems.

Performance

Client/server systems must be designed very carefully if performance improvements are to be achieved. If a monolithic application design is used (typical of two-tier systems), the net effect is to replace the powerful bandwidth of a mainframe channel with a 10MB ethernet link. For client/server systems to perform effectively, they must be designed to support parallel, asynchronous and distributed process models — much like a human organization.

Software Engineering Discipline

Some quick math reveals a little dark secret in client/server computing. Traditional computer systems achieve a reliability rating of about 90 percent.[3] If this same reliability is achieved with both client and server code in a two-tier architecture, the overall reliability of the system drops to 81 percent. Extending the math, three-tier architectures can result in 73 percent reliability. The moral in this math story is that strict software engineering discipline is required to create reliable client/server systems.

Conclusion

Patricia Seybold summarized the current state of client/server computing: "People are stampeding toward client/server because they've been told it's easy, and that's just not true. No matter what application development tools you choose, it's extremely difficult to design a high performance client/server application. It's worse than black art." [4]

User expectations are very high as a result of the current press given to client/server computing. For the most part, client/server applications have failed to live up to all the press. The architecture, development methods and tools do not provide the adaptive and robust computing environments needed in today's business environment.

An n-tier architectural model resolves several issues that currently confront the developers of enterprise-wide client/server systems. However, dividing computer systems into more and more tiers does not totally simplify client/server application development and maintenance. Conspicuously missing are the key abstractions of the business, the kind of abstractions naturally provided by object-oriented technology. The convergence of client/server and object-oriented technology provides many of the solutions to problems inherent in today's popular client/server architectures. The technology that results from this convergence is explored in The Technical Resource Connection's white paper, *Distributed Object Computing for Business.*

Client/server architectures continue to evolve in response to the demands of business. Each generation exposes users to new possibilities, new ways to take advantage of the technology. These new possibilities tend to become new expectations for client/server computing: group decisions, support systems, transaction processing and workflow. These new expectations, in turn, lead to new demands for the technology. Current client/server models have hit technical and information walls in meeting future demands. *Next Generation Computing* is needed. That generation of client/server technology is distributed object computing.

References

[1] Shelton, Robert, "Business Objects," *Data Management Review*, p. 50 (January 1995).

[2] Stikeleather, James, "What's a client, what's a server?" *Object Magazine*, p. 88 (June 1994).

[3] Putnam, Lawrence and W. Myers, *Measures for Excellence: Reliable Software On Time, Within Budget*, Yourdin Press (1992).

[4] Seybold, Patricia, "The Secret Shame of Client/Server Development," *Computerworld* (August 1993).

Suggested Readings

Orfali, Robert, Dan Harkey and Jeri Edwards, *Essential Client/Server Survival Guide*, Van Nostrand Reinhold (1994). This book is witty, approachable and comprehensive — from operating systems and communications to application architectures that incorporate database, transaction processing, groupware and distributed objects. While rich in content, it is also fun to read and contains almost 200 illustrations. More than 100 pages of the book are devoted to distributed object computing, the next generation of client/server architectures.

Berson, Alex, *Client/Server Architecture*, McGraw-Hill, Inc. (1993). Berson provides a very detailed discussion of the client/server model, its benefits, architecture, components and functions. Industry standards and products are included as well as examples and recommendations.

Boar, B. H., *Implementing Client/Server Computing: A Strategic Perspective,* McGraw-Hill, Inc. (1993).

Dewire, Dawna Travis, *Client/Server Computing,* McGraw-Hill, Inc. (1993). Dewire explains how distributed technology is evolving and offers advice on application development in distributed environments.

Distributed Object
Computing For Business

By Jim Clarke, Jim Stikeleather and Peter Fingar
In collaboration with the Object Technology Staff of The Technical Resource Connection

Contents

Someday soon you will look into a computer screen and see reality. Some part of your world — the town you live in, the company you work for, your school system, the city hospital — will hang there in a sharp color image, abstract but recognizable, moving subtly in a thousand places. This Mirror World you are looking at is fed by a steady rush of new data pouring in through cables. It is infiltrated by your own software creatures, doing your own business."

David Gelernter
Department of Computer Science, Yale University[1]

Abstract

Business applications of the future will need to be spread across multiple, and sometimes specialized, hardware that will cooperate with other hardware, as well as the legacy computer systems we have today. To meet the demands of business, the information systems we build today and tomorrow must be based upon distri-buted object computing technologies and paradigms.

The way we build systems must change because the businesses they support must change. Not only must businesses integrate islands of information internally, they must understand their position in the value chains in their industry, and establish interenterprise or virtual corporations. Extended corporations reach out to customers, suppliers, affiliates and even competitors. The airline industry exemplifies such extended business relationships: "I'm sorry, all our flights are full, but I'll be happy to book your reservation on Competitor Air flight #101."

Extended corporations reach out not only with business relationships, they must integrate their information systems. Customers, retailers, distributors and manufacturers will blur into a *business ecosystem* where it is impossible to know who is whom. Virtual corporations operate globally, 24 hours a day, seven days a week. Work and tasks follow the sun, reducing business cycle times. The resources of virtual corporations ebb and flow with the changing needs of the moment.

The only way the virtual corporation can work is through information technology. And the only way technology can work is through information systems that mirror human cognition, the way people think when accomplishing work. Information systems must be created from human-centered designs, not technology-centered designs. They must be based on human cognition — they must be based on *reality.* Human-centered, distributed object computing is the next generation of business technology. This technology will enable corporations to construct the adaptive information systems needed for 21st century business.

Business Technology: The Next Generation

The velocity of business change is increasing. Business and product cycle times are decreasing. Management is under intense pressure to streamline operations, reduce overhead and squeeze more out of production and sales channels in order to maximize shrinking margins. The global marketplace is becoming a business battleground as companies reach into all corners of the world to attract new customers.

To gain the advantage, forward-thinking businesses are redesigning core business processes. Such companies are becoming smaller and more horizontal as layers between top management and the shop floor worker or sales clerk are removed. Organizations are becoming driven by *knowledge-based* workers as people on the shop floor and in the field are empowered with information and the authority to make tactical decisions themselves.

Information is power. Corporations are grappling with exploding demands for information. Competitive pressures make it absolutely necessary to connect islands of information, resources and people together into a cohesive whole. The new business objectives demand a fully integrated information framework and infrastructure. Furthermore, the entire workforce must have access to this common information infrastructure. From a technology perspective, this means universal access that is both transparent and adaptive. This business objective has a profound impact on the

Competitive pressures have made it absolutely necessary to connect islands of information, resources and people together into a cohesive whole.

mission and on the very nature of commercial enterprise computing. Today's computing architectures and design methods for constructing information systems are simply not capable of handling the requirements of *next generation computing*. And, as Jim Stikeleather explains in an *Object Magazine* article, "There are not enough programmers in the world to meet the demands of new information systems being generated by newly reengineered businesses ... at least, not using traditional practices and technologies."[2]

Next generation information systems shift much of the business information residing in workers' heads to computers. For this to happen, the following must take place:

- The design of next generation information systems requires a new way of thinking that changes the very nature of design — a paradigm shift. Distributed object computing supplies a paradigm for building universal, transparent and adaptive information infrastructures and systems.

- As corporations become more extended and externally integrated, then the *community memory* and *organizational knowledge* become the property of the information systems, not of the people of the organization. Consequently, not only are new types of systems necessary, but also new ways of human interaction with information systems are needed. With current systems approaches, the onus is on humans to try to make sense of information from disjointed presentations of data. New types of information systems are needed that place the onus on the computer system to correctly convey information in a form that humans can process naturally. The information must reflect reality as perceived and understood by humans, not the artificial constructs of transactions, tables and spreadsheets characteristic of today's systems. Where it once stood on the sidelines, cognitive science plays a central role in new era information systems. Systems rooted in human cognition can enable instant use (no training required), correct assimilation, confirmation of user intentions and error-free communication between man and machine. Such systems are required by the extended enterprise.

The Challenge of Enterprise Computing

The recent attention and investments in client/server technologies are in response to the strategic demand for enterprise computing. However, as explained in The Technical Resource Connection's white paper, *Client/Server Architectures,* current development methods, tools and architectures have *hit technical and information walls.* Maximum limits have been reached. Today's popular development tools and techniques suffer a number of problems concerning application scalability, modularity, granularity and maintainability. In addition, they overwhelm the ability of users to assimilate diverse information. As such, these tools and techniques will not advance us much past our current position with respect to our ability to develop the necessary information systems in a timely and cost-effective manner.

Client/server technology is essential, but not sufficient. The issues limiting systems development today are not just technical. In our quest for supreme technology, business concepts have remained second-class citizens, standing in the shadow of a high performance infrastructure. Clients and servers continue to evolve technically but, in these implementations, the business itself is not *visible.* Client/server technology, by itself, does not supply a uniform cognitive model for sharing information among systems and people.

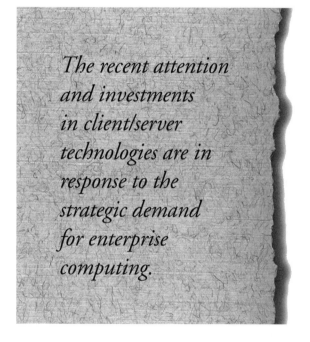

The recent attention and investments in client/server technologies are in response to the strategic demand for enterprise computing.

Jeffrey Sutherland highlights the pitfalls of the typical database server model where application logic is embedded in proprietary scripts in a user interface and hardwired to data elements in a relational database server. In what he calls the "powerblender" syndrome, business logic and interface screens are blended together resulting in redundancy and maintenance problems.[3] Sutherland maintains these and other limitations of the current client/server models "promise to make them tomorrow's legacy systems."

Even as "tiers" are added to decouple business logic, user presentation, network operations and database processing, fundamental design methods center on user screens and forms. Forms or screen-based designs do not promote reuse nor do they support workflow or other applications that are identified as a result of business reengineering. What are conspicuously missing from most client/server models are the key *abstractions* of the business. Again, the issue is assimilation of information by people. This is where object orientation adds significant value to current client/server models.

Client/server design and development needs to incorporate the power of object-oriented technology. The graphical user interface (GUI) portion of client applications may appear object-oriented, but contrary to vendor claims, client/server development needs to make much more extensive use of object technology at both the client and server level. Thus, many "object-based" tools do not allow developers to leverage object technology. Object-orientation in this context is much more than attaching procedural scripting language to graphical interface objects. It is beyond the GUI to encompass application logic that does not necessarily have a display component. In addition, object-oriented design methods produce fine-grained objects that may be distributed to any and all resources on the network.

Conversely, object-oriented technology needs to harness the power of client/server architectures. The enterprise object advantage is not realized when objects are applied "in-the-small," on the desktop, or within a department. Objects need the distribution advantages of client/server architectures if reuse is to be achieved beyond individual applications.

When the two technologies are combined as one, the next generation of business computing will have arrived. No, the next generation is not quite here, but we are standing at the threshold. When it arrives, we can meet the challenge of enterprise computing.

The challenge of enterprise computing is to support the new management structures and work procedures evolving in business today. Twentieth century technology was used to automate nineteenth century management structures. Today, progressive companies are reinventing themselves by replacing management structures and redesigning jobs. All of this redesign is aimed at adding value in a global marketplace that operates in the context of next generation information technology.

The challenge is to align information technology, business strategy, processes and organizations for a business environment characterized by rapid, near constant change. This complex environment requires very sophisticated information systems. Such systems can be built only if the complexities of the business and its underlying technology are modeled with clarity. The business and software models must be built so they are understood and owned by business professionals, not technologists. These models must reflect and support *reality* — distributed, independent, continuous and real-time business processing.

The blending of the cognitive and semantic integrity of objects with the distribution potential of client/server architectures holds great promise for meeting the challenge of enterprise computing. This new computing paradigm, distributed object computing, is explained in the next section.

Distributed Object Computing

Distributed object computing is a breakthrough framework for computing that has resulted from the convergence of *object-oriented* and *client/server technologies.* When radio and motion picture technologies converged, something completely new happened. Unlike the radio and the movies, *television* pervaded and fundamentally changed society. Television combined the distribution advantages of radio with the richness of real-world information contained in moving pictures. The result was far more than the sum of the two technologies. Distributed object computing blends the distribution advantages of client/server technology with the richness of real-world information contained in object-oriented models. Distributed object computing will fundamentally change the information landscape of business, and something totally new will start to happen. The way business software is developed will change forever.

Distributed object computing is a computing paradigm that allows objects to be distributed across a heterogeneous network, and allows each of the components to interoperate as a unified whole. To an application built in a distributed object environment, and as expressed in Sun Microsystem's slogan, *the network is the computer.*™

Business processes are essentially human phenomena. Modeling the real business processes is not a matter of modeling organization charts and company policy manuals. Real business modeling requires that we model the ways work is actually accomplished, the ways things really happen: over the phone, through e-mail, and by way of the informal human network. Successful models cut straight to the core of real business processes. They capture the real business entities and operations that accomplish work and produce value. Object orientation was developed in the 1960s to provide the capability to build models that reflect real systems.

Objects interact by passing messages to each other. These messages represent requests for information or

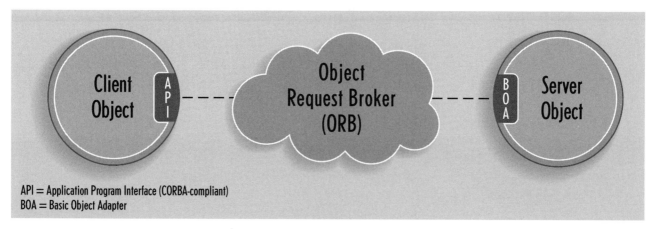

API = Application Program Interface (CORBA-compliant)
BOA = Basic Object Adapter

Figure 1
The Object Request Broker

services. During any given interaction, objects will dynamically assume the roles of clients and servers. The physical glue that ties the distributed objects together is an object request broker. The *object request broker* (ORB) provides the means for objects to locate and activate other objects on a network, regardless of the processor or programming language used to develop either client or server objects. The ORB makes these things happen transparently to the developer. Thus, the ORB is the *middleware* of distributed object computing that allows interoperability in heterogeneous networks of objects. ORBs provide a means for locating, activating and communicating with objects while hiding their implementation details from the developer. The significant benefit of ORBs is that they remove the network messaging complexity from the mind's eye of the developer. The view of the developer is refocused from technical issues to the business objects and the services they provide.

When objects are distributed across a network, clients can be servers and conversely, servers can be clients. That really does not matter since we are talking about *cooperating* objects. As shown in Figure 1, the client requests services of another object, the server object fulfills the request. Clients and servers can be physically anywhere on the network and written in any object-oriented programming language. Although

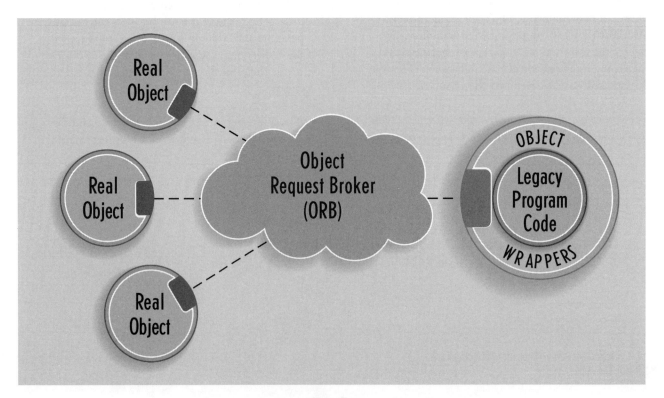

Figure 2
Incorporating Legacy Assets Into A Distributed Object Environment

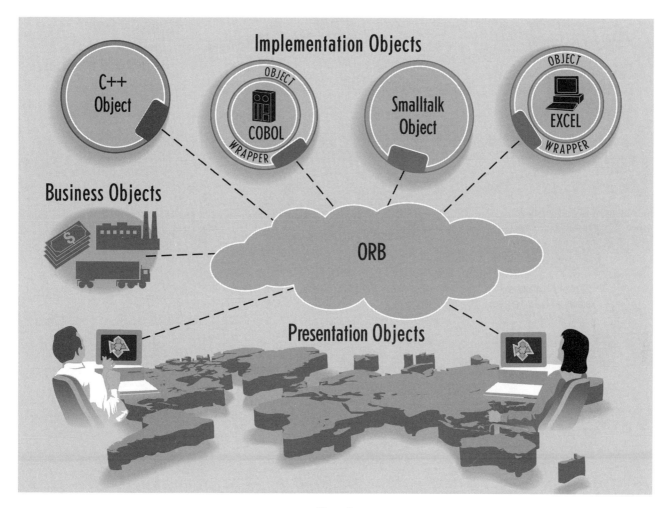

Figure 3
Distributed Object Computing With Business Objects

universal clients and servers live in their own dynamic worlds outside of an application, the objects appear as though they are local within the application since *the network is the computer*. In essence, the whole concept of distributed object computing can be viewed as simply a global network of heterogeneous clients and servers or, more precisely, *cooperative business objects.*

Furthermore, valuable legacy systems can be "wrapped" and appear to the developer to be objects. Once wrapped, the legacy code can participate in a distributed object environment as shown in Figure 2. Wrapping is a technique of creating an object-oriented interface that can access specific functionality contained in one or more existing (legacy) computer applications.

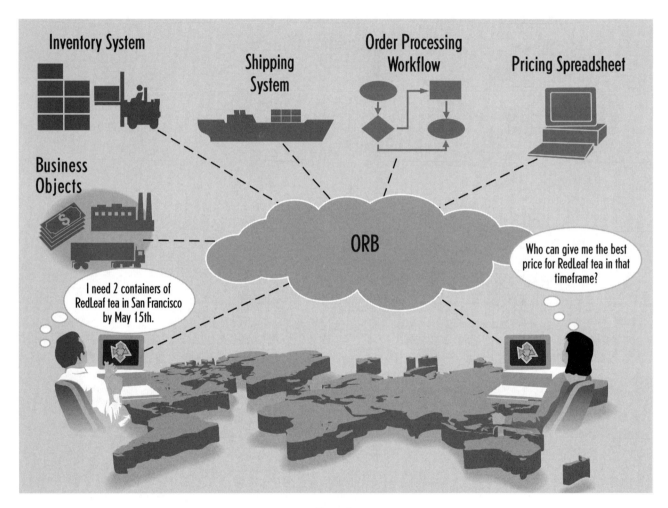

Figure 4
A Workflow Application with Distributed Objects

Each set of wrappers carves out a slice of legacy code and represents it as a real world object (person, container, shipment).

Corporations have significant investments in computer systems that were developed prior to the advent of object-oriented technology. Even though a corporation may want to migrate to object-oriented technology to derive its benefits, millions or billions of dollars of existing computing resources cannot be scrapped just because a new technology comes along. There is not a solid business case for "converting" legacy assets to the object paradigm. However, a strong business case can be made for an evolutionary approach to building new generation applications that incorporate and leverage existing assets.

Several approaches to wrapping legacy systems can be taken, from simple "screen scraping" to direct function calls to existing code. Approaches will depend on what legacy asset is being wrapped: A mainframe COBOL application, an EXCEL spreadsheet on a microcomputer, or a relational database server in an existing client/server application all require different approaches. Regardless of the means used to wrap legacy applications, the result is that existing assets can become full participants in a distributed object application as shown in Figure 2.

In a distributed object environment, an application supports a business process or task by combining active business objects. Component assembly is becoming the dominant theme for developing distributed object applications. Object interaction is accomplished through a sophisticated *messaging* system that allows objects to request services of other objects regardless of the machine or machines on which they physically reside (see The Technical Resource Connection's white paper, *Asynchronous Message Communication Between Distributed Business Objects*).

Objects only know what services other objects provide (their interfaces), not how they provide those services (their implementation). The hiding of implementation details within objects is one of the key contributions of object-oriented technology to managing complexity in distributed computing. In a distributed object environment, the application developer does not even have to consider what machine or programming language is used to implement the server objects. Figure 3, Distributed Object Computing With Business Objects, shows typical components in a distributed object application.

As shown in Figure 3, the user's view of an application consists of objects that may be written in C++ and running on one machine, a COBOL program running on a mainframe, a Smalltalk object running inside one user's workstation, and an EXCEL spreadsheet running on a microcomputer. The user is not concerned with these platforms and programming environments. The user simply sees objects interacting with one another as a unified whole.

The objects appear to the user and developer as familiar business objects, not machines, networks and programming languages. Users and developers do not have to think in terms of the technology, only in terms of familiar business objects as illustrated in Figure 4. Figure 4 shows a hypothetical workflow application for a San Francisco company that imports specialty teas. Herbal and other specialty teas have become very popular in the United States and have created a very competitive growth market. To gain the competitive edge, the company has implemented a workflow application using distributed object technology.

The company's new object-oriented inventory system is written in C++ and runs in a UNIX environment. The shipping system was developed by the company's shipping agent in COBOL and it runs on a mainframe. The San Francisco tea company's office in Hong Kong maintains up-to-the-minute pricing of Chinese tea producers in an EXCEL spreadsheet. The new order processing workflow application was developed in Smalltalk and runs on powerful workstations used by the home office purchasing agents.

This application combines radically different hardware and software technology. However, neither application developers nor users care about machines, locations, or programming languages. They view the world simply as business objects: current inventory, shipping schedules, and current pricing.

Business objects provide pre-assembled business functionality that can be used to wire together and customize applications. All the while, business objects hide the complexities of "back-end" database processing and other technologies. The Object Management Group defines a business object as "representations of the nature and behavior of real world things or concepts in terms that are meaningful to the business. Customers, products, orders, employees, trades, financial instruments, shipping containers and vehicles are all examples of real-world concepts or things that could be represented as business objects. Business objects add value over other representations by providing a way of managing complexity, giving a higher level perspective, and packaging the essential characteristics of business concepts more completely. We can think of business objects as actors, role-players, or surrogates for the real world things or concepts that they represent." [4]

Actually, business applications are just "smart" views of the business objects, not the stand alone chunks of code known as applications today. In Figure 4, the machines and programming languages that are shown in Figure 3 are replaced with business objects. These business objects model aspects of the business with *direct representation* of real business entities, concepts and vocabulary. These business objects are abstractions of *real* business rules, events, people, places and things. The order processing workflow application is in control of events needed to complete the business task: "I need 2 containers of RedLeaf tea in the San Francisco warehouse by May 15th."

In summary, distributed object computing is an extension of client/server technology. However, there is a difference in its working process and its implementation. With client/server, there is generally an application running on a client computer while another application runs on a server computer. These two applications communicate across a network and relay data to one another, usually via some middleware provided in the form of an application program interface (API) or function call library.

In a sense, client/server is a restrictive version of distributed object computing. A distributed application is made up of objects, just as any other object-oriented application. However, the objects of a distributed object application may be split up and run on multiple computers throughout a network.

Distributed object computing is not magic. It is a very complex computing environment and requires a very sophisticated and robust technology infrastructure. The information technology infrastructures of the future must be based on very sound architectures as we will discuss next.

Architecture: The Key to Adopting Distributed Object Computing

When beginning a traditional application development project, developers typically do not have an overall systems architecture from which to start. This fact is a universal problem when elevating business computing from individual applications to enterprise-wide information systems.

An architecture is a high-level description of the organization of functional responsibilities within a system. However, an architecture is not a description of a specific solution to a problem or a roadmap for success in design. It does not provide guidance in determining where functionality should reside and how to organize it. And, an architecture does not direct a designer to a successful, powerful or elegant solution to a specific problem.

The goal of an architecture is to convey information about the general structure of systems. In that sense, an architecture defines the relationship of system components, but does nothing to describe the specific implementation of those components. Client/server is an architecture in the sense that it defines a relationship between system components. It should be kept in mind that an architecture is not a solution in itself, just a framework for developing any number of specific solutions.

Computing architectures do not address the detailed design of an application. Today, most developers create an application as though it were the only one they will ever develop. There is no grand design of which technologies should be employed or why, no thought of how information should be encapsulated, accessed and assembled into applications, and no common framework for interaction with existing applications.

Effective application development projects require the definition of an architecture — an overall plan for the infrastructure of information and technologies. Although there is no single, all encompassing architecture for computing, before developing next generation applications, two architectures should be devised. These are a technical architecture and an information architecture.

A *technical architecture* provides a blueprint for assembling technology components. A technical architecture defines what tools and technologies will be used and how they will be used. The definitions may include the definition of objects that encapsulate several databases, middleware and other technologies, as well as which development tools to use and how they will be integrated to provide a complete software project support environment.

An *information architecture* describes the content, behavior and interaction of business objects. These concepts build a semantically rich model of the problem domain. The information architecture prescribes the building blocks for application development. Business objects use the services of the technical architecture objects. An information architecture provides a framework for the information components of the business: *subjects, events, roles, associations and business rules.*

A detailed view of the architecture that makes up a business object appears in Figure 5. This basic seven-layer model supports technology insulation that is necessary to provide for the business-oriented processing of the future.

As shown in Figure 5, the bottom two layers are technology insulation and implementation layers, areas into which business developers rarely venture. The basis of these layers are traditional object-oriented programming models (class/instance) and tools (C^{++}, Smalltalk).

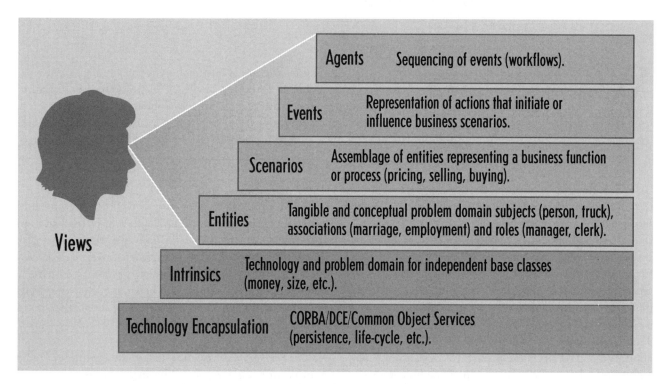

Figure 5
A Seven-Layer Object Computing Model

The bottom layer provides the infrastructure for an object-oriented environment. The second layer supplies hardware insulation and a higher level of business intrinsics, such as "money object," which includes formatting, decimal arithmetic and currency conversion.

The third layer is where the developer creates the basic "entities" of the problem domain (item, person, truck), their associations with one another (employment = person + company), and their roles in the business (a truck can be a fixed- or leased-asset). The development environment should support both text and visual programming (like OpenStep) and visual assembly.

The next four layers provide a realm for business problem domain experts and end users. With the appropriate tools, this environment permits the visual assembly of entities from the lower layers. These layers should also support visible and maintainable rules and constraints. At the "scenarios" level, for example, users can assemble entities to interact in some scenario of the business, such as sales forecasting.

The "events," or fifth, layer essentially replaces the "traditional transaction" by allowing users to define events of the business that may influence previously defined scenarios. For example, a competitor changes his price, or a new employee is hired. Such business events tend to generate many transactions that must be applied to many traditional legacy systems. In traditional systems, several transactions must be cascaded to satisfy the requirements of a single business event. In next generation systems, scenarios will subscribe to events of interest, replacing traditional transaction models.

The sixth, or "agents," layer allows the organization of multiple events into a workflow, with the seventh and final "view" layer supplying the human interface. This layer is intelligent, recognizing both the context and content of the information being exchanged with the external world and even adapting the presentation to the abilities of the outside user.

Distributed Object Computing Requires Standards

Without standards, we would not have the world's first fully automatic, universal network — the *telephone*. Likewise, we will not have interoperating networks of objects without standards. The Object Management Group (OMG) is a consortium formed in 1989 to define the standards required for distributed object systems in heterogeneous environments. OMG's objective is the definition of the Object Management Architecture (OMA), which includes four sets of standards: the Common Object Request Broker Architecture (CORBA), Common Object Services Specification (COSS), Common Facilities, and Application Objects.

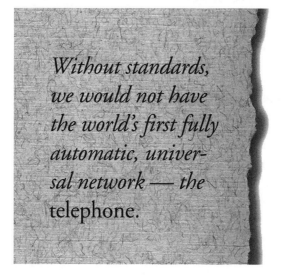

Without standards, we would not have the world's first fully automatic, universal network — the telephone.

In 1992, OMG approved a standard architecture called the Common Object Request Broker Architecture (CORBA) that defined the services to be provided by an ORB. Since then, several vendors have been working on their own distributed object computing products, primarily ORBs.

To date, there are only a handful of commercial implementations of distributed object computing products available. However, several more are in the works and should be available soon. A few of the better known ORBs commercially available today or about to become available include Expersoft's PowerBroker, IBM's DSOM, Sun's NEO, Iona's Orbix and HP's ORB+. A complete and powerful ORB implementation provides C++ developers with the ability to fully distribute application objects among various platforms and provides client access to distributed objects from Windows 3.1 and NT applications. A more in-depth discussion of ORBs is available in the book *The Essential Distributed Objects Survival Guide* (see Suggested Readings).

To date there are about a dozen ORB implementations. Some are commercially available now; the rest are expected to be released soon. Most, if not all, of these claim to be CORBA-compliant or plan to be in the near future. ORB interoperability is addressed by the CORBA 2.0 specification.

The standards that are essential to the next generation of computing are currently being written. Standards do not come easily, and at least one computer company is setting its own standards for distributed object computing. Still, the business community is under such competitive pressure and the need for next generation business computing is so pressing that standards are imminent.

Many companies are moving forward without complete standards by using the ability of object-oriented technology to hide implementation details. As standards evolve, they can undo their proprietary plumbing and plug in the standards. However, to be successful with this approach, the emerging standards must be tracked closely. Standards to watch include: Microsoft's OLE/COM; OMG's CORBA, COSS, CF, and BOMSIG; and CIL's OpenDoc. In addition, emerging technologies to watch include IBM's SOM/DSOM, Sun's NEO and Java, Taligent's Development Environment, IONA's lightweight Orbix with fault-tolerance and OCX support, NeXT's OpenStep and HP's CORBA 2.0-compliant ORB that sits on top of DCE.

The Technical Advantage of Distributed Objects

Object orientation can radically simplify applications development. Distributed object models and tools extend an object-oriented programming system. The objects may be distributed on different computers throughout a network, living within their own dynamic library outside of an application, and yet appear as though they were local within the application. This is the essence of plug-and-play software. Several technical advantages result from a distributed object environment.

Today's legacy systems can be encapsulated with multiple object wrappers to become full participants in new era information systems.

1. Legacy assets can be leveraged. Object *wrappers* (object-oriented interfaces to legacy code) may be applied to various computing resources throughout a network to simplify the means of communicating with these resources. All communication between distributed objects occurs in the form of *messages*, just as local objects within an application communicate, rather than applying different middleware and network interfaces to each legacy system. Today's legacy systems can be encapsulated with multiple object wrappers to become full participants in new era information systems. Further, a single object may represent information derived from multiple legacy systems. In this way, the massive investments corporations have made in these assets, and the associated intellectual capital, can be leveraged.

2. Since all objects — both local and remote — communicate in the same fashion (via messages), programmers have the ability to distribute components of an application to computers that best fit the task of each object without having to change the rest of the application using these objects. For example, an object that performs intense computations, such as three-dimensional renderings, might be placed on a more powerful computer, rather than on an average desktop computer, where the user interacts with the presentation objects. Such partitioning provides businesses with a new approach to manage their investment in computing resources and to match the changing needs to changing resources. Thus, hardware investments can be optimized.

3. Since objects appear to be local to their *clients*, a client does not know what machine, or even what kind of machine, an object resides on. As a result, migration of implementation objects from platform to platform is made easier. These migrations can be accomplished in steps without affecting the clients.

4. Systems integration can be performed to a higher degree. Software and hardware resources available on disparate platforms can be tied together into a single application. The goal of creating a single system image is achieved when applications can be assembled from distributed objects.

The overall technical goal of distributed object computing is clear: to advance client/server technology so that it may be more efficient and flexible, yet less complex. The benefits of distributed objects are indeed solutions to the problems with existing client/server paradigms.

The Business Impact of Distributed Object Computing

Distributed object computing, plus business objects, equals *the next generation of business computing.* New era systems are already being developed by business pioneers who understand this technology. They understand that the ultimate next generation methods and tools are still in the laboratory, but they know that sufficient standards and development resources are already in place. With a head start in their respective industries, these professionals intend to become well armed for 21st century business warfare. Time waits for no one.

The Next Generation Fuses Business and Technology

Corporations are undertaking business process redesign efforts to maintain their edge in an increasingly competitive and complex world. As experience continues to be gained, businesses are demanding that the methods and tools of business engineering and software engineering be more tightly linked.

As Dr. David Taylor points out, "Convergent engineering offers a new opportunity to create more flexible, adaptive business systems by combining business and software engineering into a single, integrated discipline."[5] New companies such as Open Engineering, Inc., are offering services and tools for object-oriented business engineering (OOBE).

Business and Software Models are Simulations of the Business

In the future, business object models likely will be developed that are simulations of the "real" business. Consider the space shuttle. Prior to the shuttle's first pieces being riveted together, the aeronautical marvel of our time was "built" in a simulator. The simulator was not discarded after the actual shuttle was built. When a shuttle is launched, the live mission includes real-time processing by the simulator. If the real shuttle encounters trouble, NASA engineers turn to the simulator to analyze the problem and simulate alternative corrective actions. Real data from the shuttle is *mirrored* in the simulator.

Space exploration is fully dependent on modeling and simulation. Such simulation makes forward and reverse engineering possible in a real-time environment. This is also true of the enterprise of the future. Simulators, in the form of business object models, will be used to design critical business processes. As innovative processes are deployed, they will provide real-time data for the business simulator. As the business encounters unexpected trouble in the marketplace, it will turn to the simulator to explore corrective action. Furthermore, with the deployment of intelligent components such as neural nets in the business model, business simulators will learn from the information fed back to them from real business activity. Buck Rogers? Not really. After all, object-oriented technology was developed in the 1960s as a natural approach to modeling and simulation. An intelligent simulator can learn from real data. Businesses that learn to deploy such technology will be first to identify market shifts and emerging patterns of demand. They intend to be first to market with innovations. They understand that to be second is to be last.

Businesses Need Intelligent Systems

The flattened organizations that result from business reengineering require that decision-making be placed in the hands of workers with direct customer contact. Systems capable of supporting this way of doing business must be intelligent. The workers have access to diverse information and decision-making tools needed for on-the-spot, quality decisions. Worker empowerment without the best available information resources will not work, and redesigned business processes will fail.

Next Generation Systems Require Next Generation Development Methods

Developing business applications from business objects is radically different from the current state of the practice of software development. Object-oriented project management approaches require different kinds of life cycles, deliverables and technology support (see our white paper, *Integrated Project Support Environments*). In his seminal work, *Object-Oriented Programming,* Brad Cox[6] spoke of a software revolution that would result from the use of Software-ICs (analogous to hardware integrated chips). A new software industry will flourish. Software factories will fabricate, customize and assemble software from standard, reusable parts. Cox's software revolution is well under way.

TQM++

With billions of objects distributed everywhere, and with atomic-sized objects being reused over and over, businesses cannot afford to have less than 100 percent reliable objects comprising their information systems. Consider the quality assurance methods that have been developed, deployed and demanded in the aeronautics field. The lives of millions of human beings depend on 100 percent quality in each atomic part of a modern airliner. At 35,000 feet, 99 percent quality in atomic parts is totally unacceptable.

What are the acceptable risks when a corporation's information infrastructure is made up of billions of objects that communicate in cyberspace? Total quality management, a buzzword of the early 1990s, takes on a very serious role in distributed object systems. To construct the new world of object-oriented information systems, defect-free components are absolutely essential. True total quality management (not the management platitude) is absolutely essential.

21st Century Corporations Will Be Learning Organizations

Arie DeGeus of Royal Dutch/Shell observed, *"We understand that the only competitive advantage the company of the future will have is its ability to learn faster than its competitors."*[7] The next generation of computing will not come easy. Both business and technology professionals must learn how to think in fundamentally new ways. Mentoring and team learning are essential to building a learning organization capable of keeping up with the rapidly evolving object technology and business engineering. In his book, *The Blueprint for Business Objects,*[8] Peter Fingar makes it quite clear that "corporate training as usual" no longer applies. As noted by Peter Senge, systems thinking is at the core of the new corporate curriculum, and business and technology professionals must learn general systems thinking.[9]

The Bottom Line

We are on the threshold of the next generation of business. The next generation of technology — distributed object computing — supplies the backdrop for the next generation of business practice. The challenge to businesses that wish to excel in the 21st century is to develop an evolutionary approach to bridge the two worlds of today and tomorrow, along with the two realities of business and technology.

References

[1] Gelernter, David, *Mirror Worlds: or the Day Software Puts the Universe in a Shoebox...*, Oxford University Press (1991).

[2] Stikeleather, Jim, "Why Distributed Object Computing is Inevitable," *Object Magazine,* p. 35 (March-April 1994).

[3] Sutherland, Dr. Jeffrey, *Distributed Object Architecture for IS Applications,* Distributed Object Computing, SIGS Publications (1994).

[4] Object Management Group, Inc., "OMG Business Application Architecture,*" White Paper Draft* (1995).

[5] Taylor, Dr. David A., *Business Engineering with Object Technology,* John Wiley & Sons (1995).

[6] Cox, Brad J., *Object-Oriented Programming, An Evolutionary Approach,* Addison-Wesley (1986).

[7] DeGeus, Arie, "Planning as Learning," *Harvard Business Review,* p. 74 (March-April 1988).

[8] Fingar, Peter, *The Blueprint for Business Objects,* SIGS Books (1996).

[9] Senge, Peter M., *The Fifth Discipline: The Art and Practice of the Learning Organization,* Doubleday/Currency (1990).

Suggested Readings

Senge, Peter M., *The Fifth Discipline: The Art and Practice of the Learning Organization,* Doubleday/Currency (1990). Senge's focus on "systems thinking" represents a discipline that is central to business processes. This work has had a major impact on business reengineering.

Tappscott, Don and Art Caston, *Paradigm Shift: The New Promise of Information Technology,* McGraw-Hill (1993). Tapscott and Caston provide an in-depth explanation of how a new era of information technology is enabling corporate rebirth. The book covers the impact of work-group computing, enterprise computing, interenterprise computing, open systems, network-based systems and the shift from software craft to software manufacturing.

Davidow, William H. and Michael S. Malone, *The Virtual Corporation: Structuring and Revitalizing the Corporation for the 21st Century,* Harper Collins (1992). The authors provide an integrated picture of the customer-driven company of the future. The book is at the cutting-edge and describes the future global marketplace that depends on corporations producing virtual products high in added value and available to customers instantly.

Gelernter, David, *Mirror Worlds: or The day software puts the universe in a shoebox ... how it will happen and what it will mean,* Oxford University Press (1991). In what could easily be mistaken for science fiction, the chairman of the computer science department at Yale University takes the reader on a whimsical ride into the future, to the day software puts the universe in a shoe box. Gelernter takes the reader on a tour of the information world being constructed with advanced networked information technology. The reader will not learn object technology, but will learn what is ultimately being built with the technology.

Mattison, Rob and Michael J. Sipolt, *The Object-Oriented Enterprise: Making Corporate Information Systems Work,* McGraw-Hill, 400 pp. (1994). This book is aimed directly at corporate information systems. Its in-depth coverage of large-scale business information systems makes the book indispensable for business and technology professionals. The book considers immediate and tactical applications of object

technology and the use of design methods and CASE tools. More than two-and-a-half years of research went into this book. The results are presented in a thorough discussion of the topic of objectification, the process of migrating to object-oriented corporate information systems. The book covers logical and physical architectures and the development of an object-oriented infrastructure.

Sims, Oliver, *Business Objects: Delivering Cooperative Objects for Client/Server,* McGraw-Hill (1994). Sims' approach is the application of business-sized objects to the user interface, where cooperative business objects correspond to an on-screen object needed by the user. The book also explains the need for middleware between applications and the operating system.

Jacobson, Ivar, Maria Ericson and Agneta Jacobson, *The Object Advantage: Business Process Engineering with Object Technology,* Addison-Wesley (1994). This landmark work provides one method to integrate the work of reengineering a business, its processes and the underlying information systems. Going beyond theory, the authors provide actual deliverables and a formal object-oriented method.

Tkach, Daniel and Richard Puttick, *Object Technology in Applications Development,* Benjamin/Cummings, 225 pp. (1994). Both authors are with IBM's International Support Center and focus on technology transfer. Their book provides a high level road map of object-oriented application development, describes the role of CASE tools and use of frameworks for reuse, and describes how legacy code can be reused in object-oriented environments.

Orfali, Robert, Dan Harkey and Jeri Edwards, *The Essential Distributed Objects Survival Guide,* Wiley, 604 pp. (1995). The authors help the Martian, Zog, on an intergalactic tour of client/server and object orientation including CORBA, Business Objects, OpenDoc, OLE, ODBMS and Component Suites. Don't let the friendly and fun nature of the book fool you. It contains serious information and in-depth coverage of the next generation — distributed object computing.

Asynchronous Message Communication Between Distributed Business Objects

By Rahul Narain, Don Rimel and Peter Fingar
In collaboration with the Object Technology Staff of The Technical Resource Connection

Contents

Alice sighed wearily. "I think you might do something better with the time," she said, "than wasting it in asking riddles that have no answers."

"If you knew Time as well as I do," said the Hatter, "you wouldn't talk about wasting it. It's him."

"I don't know what you mean," said Alice.

"Of course you don't!" the Hatter said, tossing his head contemptuously.

"I dare say you never even spoke to Time!"

"Perhaps not," Alice cautiously replied; "but I know I have to beat time when I learn music."

"Ah! That accounts for it," said the Hatter. "He won't stand beating. Now, if you only kept on good terms with him, he'd do almost anything you liked with the clock."

Lewis Carroll
Alice in Wonderland

Abstract

Today, more than anything else, each of us wants time — and more out of the time we have. Wasting time while waiting for results from others can delay or prevent us from staying on task and getting a job done.

Like people, objects can be bogged down while waiting for results from other objects. Distributed object computing requires a robust messaging system capable of eliminating time dependencies, so an object does not have to waste time attending to a message once it has been sent to another object.

An event-driven cooperative business object model requires a reliable message delivery framework that supports both synchronous and asynchronous communication between the objects. With asynchronous communication, the message sender can continue with work as soon as a message has been composed and sent. This paper illustrates the need for an effective, transparent communications framework for concurrent computing. The framework presented conforms with the Object Management Group's (OMG's) "event service specifications" — a part of the Common Object Services Specification (COSS).[1] The intended audience for this paper is senior technical managers.

What are Events and Messages?

In common language, we already know the meaning of events — incidents, occurrences and happenings that drive the world around us.

For example, Webster's dictionary defines an event as "something that happens, an occurrence." We conclude that an event occurred either because we witnessed it firsthand, or we have sufficient evidence to assume the event happened. In the world of computers, events assume exactly the same semantic role. However, in the world of computers, our definitions must be very precise.

Modeling techniques identify and define events according to their syntactic connotations or technical classification. For example, Page-Jones and Ruble[2] assert that an event must meet the following criteria:

"1.   An event occurs at a moment in time.
2.   An event occurs in the environment, not inside the system.
3.   The occurrence of the event is under the control of the environment, not the system.
4.   The system must be able to detect that the event occurred.
5.   The system is supposed to do something when the event occurs.

Failure to meet any one of these criteria is enough to send the event packing."

Page-Jones and Ruble classify events by their granularity: conceptual, business, dialogue and interface. To illustrate that events are more than input from a keyboard or a click of a mouse button, consider the *conceptual event*. Conceptual events are broad sweeping events such as: "Investor buys stock." This event can be further broken down into *business events*. The business event model consists of an event list specified in the subject-verb-object syntax as shown below. The event dictionary expands with each event that defines its business relevance and component parts that capture stimuli, activity and the response. Business events are more granular than conceptual events:

- "Investor calls broker."
- "Broker retrieves investor's portfolio."
- "Investor inquires the price of stock."
- "Investor specifies stock, quantity and price."
- "Front office confirms receipt of order."
- "Back office executes the trade"
- "Front office confirms the purchase."

These business events must be further broken down into the dialog that occurs between the system and the user in order to accomplish the business task. Human-computer interactions are the *dialog events*. To be effective, dialog events must be patterned around the ways the user thinks and acts while accomplishing the tasks: "Open a new portfolio; enter the investor profile; and so on." Human-centered design, based in cognitive science, is essential to modeling the intentions of users that interact with the system. Dialog events can be further broken down into *interface events,* then down to fine details such as "Click save on portfolio."

Events also can be classified by their sources of generation or occurrence. This creates four event groups:

- *User interaction* events
- *Temporal* events
- *Error notification* events
- *Change of state* notifications.

User interaction events are the most easily identified. They are the most physically apparent activities that result from human gestures to the system. These gestures express human intentions (what the user had in mind) and are manifest as input from a keyboard or a click of a mouse button.

Temporal events are related to time. For example, a month-end cycle is a temporal event. This may be a fixed or logical day. For example, a company may use the last Friday of the month as a date for month-end closing. However, when a Friday is a holiday, the logical closing date is the previous working day. When this day is reached, an event will be generated. Consider an automated monthly business report that is electronically mailed to a user. A temporal event, reaching the end of the month, triggers the report generation. Without any user action, the user's mailbox now contains the report.

To illustrate the relationship between events and error handling, let's consider that the user's mailbox is full. When the report is mailed to the user, an *error notification* event is generated by the electronic mail system signifying the mailbox's condition, and the report delivery is now tied to the state of the mailbox.

The user then empties the mailbox, changing its state from full to empty. Its visual representation on the screen changes from the full to empty state upon receiving the user interaction event. A *change of state* event, generated by the mailbox being emptied, is noticed by the report waiting for the mailbox. The report is now put into the user's mailbox. The mailbox changes its visual representation to indicate that there is mail in the in-box. Another example is a "trash can," which — when filled with discarded material — can change appearance to become an overflowing trash can icon. When emptied, the icon returns to a neat, closed can. The trash can icon changes its appearance because of changes of state announced by events. This example illustrates the use of events to synchronize objects that represent real world concepts with icons that present one of their aspects (e.g., full/empty).

When an event occurs, it is detected by an object which, in turn, may send a message to one or more objects. The processing of these messages may generate more events. A *message* is a communication containing information, broadcast by a sender to a receiver. *The message content is the event information.*

Each message can be broadcast openly or to a specific destination. Furthermore, the destination (also known as a recipient) can be abstract — (To: Billing Department, The Electric Company); concrete — (To: Cathy Jones); or even unknown — (To: All Subscribers). Similarly, a message can be addressed without precisely identifying the recipient. The recipient could be another object, a group of objects, another object-oriented information system, or an external system such as a legacy system. The receiving system is tasked with determining which specific object(s) needs to receive the message. The destination is defined by the system providing the service, relieving the sender of that duty. For example, the Electric Company receives our payment. It is the responsibility of the Electric Company to route it to a specific clerk for processing. On the other hand, messages posted on a public bulletin board are routed to and read by many unknown or non-specific people.

The receiving system can use header information or contents of the message to route the message to the correct object. In certain cases, the abstract recipient can be a legacy information system encapsulated by an object wrapper. For all other cases, usually at a micro level, the messages are addressed to a specific recipient. However, there are cases where the receiver is anonymous or unknown. Events that cause such messages to be generated are usually "Published," and interested objects "Subscribe" to receive the messages. In such cases, the sender does not know the recipients, nor does it even know if any object is interested. For example, software tool integration works with *publish* and *subscribe* events, and is discussed later.

Synchronous and Asynchronous Messaging

A standard CORBA (Common Object Request Broker Architecture) request results in the synchronous execution of an operation by the responding object. When a request is directed to a particular object for service, both the requester and the server must be available. If the request fails because the server is unavailable, the requester receives an exception and must take some appropriate action. This model, while otherwise easy to implement, makes concurrent computing difficult to implement. Gul Agha,[3] author of *Actors: A Model of Concurrent Computation in Distributed Systems,* states that there is no tangible evidence that such a model makes building a system simpler. Serialization is often introduced into problems that are, by their nature, parallel.

Using an asynchronous messaging approach, the *event services,* specified in the COSS standard, decouple objects while they exchange event information. *Asynchronous messaging* eliminates the need for the recipient to be available when the requester is trying to communicate with it. Event-driven business applications must be properly modeled for parallel task execution using asynchronous communication.

What is Synchronous Message Communication?

In the paradigm of synchronous communication, the receiving object must be ready to communicate with the sending object at all times. When the receiver is

> *Asynchronous messaging eliminates the need for the recipient to be available when the requester is trying to communicate with it.*

not ready to accept messages because of processing limits or other problems, an exception is raised and the sender must take some appropriate action. A telephone conversation between two people is an example of synchronous message communication. The caller makes a call, the recipient answers, and synchronous communication begins. If the receiver is not available, an exception occurs, and the caller tries repeatedly or simply gives up. The result is lost productive time. To quote Alice, "I think you might do something better with the time."

Assuming the receiver is always ready to accept messages, the sender still must get the attention of the recipient. The ringing of the phone prior to the parties conversing illustrates the *intent to communicate* prior to the occurrence of synchronous communication. A disadvantage of synchronous messaging is the required task of getting the attention of the recipient just to start communication. In addition, the attention of both sender and receiver must be maintained for the duration of message exchange. This attention is required to preserve message integrity.

Synchronous messaging implies the need for a *communications monitor* to detect exceptions and inform the sender of any errors that occur. For example, the telephone network monitors calls. If the network monitor detects an off-hook state for the recipient's phone, the network — not the recipient's telephone —

informs the caller with a busy signal.

Gul Agha states that synchronous communication is a restricted case of buffered asynchronous communication. If messages are generated by the sender at a rate faster than the recipient can process them, a buffering mechanism becomes a necessity for reliable and guaranteed transmission. In effect, this becomes a special case of asynchronous communication.

Synchronous systems are most often controlled by a global synchronizer monitoring each of the elements in the system. Each element carries out one step at a time and communicates with the global synchronizer before each step. All elements perform some predetermined number of actions, report to the global synchronizer, and wait for another "go" message from the global synchronizer before proceeding. This creates a bottleneck that can be extremely inefficient in the context of a distributed environment.

Synchronous paradigms apply to computer programming as well as to messaging schemes. Sequential programming, as a way of problem-solving, is ingrained in today's programmers: Increment the program counter — i.e., execute instruction at the current location — somewhat like a train running between two predetermined locations. Unfortunately, this mindset of a single thread of control has been carried over to the

Asynchronous message communication provides the capability for objects to send messages reliably, even without the existence of the receiving object at the instant the message is sent. The receiving object can retrieve messages at its convenience.

design of message communication systems, and productive time can be lost if each activity must wait for its turn in a sequential flow. Thus, if we can add the capability of parallel messaging and processing to the synchronous approach, we can design computer systems that can exploit slack time to optimize productivity.

What is Asynchronous Message Communication?

Asynchronous message communication provides the capability for objects to send messages reliably, even without the existence of the receiving object at the instant the message is sent. The receiving object can retrieve messages at its convenience. There is no blocking or synchronization required between objects. Asynchronous message communication is a foundation for constructing concurrent computing environments.

When communication between objects is asynchronous in nature, it is possible and perfectly acceptable that the recipient *not* be ready to accept a message when the transmission occurs. A telephone conversation between two parties requires a caller and a recipient. The need for the recipient to be available and receive the call is eliminated if a telephone answering machine is used. The caller leaves a message and the recipient listens to it later.

What if the receiver is on the phone when another caller wants to communicate? The answering machine is unable to take a message if the line is busy. The caller must call again and talk to the recipient or leave a message on the answering machine. Normally, this results in a lost or severely delayed message. Today, with the advent of electronic PBX voice mail systems, callers have the ability to leave a message even when the line is busy. Asynchronous message communication is similar.

Let's look at a business example. Extending the "Investor buys stock" scenario presented earlier, the investor calls a stock broker and places standing orders for buying and selling stocks. In the event that prices fall to the desired level, the broker buys stocks. When a particular stock climbs to a certain price, it is sold. The buy and sell orders can be canceled at any time, provided they have not already been executed. The orders can also be modified before execution. The message flow between the investor and the broker is asynchronous. The investor goes ahead with his daily routine without waiting for the orders to be processed. Information about the orders can be sent by the broker upon execution if requested by the investor, or by way of a monthly statement.

A modern software development environment provides a third example of asynchronous messaging. The environment might have an editor, a version control facility, a compiler, a project management tool, a case tool, and a source code browser. All of these tools are distinctly separate entities that can work in virtual isolation. When the source code is modified, however, the editor notifies the version control facility. Suppose the browser and the case tool have issued requests to be notified of changes to the source code. The browser now refreshes its contents and the case tool might invoke a compiler. If errors occur, the workbench is informed, and the editor highlights the offending sections.

In the preceding example, message transmission can be pushed by *senders* or pulled by *requesters*. The model in which senders initiate message transfers is referred to as a "Push" model (*Common Object Services Specification*, OMG[4]). In the "Pull" model, the receiver requests messages from the sender.

In the previous telephone example, things would change if we introduced a PBX voice mail system. For example, the voice mail system can indicate waiting messages by a different dial tone, a flashing light on the telephone, or even a small message screen. When the recipient is ready to listen to the messages, the phone mail system plays them back. In this way, the recipient "pulls" the messages.

In the "Investor buys stock" example, the broker sends notification that the trades were executed and that the portfolio has been updated. The broker does this by mailing a statement to the investor when the trades have been made. The broker "pushes" the messages. In these and other examples, we have message senders and receivers that we want to be decoupled. In addition, we want multiple senders to communicate with multiple receivers asynchronously. In order to accomplish these objectives, we introduce the concept of a message channel.

What are Message Channels?

To examine the idea of a message channel, let's consider what the newspaper delivery person does for us. Every day, the delivery person places a newspaper on our door step that contains information about events and occurrences around the globe. The delivery person can be considered an intermediate object acting as a message channel, and the messages (information about current events) are contained in the newspaper.

Introducing an intermediate object to act as both receiver and sender completely decouples the real senders and recipients. Senders consider the intermediary to be the recipient. Recipients consider the intermediary to be the sender. This intermediate object allows multiple senders and receivers to communicate asynchronously. Introducing intermediate objects allows localization of message filtering. If complex events require building a notification tree, the intermediate object provides a ready mechanism. In OMG terms, this intermediate object is an "event channel." It is the implementation of this object that determines the quality of service and persistence of messages.

Besides decoupling communicating objects, message channels also provide the ability to control the content and the flow of messages. In certain instances, an event message can be required by multiple recipients. To reduce redundant information flow (the same message sent to multiple objects one by one), the sender can deliver one message to the message channel for distribution to multiple recipients.

To take this concept one step further, what if some of the objects needed verbose event information delivered to them while others did not? Unlike in the newspaper analogy in which the carrier has no control over the newspaper's content, in the computer world message content can be controlled by the message channel delivering the message to the recipient.

> *To reduce redundant information flow (the same message sent to multiple objects one by one), the sender can deliver one message to the message channel for distribution to multiple recipients.*

Are Messages Objects?

Because messages carry only event information, they are not truly objects. Intermediate objects (message channels) that accept and deliver messages treat them as data members. This conforms to the OMG definition of event information.

Messaging and Queuing

In order to accomplish their tasks, software components must interact with each other. Traditionally, these interactions were patterned after synchronous procedure calls. Interaction through procedure calls implies that:

- each component waits on the other to complete its task
- both components are present and a connection exists between them.

Messaging and queuing work together to lessen these restrictions. Messaging addresses the waiting aspect; queuing addresses connection availability. When messaging is described, it often implies the presence of queuing.

Messaging provides for asynchronous communication. Requesting a service from another component does not block the requester. If a reply is required, then some form of rendezvous mechanism is used to notify the requester that a response is available. Traditional programming tools impose a serial and synchronous model on tasks that might be inherently parallel. Messaging helps exploit opportunities for parallel processing.

Queuing decouples message senders and receivers so they do not require a direct connection to communicate. Queuing benefits relate more to performance characteristics than to logical expressiveness. The temporary unavailability of a component is hidden from requesters since they do not require a direct connection. Queues are also used for load balancing. Multiple components may be assigned to service requests in a queue to meet overall performance objectives. Service requesters need not be aware of how many server "units" are present in the system.

How Do We Derive Maximum Benefits?

The benefits of asynchronous message communications can be achieved at all levels of granularity. *Environments, models* and *languages* for creating distributed information systems have been available for some time. Still, the market has only recently started to mature. Automated workflow environments are becoming a popular model for work unit organization. Workflow environments demand event-driven computing. Vendors provide products that help implement distributed applications in a concurrent, event-driven environment. In object-oriented environments, examples include Forté, VisualAge, VisualWorks and Distributed Smalltalk.

The actor model, introduced by Carl Hewitt, proposes the use of computational agents or *actors* that can communicate asynchronously with each other. To function correctly, this model requires guaranteed delivery of messages, but makes no assumptions about the order of message arrival.[5, 6] The actor model allows for the order of the message arrival to be arbitrary and entirely unknown. The computing actors map the events they receive into another set of events to be transferred to other actors. The original actors also can specify new behavior for existing actors. Actors can create new actors, which have entirely new behaviors. This ability is an integral part of the model.

Another model, the Real-Time Object-Oriented Modeling (ROOM)[7] method, proposes two techniques for event handling. The *preemptive* technique is synchronous and handles events based on their priority. It suspends the processing of the current events to process any new events with higher priorities. The *run-to-completion* technique queues up events and processes an event to completion before acting on the next event in the queue: It does not interrupt current event processing for a higher priority event. The techniques of this model are especially useful for designing real-time systems.

As a language example, Forté provides asynchronous event support and concurrent task execution. It can transparently deliver messages for events originating in a different part of the system. Forté classifies "business events" as client-to-server, server-to-server, and server-to-client events. Along with the support for business events, it has rich support for exception handling and generic event communication for state changes.

Today, environments, models and languages are available to construct robust event-driven systems. Event-driven systems can more closely represent the true nature of the business activity. With proper design, the benefits of asynchronous message communication can be realized by tying known states to events, without having to constantly monitor these states. For example, every manufacturing shop needs to keep track of inventory. A business event can be tied to reordering inventory. If an inventory item reaches its reorder point, this change of state creates an event that causes a purchase order to be generated. This illustrates how event handling eliminates the need for constant monitoring and, at the same time, ensures that inventory is maintained at required levels.

The benefits from asynchronous message communication do not just happen. Business applications must be *designed* to capture the benefits.

Can Asynchronous Messaging Assist in Workflow Computing?

Business object modeling allows for the clustering of related business activities into work groups patterned after human work groups. Each work group performs a unit of work and thereby adds value needed in an overall work flow. In a workflow model of computing, messages sent between work objects are of the following kinds:

- requests for a unit of work to be performed (task execution)
- information about task completion, or the output of a completed unit of work.

For the enterprise to function effectively as a whole, it must work concurrently, not like an assembly line. The chain of computing should not stop because of one point of delay or failure.

In a distributed object computing environment, appropriate actions need to be taken if a work unit object fails to perform an assigned task. Additional action is needed if the failure of one object affects the ability of several other objects to complete their assigned tasks. These dynamics require highly interactive communication between cooperative business objects. Current transaction models require transactions to be blocked and relatively short. Real business workflows are not this simple.

A situation may arise where several units of work will require hours to complete. Traditional transaction handling systems block the flow of work until the required output from the preceding activity has been committed or rolled back. On the other hand, event-driven workflow applications require a high degree of concurrent processing of transactions.

How can asynchronous communication contribute to the solution? For the enterprise to function effectively as a whole, it must work concurrently, not like an assembly line. The chain of computing should not stop because of one point of delay or failure. Defined procedures for sharing information and protocols for inter-workgroup communications must be established.

Workflow applications can be designed to use concurrent working objects with minimal interdependencies. For example, the implementation of an actor model results in a workflow management system in which business processes have been mapped to objects that communicate via asynchronous messages. This ensures a high degree of freedom and minimal interdependence. An object must be able to continue with its next task without attending to messages sent to other objects or becoming blocked if objects that represent a work unit fail. A degraded mode of operation can be designed to kick in and work around a malfunctioning work unit. A malfunctioning object picks up its messages upon recovery and continues processing. In some cases, the impact could be minimal-to-none if the message communications are reliable. Such events stop computing altogether in an assembly-line style environment.

Let's take the case of a malfunctioning print object. Objects can continue sending requests to a malfunctioning print object, and the message channel will deliver them to the print object when it is ready. The requesting objects simply continue with their other tasks. If these requests were synchronous, then the entire work flow would have been impacted by a nonfunctional printer!

However, this does not mean that asynchronous messaging will alleviate all of the problems of dependency. Sooner or later a workflow of concurrently executing tasks must be synchronized to satisfy the overall goal of the workflow.

Integrating Software Tools with Asynchronous Messages

Providers of software tools have taken advantage of asynchronous message communication to integrate pre-written software packages into higher level tools that work together as a uniform package. The following paragraphs explore offerings from Hewlett-Packard and Sun Microsystems.

HP's Broadcast Message Server

Softbench, an integrated development environment from Hewlett-Packard, provides a mechanism for the easy integration of loosely coupled, commercial off-the-shelf tools (COTS). Messages are exchanged between tools by a server known as the Broadcast Message Server (BMS)[8]. Tools registered with the server inform the server of the tool's operations or event information. These operations are classified as Requests, Notifications or Failures. Messages can contain extended information about the "context" of events.

A tool that is to exchange event information is registered with the server, and the kinds of messages the tool is to receive are specified. It is the responsibility of the BMS to propagate the information to the tools as required.

> *Providers of software tools have taken advantage of asynchronous message communication to integrate pre-written software packages into higher level tools that work together as a uniform package.*

Sun's Tooltalk Service

The Tooltalk Service[9] uses an expressive message protocol and can provide informative messages. Recipients in the communications process can be identified as specific objects or they can be anonymous objects that *subscribe* to the messages. Messages can be requests or replies, and can provide information on the event or the action taken.

The "disposition" feature of the Tooltalk[10] allows the flexibility to start a process if the recipient is not present to receive the messages, or to queue the messages up and then attempt to start a handler process. The Tooltalk service also provides information on the state of the message life-cycle. A message life-cycle is defined as created (but not yet sent), sent (but not yet handled), queued or started (a process is being started to handle the message), and one of the terminal states, such as handled, rejected (message rejected by the handler), and failed (no handler available or all handlers have rejected the message).

Implementation Tactics for Asynchronous Messages

The message delivery mechanism is affected by the frequency, content and length of messages. In addition, object communications can cross machine boundaries as well as occur within one machine. Both of these factors influence the tactics used to implement asynchronous communication mechanisms.

When communications cross machine boundaries, a network-based Inter Process Communication (IPC) is required. A network-based IPC can be implemented using streams and other communication facilities such as APPC from IBM. When message communications occur within the same machine, shared memory can be used for message transport. Asynchronous messaging within a single machine requires multi-threading. Shared memory gives rise to mutual exclusion problems, since memory is a shared resource. Mutual exclusion (Mutex) primitives must be used to preserve the integrity of the memory resource. It is possible to build a memory resource manager as an object that encapsulates mutual exclusion.

Implementations of asynchronous message communications typically utilize both shared memory and network-based inter-process communications. In addition, a facility is required to handle message queues and locate objects.

Conclusion

Event-driven business systems require a message delivery system that supports both synchronous and asynchronous communication. Implementing an effective asynchronous messaging system is crucial for achieving parallelism and cooperative computing. Environments, models and languages are available today for corporations to implement asynchronous message communications for workflow and other cooperative work group applications. However, corporations must gain the knowledge and skills needed for effective design in this advanced environment. And, as Alice would remind us, never forget that *time* is *money*.

References

[1] *Common Object Services Specification*, The Object Management Group, 492 Old Connecticut Path, Framingham, MA 01701, Vol. 1 (March 1994).

[2] Meilir Page-Jones, *Client-Server Developer,* p. 24, SIGS Publications (1994).

[3] Agha, Gul, *ACTORS: A Model of Concurrent Computation in Distributed Systems,* The MIT Press (1987).

[4] *Common Object Services Specification,* The Object Management Group, 492 Old Connecticut Path, Framingham, MA 01701, Vol. 1 (March 1994).

[5] Shriver, Bruce, Peter Wegner, Gul Agha and Carl Hewitt, "Actors: A Conceptual Foundation for Concurrent Object-Oriented Programming," *Research Directions in Object-Oriented Programming,* The MIT Press (1987).

[6] Agha, Gul, *ACTORS: A Model of Concurrent Computation in Distributed Systems,* The MIT Press (1987).

[7] Bran Selic, Gullekson and Paul Ward, "Real-Time Object-Oriented Modeling," John Wiley and Sons, Inc. (1994).

[8] "The H.P. Softbench Environment: An Architecture for a New Generation of Software Tools," *Hewlett-Packard Journal,* pp. 41-43 (June 1990).

[9] *Tooltalk 1.0 Programmer's Guide,* Sun Microsystems, 2550 Garcia Avenue, Mountain View, CA 94043.

[10] *Application Integration with Tooltalk — A Tutorial,* Sun Microsystems, 2550 Garcia Avenue, Mountain View, CA 94043.

Integrated Project Support Environments

By Rahul Narain, Jim Clarke and Donald E. Rimel, Jr.
In collaboration with the Object Technology Staff of The Technical Resource Connection

Contents

Managed evolution is the use of a new product, process or service to spawn an even newer product, process or service. Its motto is "each successful new product is a stepping stone to the next."

Peter F. Drucker
"The 10 Rules of Effective Research"[1]
Managing for the Future: The 1990s and Beyond

Abstract

Every software development manager wants his or her organization to produce a better product. It must be produced faster than the one built yesterday and delivered ahead of the one that the competition is building. Yet most software development projects today lack quantitative measurements for their processes. This hinders the timely delivery of high-quality software products. The lack of accurate and timely information from project environments prohibits organizations from taking corrective actions that can prevent delays, poor quality, mismatched expectations and poorly defined requirements. As a result, software development organizations deliver software products that do not meet user expectations or requirements.

Software development organizations must learn from their successes and failures. Successes should be made repeatable. Processes, or their absence, that led to past failures should be analyzed to prevent their recurrence. Information about what can be done better-faster-cheaper can be extracted from projects executed by the organization and applied to the next product being built. The software development process should be evolutionary and must accurately fulfill dynamic business requirements of today and tomorrow. This cannot happen without process monitoring, analysis and continuous improvements. A suitable framework must be defined to support quality software production.

Integrated Project Support Environments (IPSE) provide the strong structural foundations for building software. An IPSE is an essential part of an organization's technical architecture. An IPSE allows the software development manager to analyze and improve development processes before it is too late.

An IPSE can improve development efficiency, product effectiveness and software processes. An IPSE provides improved information gathering about each development process contributing to the product delivery. With an IPSE, *"... each successful new product is a stepping stone to the next one."*[1]

Why Process Improvement in Business?

The velocity of business change is increasing. Product cycle times are decreasing. Management is under intense pressure to streamline operations, reduce overhead and squeeze more out of production and sales channels in order to maximize shrinking margins. The global marketplace is becoming a strategic battleground as companies reach into all corners of the world to attract new customers.

Significant business reengineering efforts are under way in corporations that have recognized the need for major change. Some companies have undertaken radical change efforts, while others have sought a gentler approach through continuous process improvement. Regardless of the approach, forward-thinking companies are redesigning core business *processes* to gain the competitive advantage. Such companies are becoming smaller and more horizontal as layers between top management and the shop floor worker or sales representative are removed.

Forward-thinking companies are redesigning core business processes to gain the competitive advantage.

Radical or Continuous Process Improvements

Regardless of approach, companies wanting to survive are looking at their business from a process perspective. Some companies have taken radical approaches to business process improvement. The radical approach is articulated by Michael Hammer and James Champy in their widely read book, "Reengineering the Corporation."[2] This radical approach to business process improvement is often referred to as business process reengineering (BPR). The themes are "don't automate, obliterate" and that traditional *functional management* should be transformed to *process management.* Other recognized authorities on business management recommend less disruptive strategies to process improvement. Thomas Davenport places both approaches in perspective in his widely acclaimed work, "Process Innovation."[3]

Roots in the Quality Movement

Every organization has fundamental business processes. The processes may not be visible, but they exist just the same. Process-focused thinking grew out of the total quality movement. When Dr. W. Edwards Deming, father of total quality management, pronounced that the improvement of quality is 90 percent centered on the system, on processes, the bell tolled for the business world. Those companies that have transitioned to process management essentially have adopted a view of the business that makes processes clearly visible. Some companies reject the notion of process management and maintain a functional management view. However, they are just as much driven by processes.

A Shift in Focus

What is a business process? Simply stated, *a business process is a series of steps or activities that produce a product or service.* What's so radical about that? According to Davenport, "Adopting a process view of the business represents a revolutionary change in perspective: It amounts to turning the organization on its head, or at least on its side. A process orientation to business involves elements of structure, focus, measurement, ownership and customers. It implies a strong emphasis on *how* work is done within an organization, in contrast to a product focus' emphasis on *what*."

One way a business can make processes visible is the use of workflow automation. Workflow is the structured flow of information through a series of well-defined steps of a business process. In a workflow, tasks are performed on elements of the information. Workflow provides a picture of how processes are used and by whom. Since the processes are made fully visible, measurements can be developed for them. These measurements become the foundation for process improvement.

IS organizations are tasked not only with automating business processes, but also with providing leadership in business process improvement. Successful companies recognize that processes of the business need to be improved continuously, whether through planned reengineering efforts or as a fundamental part of the company's culture.

Is Software Development Different?

The critical challenge facing today's IS organizations is to provide leadership in business process improvement. While assisting the larger business organizations with redesign of core processes, what has the IS organization done to make visible and improve its own core processes? Why is the software development process any different from other business processes? In many ways, it is not.

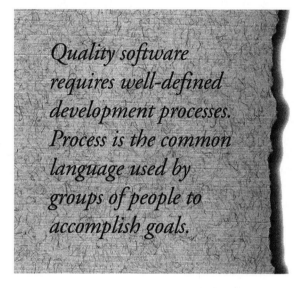

Quality software requires well-defined development processes. Process is the common language used by groups of people to accomplish goals.

workflow, software might be installed before being tested. Workflow for software development identifies the same who, what, where, when and why as business workflows.

Quality software requires well-defined development processes. *Process* is the common language used by groups of people to accomplish goals. A group of people function together as a team when process is defined. *Process* increases the group's efficiency and effectiveness, thereby positively impacting cost and quality.

Software development requires effective processes to complete tasks just as other business workflows do. Unlike workflows that create products, software development workflows are not tangible. So it is even more important for software development processes to be visible if they are to be improved.

Workflow defines the interaction and cooperation among processes. Workflow provides the who, what, where, when and why of processes. Processes developed without workflow have a high risk of not enabling all the required tasks to be accomplished. For example, consider a simple accounting system that includes receiving inventory, accounts payable and general ledger. The financial picture of a company can be misstated if the accounting workflow is not defined. The interaction of the receiving process with the accounts payable process could result in duplicate payments, erroneous encumbrances and an inaccurate general ledger. Software development can have similar problems. For example, without a properly designed

The accounting profession, for example, uses standard processes to ensure common communication and representation of information. Generally Accepted Accounting Principles (GAAP) and the Financial Accounting Standards Board (FASB) provide frameworks for accounting. GAAP and FASB create common visible abstractions of accounting that are used by business. These common abstractions allow the business to hire accountants who already understand the accounting principles being used by the company. This standardization reduces the cost of training new personnel. Risk is reduced because all the accountants in a company use the same processes. Communication improves through the use of common principles.

Similarly, the Software Engineering Institute (SEI) and the International Organization for Standardization (commonly referred to as ISO) provide frameworks for software development. Software development standards can provide benefits similar to accounting standards for software development organizations. However, the focus of the SEI and ISO standards is on the software development *process* rather than proposing a *standard* development method. Process improvement is the goal.

A defined software development process provides a foundation for reliability and reduction of cost. Reliability is important in reducing the costs of maintenance and support. Since the costs of maintenance and support are greater than the cost to develop software, reducing these costs can have a greater business impact than reducing initial development costs.

Perhaps because development enjoys higher visibility, many firms have concentrated on reducing development costs. Reuse of the artifacts of development—the deliverables of the software development process—can reduce the time and cost of a software product's creation. Artifacts include the requirements specification, analysis, design, code, test plans and documentation. Reuse is commonly referred to as code reuse. However, program code is only one of the artifacts of software development.

Reusing requirements, analysis and design artifacts can provide greater impact on cost and quality than code reuse. The reuse of one analysis artifact can reduce the analysis phase of many other projects. A significant benefit of reusing software development artifacts is a subsequent reduction of the cost of development. These savings can offset additional testing and research, thereby impacting reliability. Increased reliability reduces the maintenance and support costs. Indeed, the arguments for reuse are so compelling that reuse is often considered the holy grail of software development.

Reliability can be attained through the deployment of quality assurance and configuration management processes. Quality assurance processes reduce the number of defects through testing and reviews. Configuration management increases reliability through processes that guarantee the consistency of the code. Only tested and approved changes are applied to the baseline, ensuring that each programmer's work is consistent with that of all the other programmers.

Reuse of software development artifacts can be achieved through effective configuration management processes, which can be applied to all of the software development artifacts including program code. An Integrated Project Support Environment (IPSE) provides a secure repository for software artifacts and design documents that can be used with other projects.

A Software Assembly Plant

A software organization can emulate a product assembly plant. It can produce high-quality products at a low cost by adhering to process management and improvement models specifically designed for software development organizations. As such, a software assembly plant should:

- leverage state-of-the-art technology
- adapt to industry changes
- provide for low component failure
- maintain just-in-time component inventory
- leverage the existing technology infrastructure.

A software organization can emulate a product assembly plant. It can produce high-quality products at a low cost by adhering to process management and improvement models.

specific needs. An IPSE provides the framework to monitor and control a software assembly plant.

Well-defined software development processes and an IPSE allow a software development team to adapt faster to industry change without suffering reduced quality. An IPSE helps ensure that the appropriate processes are being accomplished and associated metrics recorded.

By providing a mechanism to validate and monitor software development processes, an IPSE can lower component failures. For example, if milestones are required throughout a process, they cannot be ignored, which reduces a natural human tendency to abandon established processes when faced with a crisis.

Software development organizations often focus on leveraging state-of-the-art technology. Unfortunately, technology advertised as leading edge is often actually bleeding edge. Until a so-called leading edge technology is successfully employed in its intended role by at least one firm, it remains bleeding edge. Leveraging state-of-the-art technology implies the use of the most up-to-date tools to reduce costs, time to market and risk. If a claimed state-of-the-art technology cannot be backed up by real world implementations, corporations should be leery. Businesses should not be enamored with technology for technology's sake.

In emulating a product assembly plant, a software assembly plant uses the same principles, adapted to its

An IPSE also provides a framework for just-in-time component inventory. A key factor in a just-in-time inventory environment is knowing when the next component is required, and a tightly coupled IPSE updates the project plan as work on components is started, modified and completed.

The use of an existing technology infrastructure is maximized by an IPSE, which uses all the components of the infrastructure during software development. The metrics captured by an IPSE document infrastructure use.

The Business Value of an IPSE

In the work *The Cultural Dimensions of Technology-Enabled Corporate Trans-formations,* cultural anthropologist Marietta Baba and her colleagues suggest that successful reengineering of basic business processes requires application of the *science of culture.* These researchers maintain that "Many American corporations tend to view information technology as a solution to their business process integration problems without recognizing that processes are fundamentally human phenomena. Unfortunately, an investment in information technology does not guarantee automatic redesign, or its benefits.

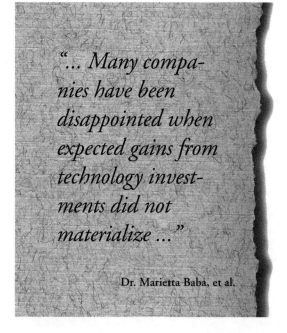

"... Many companies have been disappointed when expected gains from technology investments did not materialize ..."

Dr. Marietta Baba, et al.

"Many companies have been disappointed when expected gains from technology investments did not materialize. While there is considerable debate concerning the causes of these limitations, few dispute the conclusion that such poor returns from investments of such great magnitude represents a serious and worrisome problem. Among the hypotheses advanced to explain disappointing results from technology investment, one that is gaining widespread acceptance is the argument that information technology is only an enabler; as an enabler, it cannot achieve process improvement on its own." [4]

Continuous software process improvement (SPI) is the key to realizing returns on technology investments. For example, investing in object-oriented technology will

not yield the desired results if an IPSE and continuous process improvement are not applied. Software process improvement programs have been implemented by quality and cost-conscious organizations around the world. To make process improvements, however, the current state of affairs must first be assessed.

James Herbsleb and his colleagues[5] documented such assessments for SEI. They also documented cases where management is reluctant to commit resources without any data to support a business case. The Herbsleb survey identified thirteen organizations that represented varying levels of sophistication in process management. The application areas included domains such as telecommunications, embedded real-time systems, information systems and operating systems. The results of the study clearly indicate that potential gains can be produced in the following areas:

- cost of process improvement
- productivity
- calendar time
- quality
- business value (Return on Investment).

The results are shown in Table 1 on the following page.

Opinions differ as to whether productivity gains and early detection of errant processes are by themselves sufficient criteria for investing in process improvements. Most agree, however, that reducing the time needed to produce a quality software product, and hence a reduction in the time needed to bring a product to market, is reason enough to justify investing in process improvement. The study further demonstrates the benefits of process conformance, which are reflected in lower post-release defect reports. An IPSE provides the mechanism for process conformance.

	Category	Range	Median
1	Total Yearly cost of SPI activities	$49,000 - $1,202,000	$245,000
2	Years engaged in SPI	1-9	3.5
3	Cost of SPI per software engineer	$490 - $2004	$1375
4	Productivity gain per year	9% - 67%	35%
5	Early detection gain per year	6% - 25%	22%
6	Yearly reduction in time to market	15% - 23%	19%
7	Yearly reduction in post-release defects reports	10% - 94%	39%
8	Return on Investment	4.0 - 8.8	5.0

Table 1
Results from the 1994 Herbsleb Study

Process Models

A software process model represents the software development tasks required to implement a business solution. Each process model emphasizes continuous process improvement for the software organization to achieve the creation of high-quality products. A repeatable and measurable process model can help improve software quality.

A process model breaks down the software development process into a collection of tasks. Subprocesses focus on analysis, design, implementation, testing and documentation. Software measures or metrics gathered from the subprocesses can be used to drive process improvement.

Two software process models are provided by the Software Engineering Institute and the International Organization for Standardization.

The Software Engineering Institute

The Software Engineering Institute at Carnegie Mellon University has developed a Capability Maturity Model[6] (CMM) for software development, which focuses on the

Level	Description
1. Initial	The organization has no or few defined processes in place. This level could also be referred to as ad hoc. At this level, software development is often chaotic.
2. Repeatable	Basic project management processes are established to track costs, schedules and functionality. The organization can control the establishment of its plans and commitments. Software development process is defined and repeatable.
3. Defined	The organization has integrated both engineering and management into standardized software processes. The foundation has been established for continuing process improvement.
4. Managed	The organization collects detailed measures of software process and product quality. Software processes and products are quantitatively understood and controlled. Proactive process design and problem-solving are based upon measurements.
5. Optimizing	Continuous process improvement is provided by quantitative feedback from the process. Note that eventually optimization can only come from piloting new technologies and innovative ideas. These are integral processes at this level of maturity.

Table 2
The Capability Maturity Model

concerns of software quality and the importance of process management within the software development process. The CMM identifies five levels that define the state of maturity in "Key Process Areas" of a software organization. These levels are summarized in Table 2.

An Integrated Project Support Environment includes the key processes of "Integrated Software Management" found at maturity level 3. "The purpose of Integrated Software Management is to integrate the software engineering and management activities into a coherent, defined software process that is tailored from the organization's standard software process and related process assets."[7]

ISO 9000

The International Organization for Standards in Geneva has issued several quality standards. ISO 9000 provides guidelines for the selection and use of a series of standards on quality systems. The ISO 9001 specification, "Quality systems — Model for quality assurance in design/development, production, installation and servicing," describes 20 ingredients necessary to produce a quality system.[8]

A tightly coupled IPSE supports 12 of the 20 ingredients of the ISO 9001 as shown in Table 3. These 12 are the repeatable processes that can be automated.

IPSE Support	ISO 9001 Ingredient	IPSE Support	ISO 9001 Ingredient
	Management responsibility.	X	Quality system.
	Contract review.	X	Design control.
X	Document control.		Purchasing.
	Purchaser supplied control.	X	Product identification & traceability.
X	Process control.	X	Quality records.
	Internal quality audits.		Training.
	Servicing.		Inspection testing.
X	Inspection, measuring & test equipment.	X	Inspection & test status.
X	Control of non-conforming product.	X	Corrective action.
X	Handling, storage, packaging & delivery.	X	Statistical techniques.

Table 3
The ISO 9001 Specification

Other Process Models

Other process models are available for adoption by software development organizations. The "IEEE Standard for Developing Software Life-Cycle Processes"[9] provides a set of processes and activities that are required to develop and maintain software. The military standard, *Defense System Software Development,* "MIL-STD 498,"[10] also specifies the processes required for software development.

The process models for software development provide the foundation for developing an Integrated Project Support Environment, which ensures conformance with the standards contained in the process models.

An Overview of an Integrated Project Support Environment

The business world, seeking tangible financial benefits, strives for perfection in product quality. But today, quality alone will not make the product attractive to the consumer. It must also be cost-effective and cater to the consumer's specific needs. For a software organization, like any other manufacturing organization, these issues essentially boil down to better, cheaper, faster software products filling the immediate and future needs of the consumer.

The environment allows a project's defined software processes to mirror the organization's standard processes.

With an IPSE, software organizations can realize the benefits from process management. The support environment integrates the people in a software development organization with the development process. IPSEs provide an integrated set of tools and components to support all phases of the software organization's processes. An IPSE deals directly with tools in a heterogeneous environment. The environment allows a project's defined software processes to mirror the organization's standard processes. Thus a project can be planned and managed according to the organization's defined processes and goals. An IPSE should be designed to be process-oriented and vendor-independent. A successful IPSE implementation should allow tool changes with little or no impact to the developer while preserving the structure and interaction of the process areas.

Problems arise when improper processes are introduced into an organization. Problems can also result from adhering to processes that have decayed over time or have simply outlived their usefulness. These problems can be identified through their associated symptoms, which — in the domain of software organizations — manifest themselves as increased costs and delayed deliverables. Incorrect software functionality can be measured by an adverse impact that increases costs and delays delivery schedules. However, costs attributed to lost opportunities from delayed implementation and from "bugs" or errors in the software can remain hidden. By building an IPSE, software organizations can implement and track the necessary processes and tools to avoid these adverse effects. In addition, the hidden costs associated with delayed deliverables can be monitored by the IPSE.

As the framework for control in the software development process, an IPSE should provide the following components and capabilities:

> *Quality Assurance* — The IPSE can include tools to build and execute test suites against common components and new applications. The test suites can be managed via configuration management to provide automatic

regression testing as software or hardware changes are made. Additionally, tools can be integrated into an IPSE to parse and analyze code and insert run time checking and monitoring routines. These routines look for and identify common coding errors, run time errors and potential coding practices violations. Quality assurance standards define the measurement criteria to be used by other components of the IPSE that accomplish tasks (project management, CASE, tools and environment, and common services).

Metrics — As part of the code "check-in" process and overall configuration management, an IPSE can utilize software to calculate metrics associated with the code, such as function points and McCabe complexity indices[11] (see Caper Jones' book in Suggested Readings). Metrics provide the feedback needed to determine how well quality assurance criteria are being met.

Project Management and Estimation — An IPSE can provide common tools for tracking and managing software development projects. Metrics supplied by an IPSE can assist managers in the development of project plans and estimates. Integration with the CASE components and repository of reusable objects can make it possible to automate some of the management process (see Watts S. Humphrey's books in Suggested Readings).

CASE Tools — One or more CASE tools can be selected, implemented and integrated to provide analysis, design and code generation capabilities. Further, a CASE repository can contain reusable classes for use throughout projects, along with a capability for locating and incorporating the pre-developed classes into new application designs. A CASE tool should be carefully evaluated and selected to support the analysis and design method chosen for development.

Development Tools and Environment — Compilers, class and application assemblers, frameworks, debuggers and class browsers can be included as part of an IPSE. They can provide developers with a complete environment for assembling object-based applications using the common class libraries, common services and their in-house developed classes. The goal is to seamlessly integrate the development environment with other components of an IPSE.

Configuration Management — Tools included with an IPSE, either developed or purchased, can manage the software development life cycle, providing version and release control, assuring that all quality assurance is executed and that all automated standards reviews are completed. In addition, configuration management can be the vehicle for software distribution, assuring that the correct versions and releases are distributed for production. Configuration management is used to synchronize other components of the IPSE that are used to accomplish tasks (project management, CASE, tools and environment, and common services).

Common Services — Classes provided within the common class libraries can take advantage of common services developed as part of an IPSE. These common services include such things as standard Error, Help and support interfaces to network and systems management software, and object distribution and management services.

IPSE components and their relationships are shown in Figure 1.

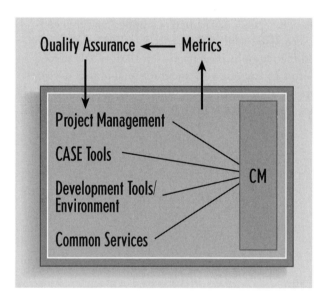

Figure 1
Components of an IPSE and Their Relationships

An IPSE can notify the appropriate members of the software development organization when quality assurance activities are required and provide metrics for quality assurance activities. Process automation reduces the risk of excluding these vital software development processes.

The automated processes, configuration management and quality assurance components that are incorporated in an IPSE provide control to the project manager. Process is *enforced* and information is provided to the project manager in a consistent and timely fashion.

A Weak IPSE

A weak IPSE results from selecting tool sets for their specific functionality and not their ability to be integrated. A project manager typically selects the project management tools, an analyst selects the CASE tools, developers select the development tools, and the configuration manager selects the configuration management tools.

The typical messaging system used in a weak IPSE is paper. The project manager creates the project plan for the rest of the team. The analyst uses CASE tools to generate designs and posts them for viewing. The developers use the designs and create the product. The configuration manager is informed when the software is ready to be checked in with the check-in document. Metrics may or may not be captured using the paper messaging.

Some software development organizations have integrated their tools without creating a true IPSE. Such systems point the user to the appropriate tool instead of bringing the tool to the user. Such environments still require the user to provide information when certain tasks have been completed. The metrics from this type of environment are typically incomplete or inaccurate, and contribute little to effective project management or process improvement.

A Strong IPSE

A strong, or tightly coupled IPSE, brings the appropriate tool to the user. The configuration management rules are applied to any activity that is being done within the framework of the IPSE. This means the prerequisites are checked before a subprocess is started and requisites are checked before a subprocess is completed.

Since a strong IPSE is integrated, metrics are systematically captured. These metrics can be used to monitor the work-in-progress and to foster process improvement. The weak IPSE can capture the same kinds of information but the metrics cannot be guaranteed. Metrics are not guaranteed in the weak IPSE because they require the user to provide information manually, and stated configuration management rules might be bypassed.

A Simple IPSE Example

A simple example of an IPSE is the Emacs editor. Although Emacs does not capture metrics, this example is presented to illustrate tool integration. Emacs is an editor that was originally developed for the DEC PDP-10. Today, it is a popular editor for UNIX systems. The Emacs editor supports access to e-mail, compilers and source code control.

Most traditional editors perform the single task of editing. The additional tasks of e-mail, compiling and source code control require that the tasks be started from outside the editor. The common method of developing a program is to edit, compile and test. The integration of the tools in Emacs allows the developer to edit code and compile from the editor. Emacs also uses the source code control system (SCCS) for configuration management. Traditional editors require an additional step to use SCCS.

Emacs is an example of a software development process that was improved by integrating tools. The developer became more productive because work occurs inside one environment and the developer was no longer required to start other processes outside that environment. Emacs was not originally developed as an IPSE, but evolved over time to simplify the program development process.

Summary of Software Process Models and IPSE

A variety of software development life cycle models, methods and tools support software process models. For example, a project manager may use Microsoft Project or Project Workbench for project tracking. A CASE tool may provide support for analysis and design. A C++ or Smalltalk compiler can produce executables, while PVCS, SCCS or RCS might provide configuration management. An IPSE ties these tools into a coherent environment for total project development. Integration varies from weakly coupled to tightly coupled sets of support tools.

Integration and Tool Set Options

An IPSE needs to be extensible to keep pace with the continual improvement of software development processes. The integration of the tools does not start from scratch. Products like Pure Software's PureDDTS provides a foundation for creating an IPSE, providing the documentation of the software development processes and configuration management. Since it is an extensible product, it can be modified to keep up with software development process improvement.

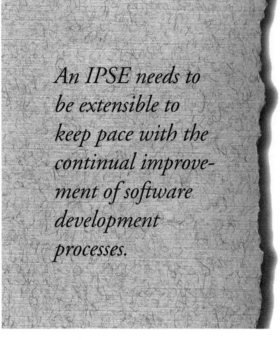

An IPSE needs to be extensible to keep pace with the continual improvement of software development processes.

ments (PCDE). "A Process-Centered Environment (PCE) is a software specification that includes the facilities of a Process-Centered Framework (PCF), as well as application tools. Examples of applications that these tools may support are: metrics collection, project management and software development. A PCF provides the functionality necessary for the definition and enactment of a process. It includes a process enactment language, mechanisms for process enactment, a means to invoke tools, support for communications (between persons and tools) and capabilities to support the debugging process

Some organizations require tool integration facilities, as opposed to a single-tool or a suite of tools. With tool integration services, project tools from different vendors become plug-and-play solutions. If an organization has certain requirements that cannot be met with existing tools, the organization can build its own. Sun Microsystems' Tooltalk and Hewlett-Packard's Broadcast Message Server (BMS) are tool integration services for software development environments.

Emerging Environments

As software development organizations recognize and adopt process-centered environments, these environments will mature and evolve. The Software Engineering Institute is currently conducting research in advanced Process-Centered Development Environ-

models described within the process enactment language."[12] Some vendors have already provided support for PCFs. These products include Life*Flow from Computer Resources International A/S, Process Engineer from LBMS and ProcessWeaver from Cap Gemini America.

PCD provides more than a framework for integrating project management, configuration management and development tools. "Automation of the process includes, but is not limited to, providing software organizations with appropriate tools to perform specific tasks, relieving developers and managers of as much tedium as possible, eliminating error-prone activities and guiding process-critical tasks."[13]

How to Get There from Here

Moving an organization from chaos to a managed process (SEI level 4) cannot be done in one giant leap. The organization and people need to improve step by step. The organization needs to have basic project management processes established. Once these processes are in place, software development processes can be defined and implemented. At this point, an IPSE can be introduced into an organization.

An IPSE provides the foundation for moving an organization from a repeatable (SEI level 2) to a defined (SEI level 3) process level. The integrated software development tools provide the developer with a process for development and a means to gather metrics for the project planning processes. These metrics can be used to improve development processes.

An IPSE is not an absolute guarantee for achieving SEI level 3. However, without an IPSE, the development process can be more work intensive, and the quality of metrics is at risk. Further, the flow of information back to the project planning processes may not be timely.

To create an IPSE, the following steps are required:

- Establish project planning processes. Make sure these processes include scheduling and cost tracking.

- Define the software development process.

- Identify the software development tools with integration capabilities.

- Make a "build or buy" decision for the IPSE.

- Implement the organization's software development processes into the IPSE.

- Provide IPSE training to the members of the software development team.

The definition of an organization's software development processes are key to defining a pertinent IPSE. The IPSE needs to reflect the specific software development processes of an organization. The fundamental software development processes of requirements specification, analysis, design, implementation and testing are part of the software development process. Specific methods and tools will define the requirements of the IPSE.

Should the software development organization build or buy an IPSE? The build or buy decision is often a difficult one. If a software development organization does neither, however, development efforts will probably never mature beyond SEI's level 2, repeatable processes.

> *Moving an organization from chaos to a managed process (SEI level 4) cannot be done in one giant leap. The organization and people need to improve step by step.*

Conclusion

*P*rocess management is the key to the future for both business and software development organizations. A software development organization should define, implement and automate development processes. This is not a technical decision, but a business decision based on the return-on-investment from the processes being implemented. Progressing along SEI's CMM levels depends on the implementation of project management and quality software development processes. The efficiency and effectiveness of the software development organization improves with each CMM level.

Organizations should adopt a software process model for software development. An IPSE is critical for adopting the SEI CMM, ISO 9000, IEEE and MIL-STD 498 models.

An IPSE provides the framework for automating the key software development processes. Metrics for process improvement are provided by an IPSE. Management can be better informed with timely and meaningful project information. Quality and configuration management can be incorporated in an IPSE, improving the productivity of developers. An IPSE is a necessity for a mature software development environment.

Integrated software development tools in an IPSE will reduce development, maintenance and support costs. The product will be developed in a shorter time and have fewer defects because of quality assurance and configuration management processes. The business justification for an IPSE is faster, cheaper and better production. In software development, faster, cheaper and better directly affect the bottom line of the business.

References

[1] Drucker, Peter F., *"Managing for the Future: The 1990s and Beyond,"* Butterworth-Heinemann Limited, Oxford, U.K. (1992).

[2] Hammer, Michael and James Champy, *Reengineering the Corporation: A Manifesto for Business Revolution,* Harper Business (1993).

[3] Davenport, Thomas H., *Process Innovation: Reengineering Work through Information Technology,* Harvard Business School Press (1993).

[4] Baba, Marietta, D. Falkenberg and D. Hill, "The Cultural Dimensions of Technology-Enabled Corporate Transformations," research paper (March 28, 1994). Published in *Technological Innovations and Cultural Processes: New Theoretical Perspectives,* edited by Santos, M. Josefa and R. Diaz Cruz, National University of Mexico, Mexico, D.F. (1994).

[5] Herbsleb, J., A. Carleton, J. Rozum, J. Siege and D. Zubrow, *Benefits of CMM-Based Software Process,* CMU/SEI-94-TR-13, Software Engineering Institute, Carnegie Mellon University, Pittsburgh, PA (March 1994).

[6] Paulk, Mark C., Charles V. Weber, Suzanne M. Garcia, Mary Beth Chrissis and Marilyn Bush, *Key Practices of the Capability Maturity Model, Version 1.1.* CMU/SEI-93-TR-25, Software Engineering Institute, Carnegie Mellon University, Pittsburgh, PA (February 1993).

[7] Paulk, Mark C., Charles V. Weber, Suzanne M. Garcia, Mary Beth Chrissis and Marilyn Bush, *Key Practices of the Capability Maturity Model, Version 1.1.* CMU/SEI-93-TR-25, Software Engineering Institute, Carnegie Mellon University, Pittsburgh, PA (February 1993).

[8] Van Vilet, Hans, *Software Engineering Principles and Practice*, John Wiley & Sons LTD, p. 81, West Sussex, England (1993).

[9] IEEE (1993), IEEE Std 1074-1991, *IEEE Standard for Developing Software Life-Cycle Processes.*

[10] Military Standard *Software Development and Documentation*, MIL-STD 498 (December 5, 1994).

[11] Jones, Caper, *Applied Software Measurement,* McGraw Hill (1991).

[12] Christie, Alan M., *A Practical Guide to Technology and Adoption of Software Process Automation,* Appendix D, p. 110, CMU/SEI-94-TR-007, Software Engineering Institute, Carnegie Mellon University, Pittsburgh, PA (March 1994).

[13] Christie, Alan M., *Process-Centered Development Environments: An Exploration of Issues,* p. 1, CMU/SEI-93-TR-4, Software Engineering Institute, Carnegie Mellon University, Pittsburgh, PA (June 1992).

Suggested Readings

Reference Model for Project Support Environments (Version 2.0), CMU/SEI-93-TR-23 ADA275169, Software Engineering Institute, Carnegie Mellon University, Pittsburgh, PA (1993). Part of the Next Generation Computer Resources (NGCR) program of the US Navy, this paper describes a model for project support environments and specifies interface standards for tools integration. The objective of this program was "to restructure the Navy's approach to take better advantage of commercial advances and to reduce cost and duplication of computer resources."

Humphrey, Watts S., *Managing the Software Process,* Addison-Wesley (1990). Humphrey, formerly with IBM and later head of the Software Engineering Institute, describes his observations on the software process and his method for evaluating the five stages of maturity of software development organizations.

Humphrey, Watts S., *A Discipline for Software Engineering,* Addison-Wesley (1995). Humphrey's new book scales down the methods described in the first book to a personal level, helping software engineers develop the skills and habits needed to plan, track and analyze large, complex projects.

Jones, Caper, *Applied Software Measurement: Assuring Productivity and Quality,* McGraw-Hill (1991). Without measurement as the guide, significant improvements in software performance are unlikely, if not impossible. Jones provides a complete guide to the latest methods for accurately measuring software quality and offers a battery of tools for improving scheduling, costs and quality software projects.

Putnam, Lawrence H. and Ware Myers, *Measures for Excellence: Reliable Software on Time, Within Budget,* Yourdon Press (1992). Putnam and Myers offer readers an extensively researched, systematic look at the basis for the life-cycle method. They discuss life-cycle models, cost estimating, life-cycle management, productivity analysis, tracking and control. Details are provided on the *Software Life-Cycle Model* developed by Putnam.

Rader, J., A. Brown and E. Morris, *An Investigation into the State of the Practice of CASE Tool Integration,* CMU/SEI-93-TR-15 ADA272441 Software Engineering Institute, Carnegie Mellon University, Pittsburgh, PA (1993). This report illustrates the current state of CASE tool integration and explains why the state of integration has remained modest.

Zarrella, P. and A. Brown, *Replacing the Message Service Component in an Integration Framework,* CMU/SEI-94-TR-17, Software Engineering Institute, Carnegie Mellon University, Pittsburgh, PA (1994). This report discusses requirements for integrating tools via asynchronous message communication and the steps needed to implement and benefit from tools integration.

Leveraging Legacy Assets

By Ronald C. Aronica and Donald E. Rimel, Jr.
In collaboration with the Object Technology Staff of The Technical Resource Connection

Contents

Abstract

L egacy systems are valuable assets that can be leveraged and integrated into next generation business systems. *Leveraging Legacy Assets* describes how. It provides a broad definition of legacy systems and discusses various approaches for dealing with them including replacement, extension and integration. Legacy integration strategies have great potential for recapturing the investment in existing system assets while managing risk. Legacy integration explicitly acknowledges that legacy systems are valuable resources — resources that should be part of an enterprise-wide systems architecture. They provide a base for the architecture.

This white paper presents three examples of successful legacy integration projects. The first example is a CICS system, the second is a heterogeneous system environment, and the third is a UNIX-based system. The examples are, at first, very different. They are, however, all legacy system environments and addressing them as such was important for obtaining maximum benefit.

The Role of Legacy Assets in Next Generation Systems

Today's IS managers are being buffeted on all sides by conflicting demands and by conflicting solutions for addressing these demands. Business is changing at increasingly faster rates. Product and service life cycles are decreasing. The global marketplace is a major business battleground as companies try to attract customers and suppliers from all corners of the world. To gain an advantage, progressive companies are reengineering and redesigning their most fundamental business processes. In response to these business changes, companies are developing new information architectures and systems that place more demand on data integration and the ability to communicate and to share information and knowledge.

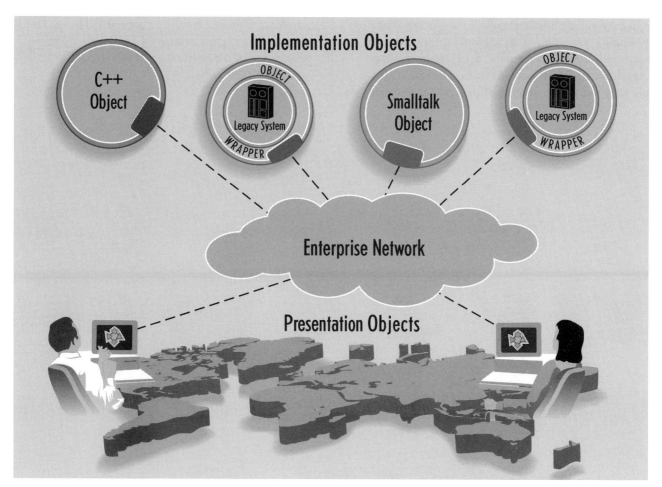

Figure 1
Distributed Object Computing with Legacy and Next Generation Systems

Managers know this is the world into which they want to bring their organizations, but the question is: How? Add to this the pressures many IS managers are receiving from their users to develop new applications, and it is no wonder they agree with the manager who said, "The faster I run, the farther behind I get."

Businesses are reluctant to abandon their investments in proven applications, but some believe — incorrectly — they must discard their existing systems before they are able to enter the brave new world of client/server and distributed object technologies — the world of *next generation computing*. They are looking for ways to meet their users' needs without being forced to scrap everything that they currently have. They are struggling to find ways to leverage their legacy assets when designing and implementing new architectures and next generation systems. The task is daunting, but proven solutions exist.

Many companies are finding that, by using appropriate methods, they can actually increase the useful lives and returns-on-investment (ROI) of their legacy assets while satisfying their longer-term objectives. They help reduce risk by using existing, functional systems and code as components in new systems. As shown in Figure 1, both legacy and next generation users and systems can interact and fully cooperate. The goal is to reuse the "best" parts of their legacy systems. The bottom line of the business is the motivation for leveraging these assets.

What is a Legacy System?

Most older information systems were developed using architectures very different from those in use today. Common characteristics of these older systems are:

- They are domain-specific.

- They use traditional database services or no database management systems at all.

- They are large, complex monoliths.

- They are "mission critical."

- They typically have mainframe hosts and have large, centralized, in-house staffs for their development, maintenance and support.

These characteristics, while not universal, represent the state of many older systems.

Legacy System Characteristics

The majority of legacy systems are domain-specific; they and their designs support the needs of individual functional business domains, not those of the entire enterprise. As a result, such systems have a limited focus — that of the domains for which they were developed initially — and are unable to grow or to evolve easily as the business changes. Rather than being developed by first building *business models*, most legacy system architectures — if architectures were developed — were developed from *technical models*. Using technical models as the basis for implementing systems

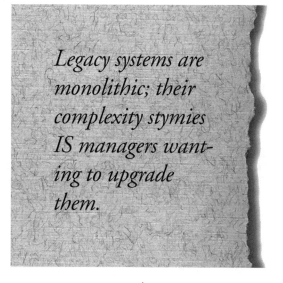

Legacy systems are monolithic; their complexity stymies IS managers wanting to upgrade them.

is similar to constructing a building using only electrical, plumbing, and heating and air conditioning blueprints: The "big picture" — the building itself — as shown in the architectural renderings is lost.

Companies continue to have large amounts of data residing in legacy databases. Elizabeth Harding reports that, according to an IBM survey, "Ninety percent of Fortune 1000 companies use IMS. Today, the database manages an aggregate of 12 million GB of application data and processes 7.7 billion transactions per day."[1] Data integrity in many of these systems is surprisingly poor. Thomas Redman cites studies that report data error-rates approximating 75 percent.[2] Lack of a shared business vocabulary, using application-specific information and using "codes" to represent technical rather than business information all contribute to the extraordinarily high error-rates. Notwithstanding the data quality problems, some IS managers are loath to change their database systems. Besides dealing with the prevalent attitude of "if it ain't broken, don't fix it" and with the size of the migration task, they are concerned about resources and new skills required to do it.

Many legacy systems were developed as single monoliths rather than having their functionality divided into smaller, more manageable parts. It is common to find systems containing hundreds of thousands of lines-of-code, which cost millions of dollars and took multiple years to develop — this does not even include the impact of maintenance. Monolithic applications lead to multiple application system interdependencies. Changing any one system affects others in often unpredictable ways. IS managers are stymied in their desires to upgrade; the systems are too entangled for them to know where to begin.

The "mission critical" nature of many legacy systems is a "two-edged sword." One edge is that doing anything that makes these systems more responsive to changing business needs is beneficial and important. The other is that businesses are unwilling to incur the risk of

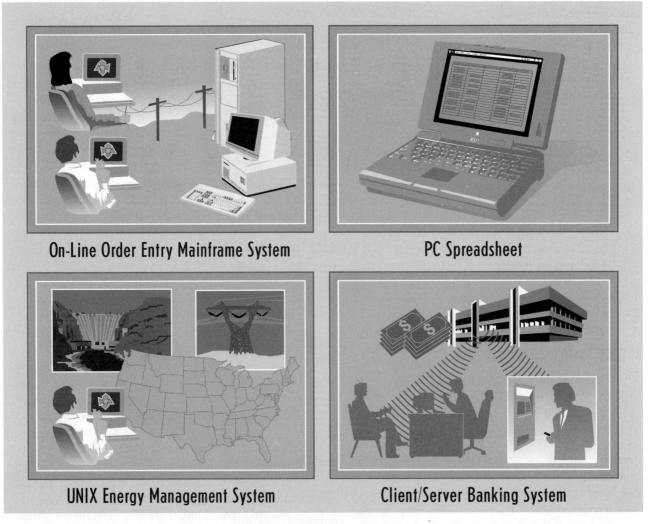

On-Line Order Entry Mainframe System

PC Spreadsheet

UNIX Energy Management System

Client/Server Banking System

Figure 2
Example Legacy Systems

errors that can come with reimplementing these systems.

The majority of legacy systems are host-based and, depending on a system's age, are:

- *non-distributed batch systems* that share data by passing it from one system to another, usually through interface files

- *on-line inquiry,* batch systems that allow on-line queries but continue to do most of their processing in a batch mode

- *transaction-based systems* that allow direct inquiry and possible update to information.

Many systems use a combination of these techniques and use technologies developed in the 1970s. These technologies do not facilitate integration, and they reinforce the use of domain-specific systems models. Systems were principally batch-driven and piped data from one system to another.

A Broader Definition of a Legacy System

Most discussions of legacy systems focus on — and most legacy systems are — systems with the above characteristics. By themselves, however, these characteristics are inadequate for identifying all legacy systems. *The American Heritage Dictionary* defines *legacy* as "something handed down ... from the past" and *heritage* as its synonym.[3] This definition helps broaden the view of legacy systems: A legacy is not necessarily old, but it is from the past and is part of today's heritage. Within this definition, a legacy system is any system that, regardless of age or architecture:

- has existing code

- is a useful asset, i.e., is still useful today.

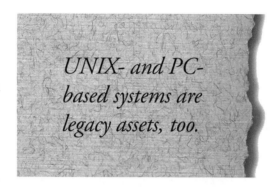

UNIX- and PC-based systems are legacy assets, too.

This broader definition includes not only traditional mainframe-based systems but, for example, UNIX-based systems written in C, C++ or other languages; PC-based systems operating either as standalone systems or as part of a network — consider the number of Windows applications that became legacy systems with the advent of Windows 95; client/server-based systems; and personal productivity tools such as Lotus' 1-2-3 and personal information managers (PIMs). Figure 2 illustrates some of the variety of legacy systems.

Legacy systems, no matter what their history, represent a significant investment and still provide value by supporting current business operations.

Integration is the Best Strategy

Managers responsible for IS organizations generally use two methods for trying to get maximum benefit from their legacy systems: *legacy extension* and *legacy integration.*

Legacy extension modifies legacy systems without significant regard for determining how the system fits into and contributes to the enterprise's overall requirements and information architecture. The focus of legacy extension is on correcting system deficiencies and enhancing the system while, at the same time, addressing the short-term needs of the business.

Legacy integration uses legacy systems and legacy data in the broad context of the business and of its information architecture. The principal focuses of legacy integration are the business, business processes, the information architecture and how a legacy system, as a business asset, can contribute to implementing the architecture without propagating the weaknesses of past designs and development methods. Integration hides (encapsulates) legacy systems behind consistent interfaces that (1) more closely relate to business processes and vocabulary, (2) hide implementation details, and (3) allow changing or replacing implementations without affecting other systems.

There's Always Replacement

Of course, replacement is always an option — frequently the option IS managers first consider. Re-

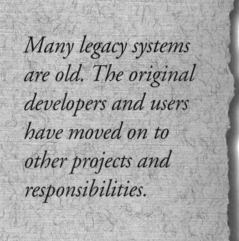

Many legacy systems are old. The original developers and users have moved on to other projects and responsibilities.

placement, however, is an "all or nothing" approach, and managers find that escaping from legacy systems is always more costly and complex than was planned initially; legacy data has more anomalies and special cases than considered even in their most pessimistic plans; and errors keep occurring long after replacement systems are operational.

Many legacy systems are old. The original developers and users have moved on to other projects and responsibilities. They are the people in whom the institutional or *communal memory* resides about how and why they developed these systems. The lack of communal memory significantly contributes to the inability to understand the subtleties of the systems and what capabilities replacement systems must possess.

Equally important, replacement runs counter to the principal goals of leveraging legacy assets — increasing the ROI of legacy assets, reducing initial and ongoing costs, and reducing risk.

Extension Appears Seductively Easy

Many organizations consider extension to be a low cost, relatively painless and quick method for adding new functionality to existing systems. Extension keeps the system's existing architecture — however limited it may be — without incorporating it into a larger, enterprise-wide information architecture. It treats each system as a separate domain and extends multiple systems independently without allowing for systems to cooperate. The result is the "spaghetti and meatballs" approach to interconnecting systems shown in Figure 3.

The basis of legacy extension is, in part, similar to the business model that organizes companies into divisions and minimizes interactions between them. Many businesses no longer use the division model; they are finding that, to be competitive, they are having to be "virtual," extended corporations. Their organizations are flatter, with more cooperation between people. Cross-discipline, *ad hoc* teams are becoming the new organizational model. Today's information systems must support a similar model. They must present consistent semantics and be so easy that novice users can quickly assimilate, understand and use their information.

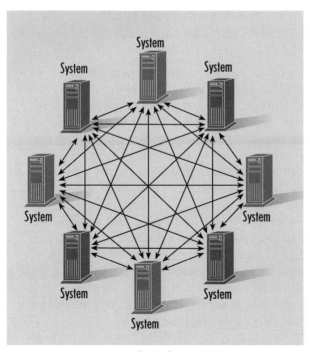

Figure 3
The Spaghetti and Meatballs of Legacy Extension

As described in The Technical Resource Connection's white paper, *Getting Started With Object Technology,* "the critical challenge facing today's IS organizations is to provide leadership in business process improvement. … The overall goal is to realign technology with the business."[4] Extension makes no changes to a legacy system's fundamental architecture and does nothing to incorporate these systems into a larger information architecture. Legacy systems do not "map" well to cross-functional business processes. Extension addresses neither realigning technology nor mapping legacy systems to business processes. It keeps the legacy system's existing technology and architecture while only incrementally adding new functionality and, in doing so, creates a maintenance nightmare.

Integration is the Solution

The objective of legacy integration is to take advantage of a legacy system's information and code-base when developing enterprise architectures. Legacy systems must be able to cooperate with next generation and other systems. Defining the type and level of cooperation requires IS organizations to develop information architectures in which legacy systems are resources available during both the architecture's design and its implementation. These are architectures in which legacy systems participate, and which decouple and decompose legacy systems into their service-based components and partition business processes into distinct, cooperating domains.

Repartitioning legacy systems into domains able to cooperate among themselves requires (1) understanding the *semantic contents* and *usage patterns* of the systems, and (2) implementing abstract interfaces that make the semantic contents and usage patterns available in other domains.

Semantic content refers to business rules and other logic the system contains within its code and data. For example, a Sales Order System may contain rules that determine an order's discount depending upon the order's value and upon the specific customer.

Usage patterns describe how users informally use and extend a system. Usage patterns are not visible when studying a system's documentation, data or code. A Sales Order System may, for example, support only one *ship-to address* per customer even though some customers may have multiple ship-to addresses. Though the system does not directly support multiple ship-to addresses, a clerk may enter customers into the system multiple times, once for each ship-to address.

The Therac-25 software error described in the inset exemplifies the disastrous consequences of not fully understanding usage patterns. Unfortunately, lack of understanding usage patterns and its consequences are not unique to medical systems. Brokerage and asset management systems responsible for time-critical assets, such as derivatives, have encountered similar problems.

An example of a more pervasive usage pattern is the use of "code" fields either within databases or within input forms and screens. Many systems use code fields as fields with undefined meanings; users can use these fields however they choose. The software neither verifies the data nor does processing based upon the fields. Nowhere within the system's source code or documentation exist definitions of these code fields or how to use them, but they, nonetheless, contain information important to the system and to its use. A more insidious version of code fields is a field (for example, a *ship-to name* field) that has a defined purpose but is used for other purposes (for example, using variant spellings to indicate the shipping method).

Exporting the contents of systems through abstract interfaces provides an opportunity to include the

Nancy Leveson and Clark Turner analyzed a software error that was responsible for the Therac-25, a software-controlled radiation treatment unit, causing several deaths. Simply stated, the "problem" — calling it a problem is a gross misstatement considering that people were killed — was that two processes controlling the X-ray beams had a subtle error. The designers tried to consider all operating conditions, but inadequately considered the implications of the processes operating asynchronously. Under certain circumstances — circumstances that occurred all too often — both processes processed their critical code simultaneously. The existence of the error was unexpected because the same code had successfully controlled the predecessor unit, the Therac-20. The legacy code that worked properly in one environment failed when put into a new environment with new usage patterns.

systems' semantic contents and usage patterns in their public definitions. The abstract interface encapsulates or hides the actual system implementation. Clients (users and other systems) see the system only by way of its abstract interface and access it only through this interface. *Wrapping* the system is the process of defining and allowing access to a legacy system through its abstract interface.

Figure 4 illustrates the difference between extension and integration. It shows how extension treats each legacy system as independent stove-pipe systems, building on each system's existing code-base. It also shows how integration treats legacy systems as components of an overall architecture by providing service interfaces on an enterprise network.

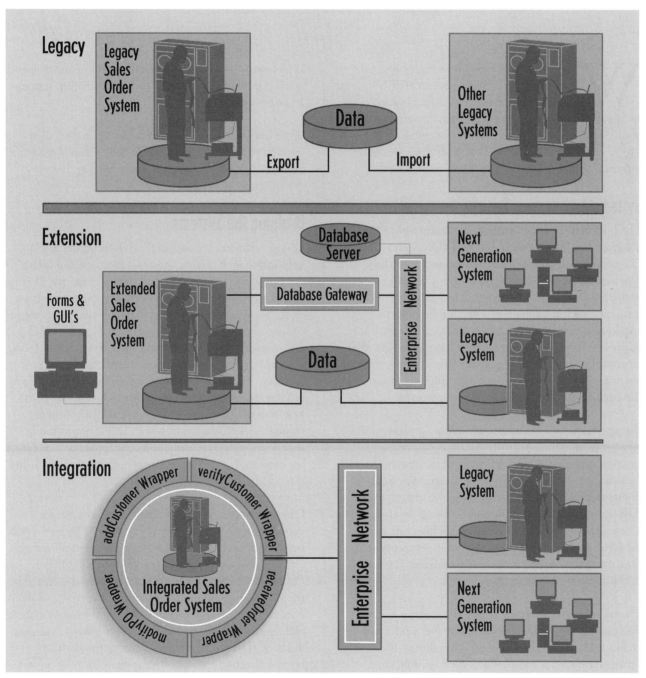

Figure 4
Extending and Integrating Legacy Assets

Integrating Legacy Systems by Using Object Wrappers

We have been describing how legacy systems fit into enterprise-wide systems architectures, but we have not defined systems architecture and how to integrate legacy systems within one. A systems architecture has several components, which are, themselves, subarchitectures; they are the *information, application* and *technical* architectures.

Systems Architecture Basics

The information architecture describes the content, behavior and interaction of business objects. It models the information and activities of the enterprise and provides the organizing abstractions in the business domain for solving business problems. The information architecture defines the building blocks for application development and provides a framework for business information components. More generally, the information architecture's primary role is to provide an environment and overall structure to support modeling the information and activities of the enterprise.

The application architecture defines the fundamental services required to construct solutions within the business domain and is at the heart of the systems architecture. The services provide an abstract, business-domain-oriented interface that hides the underlying implementation from application software developers. The components of an information architecture are modeled, designed and implemented in terms of the fundamental roles and processing paradigms developed in the application architecture.

The technical architecture defines the tools or *engines* that provide the services identified by the application architecture. It specifies, among other things, the actual technologies and products used to implement

applications. The technical architecture considers legacy systems potential "products" for implementing systems architectures.

More information about systems architectures, their importance to business, and how to develop them is available in the white paper, *Understanding Systems Architecture: A Business Brief.*

Bridging the Systems

Object wrappers are one method for bridging the application architecture's abstract interface and legacy systems identified by the technical architecture. On one side of the bridge, the wrapper presents systems with a clean, abstract interface. On the other side, the wrapper communicates with legacy systems using their existing facilities. Object wrappers and their abstract interfaces present a system view that is implementation-independent. Using *object wrappers* provides a natural way of integrating legacy systems with each other and with new systems. They provide access to legacy systems through an encapsulation layer. This is not to imply that developing and using object wrappers is easy; rather, the message is that significant benefits come from using this approach.

Object wrappers allow next generation systems to cooperate with wrapped legacy systems. Once wrapped, legacy systems can participate in distributed object environments using object request brokers (ORBs). Distributed objects and ORBs are described in detail in the white paper, *Distributed Object Computing.* Other systems that used services provided by the legacy systems will continue to use the same abstract interfaces as they did with the legacy systems. Keeping the abstract interface constant keeps other systems from being aware of changes and eliminates the need for modifying these other systems.

The legacy Sales Order System that was shown in Figure 4 operates in an integrated environment using object wrappers to present services to other client systems. The original system is wrapped to present an abstract service interface to enterprise business objects and processes.

The original legacy system may have been constructed from statements, such as *READNEXT, START, XCTL* and *GU.* These are low-level, implementation- and domain-specific constructs that have little or nothing to do with the business and its processes. Object wrappers raise the level of abstraction to the level of business objects. The example Sales Order Systems uses multiple wrappers and has service interfaces such as *addCustomer, verifyCustomerCredit, modifyPurchaseOrder* and *receiveOrder.*

Depending on the functionality of the original Sales Order System, the new interface may interact with only this one system or it may need to interact with other systems such as an Accounts Receivable System. Wrappers encapsulate the details of which systems contribute to satisfying requests and the methods by which they are satisfied.

Object Wrapper Techniques

The key benefit of object wrappers is that they provide consistent services to both legacy and next generation systems. Client objects are unable to determine how server objects are implemented. Thomas Mowbray and Ron Zahavi[5] identify several approaches to object wrapping. Some are:

- *Layering,* the most basic type of wrapping, maps one form of interface onto another form. The functionality provided by layering depends on the

sophistication and availability of legacy system APIs (application programming interfaces). If a legacy system has no API or just a minimal one, there is little that can be done using layering techniques.

Layering can be used to aggregate multiple legacy systems. In the Sales Order System example, the service, *verifyCustomerCredit,* may require information from both the Sales Order and Accounts Receivable Systems. A single, layered object wrapper can encapsulate both systems such that other objects are unaware of how the wrapper determines to grant a customer credit and from which systems the wrapper gets and updates its information. Inversely, layered object wrappers can partition a complex legacy system into multiple business objects.

- *Data migration* maps the existing data model onto a different model. Many systems use multiple databases controlled by legacy database systems or traditional file structures. Wrapping involves adding a layer that bridges the new data model and the legacy database. The complexity of the data migration wrapper can range from a simple API to sophisticated data mining.

Goals for data migration wrapping are to map legacy databases onto data objects and to encapsulate specific database mechanisms. Data migration wrappers allow changing database schemas and the databases themselves without affecting the objects that use these wrappers.

An alternative to mapping the existing data model onto another model is to build a new data store and then to build an API that allows the legacy systems access to the new data store. This technique works well for flat- and indexed-file systems, but is difficult to implement for data stores — like IMS and DB2 — because a significant amount of access logic is embedded within the application.

- *System reengineering* is reengineering and replacing legacy systems either *in toto* or one component (subsystem) at a time. Organizations usually use reverse system reengineering to reduce cost, to enhance maintainability, to increase performance, and to increase congruency between the system's model and the information architecture.

  The information architecture is the usual starting point for a reengineering project. After analyzing the legacy system to better understand its operation, the information architecture and its business objects are mapped onto the existing system's components. Based on the reengineering objectives, parts of the systems will be reimplemented.

- *Middleware* is system integration software for distributed processing and for database and user interfaces. Distributed processing middleware is rapidly migrating toward supporting the Object Management Group's CORBA. Other distributed processing standards, such as Microsoft's Object Linking and Embedding (OLE), are developing CORBA support.

  Database middleware provides common access mechanisms for using a variety of database systems and file structures. Some database middleware products map legacy database systems, such as IMS, onto relational or object models. Database middleware allows a system to issue a single information request and to access, in turn, several data sources that can each be using a different vendor's database system.

  Some database middleware products are closed systems that have little or no external software interface support. A key indicator of such a system is the lack of a robust, well-documented client/server API or abstract interface. Systems without such interfaces are difficult to wrap properly and limit the ability to easily replace

them in the future. They are a step backward and present similar problems to those encountered with legacy systems.

User interface middleware provides a common API for developing user interfaces — usually graphical — that operate on multiple platforms and operating systems. Most products provide rich APIs that may or may not be object-oriented. Most are at low levels of abstraction, and while they are fairly consistent across different environments, they are proprietary to each vendor. Wrapping user interface middleware can raise its level of abstraction and allow replacing one product with another.

- *Encapsulation,* the most general form of object wrapping, separates interface from implementation. Encapsulation treats systems as black box abstractions in which the interface hides the implementation details. All accesses, including direct and indirect accesses to state variables, are performed through interface methods. Using interface methods allows changing implementation details without requiring other changes.

  CORBA and its Interface Definition Language (IDL) allow encapsulating systems that hide differences in programming languages, systems locations, operating systems, algorithms and data structures. Using the IDL allows defining object encapsulations that are free of implementation details.

  Encapsulation can be used with legacy systems where the source code is no longer available. The wrapper can access legacy files and databases directly. If the legacy system has a reasonably robust API, the wrapper can use it to perform most functions. Screen scraping, using products such as 3270- and 5250-class emulators and EHLLAPI (Enhanced High-Level Language Application Programming Interface) programs, can be used to add information to and request information from legacy systems. A single object wrapper can use multiple screens and even multiple systems to provide its services.

Encapsulation is also useful for decomposing and decoupling large legacy systems into separate components. Each component can have its own wrapper assuming that the system's architecture supports it. This allows reusing and upgrading each component independent of others. *Dividing* legacy systems into components permits *conquering* them incrementally.

- In the context of a *systems architecture,* wrappers provide the translation between the architecture and legacy systems. Wrappers should implement the architecture in all its details including providing metadata and data conversion.

Object wrappers are important tools for successfully integrating legacy systems into next generation architectures and are the basis for most successful integration projects.

Successful Legacy Integration Projects

Successful legacy integration projects do not lend themselves to "cookie cutter" approaches. Managers must analyze their own environments before determining the "best" methods for integrating their legacy systems into their systems architectures.

The following sections describe three very different organizations, each with its own unique requirements and constraints, and how each integrated its legacy systems into its next generation computing environment.

Mainframe-Based Transaction System

A large chemical company originally developed a manufacturing control system in 1973. Numerous changes have been made to the system during the intervening years. Some changes were to allow the system to continue to operate as the processing envi-

ronment changed. Most changes, however, reflected changing business requirements.

Originally, it was a batch system written in COBOL, and it used VSAM file access. Over time, the staff added a CICS front-end and the ability to access IMS databases. The IMS databases contained data that were, for the most part, duplicates of the VSAM data.

The IS organization started reengineering its systems in 1993. This was part of a company-wide reengineering effort. The team responsible for developing the systems architecture determined that a distributed information infrastructure was the best method for supporting the company's objectives and for providing the flexibility required for responding to future business events and conditions.

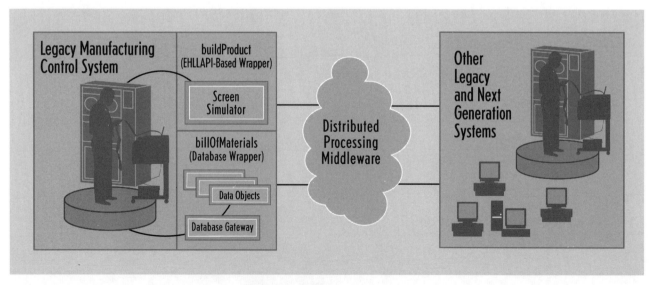

Figure 5
Wrapped Manufacturing Control System

After taking an inventory of all legacy systems, the architecture team determined that the manufacturing control system was key to the company's daily operations and decided to use as much of the existing system as possible. The team developed a mapping of the previously identified business processes onto the system. Object wrappers corresponding to each process were developed.

Since the system did not have a robust API, a variety of implementation strategies were required to keep the object wrapper interfaces at high levels. CICS inquiry and data entry were originally done using 3270-type terminals; the wrappers simulated these terminals using EHLLAPI routines. The data in the IMS databases were directly accessed when necessary using a database gateway.

The company purchased a distributed processing middleware product for use with its enterprise-wide environment. Even though the objects represented by the manufacturing control system's wrappers resided on one processor, they communicated using the middleware. This was done to allow easy future replacement of parts of the system.

Figure 5 shows some of the object wrappers around the legacy manufacturing control system.

Event-Driven Migration

An international electronics manufacturer had more than 650 in-house business applications. Many of these were global applications that were tied together using

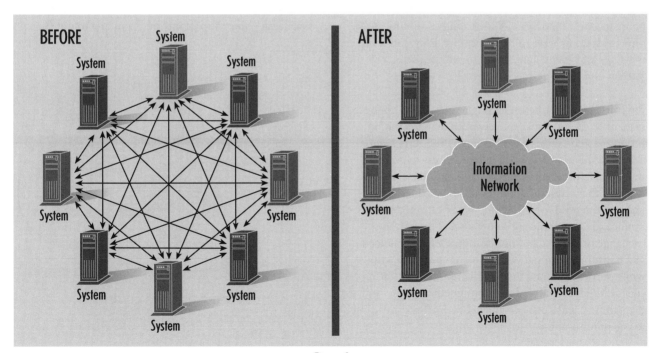

Figure 6
Publish-and-Subscribe Network

point-to-point interfaces. Interfaces were hard-coded to work with specific hardware platforms, languages, networks and data formats. The applications formed a lattice of point-to-point interfaces similar to the "spaghetti and meatballs" of interdependent systems shown in the *before* diagram in Figure 6.

The design caused problems common to most legacy systems: (1) changing one application caused changes to multiple, interdependent applications; (2) the lack of institutional memory about the applications caused the changes to be more complex than would otherwise have been the case; (3) the number of changes affected the entire IS organization, which became bogged down trying to keep its applications in synch; and (4) IS became a bottleneck for new development.

As part of the company's business reengineering efforts, the IS organization developed a plan to remove all point-to-point interfaces. Rather than communicating directly, systems were to communicate using common messages and events (an API) through the use of a *publish-and-subscribe* mechanism.

Publish-and-subscribe uses a single interface to connect systems to the information network. Systems can be producers and consumers of events. Producers *publish* events to the network, which then delivers them to those consumers who have *subscribed* to them. Events can be either requests or notifications. Requests indicate the need for an action. Notifications announce the occurrence of something. Through the exchange of request and notification events, producers and consumers can participate in complex interactions while remaining anonymous. The resulting execution style is highly decoupled and configurable. The *after* diagram in Figure 6 shows the network after converting to the publish-and-subscribe paradigm.

Wrappers were used for legacy systems that were unable to use the publish-and-subscribe API directly. Systems

for which wrappers were required tended to be old COBOL systems, or database or data-generating systems, such as those using EDI (electronic data interchange). The wrappers transform raw data formats into business events using the publish-and-subscribe API. The company developed wrappers for 3270-data streams, flat files, e-mail and EDI systems.

Behind the network was message-oriented middleware (MOM) that the company also developed. The MOM resided on each processor and was responsible for broadcasting events to all subscribing systems. The MOM kept track of all subscription requests and routed all messages and events.

The company found that publish-and-subscribe allowed it to integrate its existing and new systems in an evolutionary manner. Systems no longer had complex interactions and the effects of changes were localized. Most important, the company found the

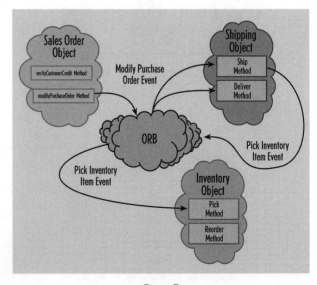

Figure 7
Objects Communicating Through an ORB

legacy systems and their components were more consistent with the business objects identified during the company's business reengineering activities.

The conversion from point-to-point to publish-and-subscribe was started prior to the availability of commercial ORB products and standards. The company is replacing its publish-and-subscribe mechanism with a CORBA-compliant ORB with *Event Services* and its *event channels*. The Event Service allows objects to register and unregister their interest in specific events. The event channel is the path by which multiple event producers communicate with multiple event consumers without explicitly knowing about each other. Figure 7 shows an example of how the company expects objects will communicate within an ORB environment.

UNIX-Based Trading System

A major investment bank had a derivatives trading system written in C++, using the relational database system, Sybase, and operating under UNIX. The system performed the required business functions, but was unable to keep up with the increasing transaction volume. The system initially supported only four traders; as the business grew, it had to support approximately 400 traders. The new traders were located in four cities scattered around the globe.

The bank wanted to continue to use its existing system because it met its business needs, interfaced well with other financial systems, and traders liked using it. The

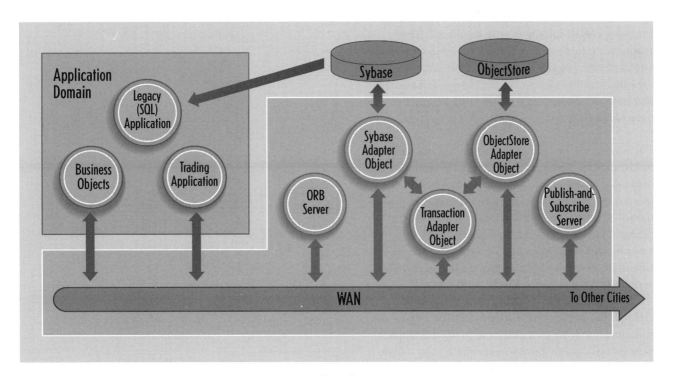

Figure 8
Revised Trading System

challenge was to increase its capabilities by two orders of magnitude.

The bank developed a new architecture for the system. The architecture used XShell as the middleware ORB. It also used an object-oriented database manager, ObjectStore, to augment the Sybase database and to provide the required performance.

Rather than replacing the existing database with an ObjectStore database, the revised system kept two copies of the information, one copy in each database. This allowed existing "back office" applications to continue to use the legacy Sybase database while the revised derivatives trading system used the ObjectStore database and its increased performance.

Sybase and ObjectStore *adapter* objects were created to control access to their respective databases. The adapters notified a *transaction adapter* object whenever one database changed. The transaction adapter notified the other database adapter of the change and assured that both databases stayed synchronized using two-phase commit.

The revised system used XShell's publish-and-subscribe mechanism to communicate changes throughout the network. Whenever there was a change, the changed site published a notification event. Other sites subscribed to specific events and locally replicated the change. The objects were intelligent enough to replicate data only when needed, which helped eliminate unnecessary network traffic and improved overall performance.

Figure 8 shows the revised system, how individual sites communicate with each other and how other applications directly query the Sybase database. The derivatives trading system is an example of a legacy system that uses contemporary languages and technologies but needed to be integrated into a broader, distributed environment to meet changing business needs. Its architecture and the use of object wrappers and an ORB allow it to adapt and to grow in response to new business requirements.

Conclusion

The changes forcing businesses to reengineer their most basic processes are forcing IS organizations to do the same. The bind in which IS organizations find themselves is the result of their users' demands for new, more responsive systems and their recognition that they do not have the resources required to replace their existing systems. The issue may appear to be technical, but it is, in reality, a business issue. Legacy systems are the life-blood of current business operations and represent assets that businesses cannot afford to write off. Businesses must gain maximum benefit and better value from these assets.

Distributed objects is a key technology for integrating legacy systems with new architectures and systems. The ability to replace individual system components gives IS organizations flexibility. They can upgrade or reengineer selected components as business needs dictate and when resources are available. The task is considerably simplified; changes to individual components do not affect other components.

Developing system architectures, designing object wrappers and implementing distributed computing are complex processes. This paper described some of the issues to consider and techniques to use when developing strategies for next generation systems. Success depends in no small part on having experienced system architects guide these activities. Although an organization can go it alone, an experienced guide can show the way and allow a company to maintain its business focus during the journey.

References

[1] Harding, Elizabeth U., *Older Databases Hang In: How can We Miss Them When They Won't Go Away?* "Software Magazine," Vol. 15, No. 7, pp. 22+ (July 1995).

[2] Redman, Thomas C., *Data Quality: Management and Technology,* Bantam Books, (1992). Referenced in Ganti, Narsim and William Brayman, *The Transition of Legacy Systems to a Distributed Architecture,* John Wiley & Sons (1995).

[3] SoftKey International, *The American Heritage Dictionary,* 3rd. ed., SoftKey International (1994).

[4] Fingar, Peter and Jim Stikeleather, *Getting Started with Object Technology: A TRC White Paper,* The Technical Resource Connection (1995).

[5] Mowbray, Thomas J. and Ron Zahavi, *The Essential CORBA: System Integration Using Distributed Objects,* John Wiley & Sons (1995).

Suggested Readings

Brodie, Michael L. and Michael Stonebraker, *Migrating Legacy Systems: Gateways, Interfaces & the Incremental Approach,* Morgan Kaufmann (1995). This thorough, well-written book centers on an 11-step migration approach the authors dub the "Chicken Little Approach." It is a step-by-step approach that controls risk throughout the process. The book includes case studies and discusses available tools.

Ganti, Narsim and William Brayman, *The Transition of Legacy Systems to a Distributed Architecture,* John Wiley & Sons (1995). Both Ganti and Brayman have substantial experience at the Boeing Company with moving from legacy systems to systems developed using formal architectures. They describe an architecture-based approach to migrating legacy systems, outline a series of steps that can be used to realign information technology with changing business strategies, and provide guidelines for visualizing the transition.

Graham, Ian, *Migrating to Object Technology,* Addison-Wesley (1995). This book is really two books in one: It is first a book about strategies for migrating legacy systems to distributed object-based systems, and it is second a book describing the author's Semantic Object Modeling Approach (SOMA). SOMA is a development method, which is organized similarly to the OMG's reference model. The first part of the book is of most interest to organizations migrating their legacy systems.

Jackson, Michael, *Software Requirements & Specifications: A Lesson of Practice, Principles and Prejudices,* ACM Press: Addison-Wesley (1995). The author is best known for his work on developing the JSP program design method. This new book presents principles and techniques for requirements analysis, specification and design. While not explicitly about legacy systems, many of the principles and techniques are useful for addressing the issues of legacy and next generation systems integration.

Mowbray, Thomas J. and Ron Zahavi, *The Essential CORBA: System Integration Using Distributed Objects,* John Wiley & Sons (1995). Mowbray and Zahavi worked together at The MITRE Corporation on the DISCUS project. They use this project as the basis for explaining the OMG's object request broker, CORBA, and how to use it for developing next generation systems. They explain techniques for wrapping legacy systems and integrating them into next generation systems architectures. The book provides both an introduction to CORBA and examples of using it during system implementation.

Object-Oriented Knowledge Transfer

By John Cribbs, Peter Fingar, Samuel Joseph and Ron Schultz
In collaboration with the Object Technology Staff of The Technical Resource Connection

Knowledge Systems Corporation (KSC) is recognized as the company that formalized the apprenticeship and mentoring approach to object-oriented technology transfer.

The Technical Resource Connection gratefully acknowledges its contributions to this white paper.

Contents

Abstract

O bject-oriented information systems promise to make building and using technology easier for business and technology professionals. But first, developers and users of the technology must learn to think in fundamentally new ways. Object orientation is a paradigm shift as clearly defined in Joel Barker's 1992 book, *Future Edge.* It is not just a new tool or technique, but an entirely new framework for defining and solving problems.

The problem with a paradigm shift is that years of accumulated knowledge, skills and experience cannot be directly applied to the new paradigm. Not until the enlightenment or "aha" stage is reached (where an intuitive understanding of the new paradigm is gained) can past skills be adjusted and applied in the new framework. Transitions to the new paradigm must account for these human factors. These issues are addressed in this paper in order to provide insight for companies planning their migration strategies.

This paper focuses on the role of mentoring and multi-step training during initial technology transfer projects. Mentoring and team learning are essential to making successful transitions and in developing an organization that is capable of keeping up with the rapidly evolving technology. The paper concludes by outlining strategies for continuous learning.[1]

---

[1] Some of the materials included in this paper have been adapted from the book *The Blueprint for Business Objects,* SIGS Books, New York, 1996 (see Suggested Readings, page 176).

Next Generation Computing Know-How

New Disciplines for IS

"Our industry is on the verge of massive upheaval and change. The nature of the problems we are trying to solve cannot be fixed with the tools we currently use or with the problem-solving paradigm we have in our heads. The systems we need to build in the future are real-time, event-driven simulations of the business, not the transaction-processing, record-keeping reporting systems we built over the last 30 years." — Jim Stikeleather, *Computerworld Client/Server Journal.*

Robust, intelligent and human-centered information systems, the type needed for the competitive edge, cannot be designed and developed with the traditional data processing skill set. The next generation of computing will not come easily. Business and technology professionals must learn how to think in fundamentally new ways. Mentoring and team learning are essential to building an IS organization capable of keeping up with the rapidly evolving object analysis and design methods and the *new era* applications resulting from business engineering initiatives.

There are no short-cuts and no one-week programmer classes that bring about transformations. The knowledge needed to conceive, develop and implement next generation information systems is much broader and far more specialized than the knowledge needed for traditional data processing applications. Essential

The next generation of computing will not come easily. Business and technology professionals must learn how to think in fundamentally new ways.

systems development knowledge must be expanded to include:

- general systems thinking, modeling and simulation
- human-centered design
- self-directed team management
- object-oriented software engineering.

It's a whole new ball game with new players and roles.

General Systems Thinking, Modeling and Simulation

Except for today's programmers and developers of real-time systems, modeling and simulation skills are not part of most commercial IS organizations. Yet it is precisely these skills that are needed to conceive, design and construct event-driven, distributed object computing applications. Disciplines taught in mathematics and science provide the backdrop. As Professor Lewis Pinson explains, "Herein lies the problem: All too frequently, the COBOL programmer does not have the background required to be successful in the [C and C++] culture." He maintains that it is the "science" in computer science that is missing from many commercial developers today. "Consequently, the transformation of programmers without the prerequisite science background is slow, difficult and extremely painful."[2]

Rather than develop point solutions or single purpose applications, object-oriented systems development relies on a new style in which developers are constantly building upon architectures and infrastructures to achieve productivity and reuse. Systems thinking is a core discipline for designing and constructing such infrastructures.

Human-Centered Design

The information systems of the future must be simple to use, yet powerful. "Complex is easy; simple is difficult."[3] The corporation of the future will rely on advanced information technology. And the only way technology can work is through information systems that *mirror* human cognition — the way people think when accomplishing work. Information systems must be created from human-centered designs, not technology-centered designs. They must be based in human cognition — they must be based in *reality*. Nippon Telephone and Telegraph (NTT), the Japanese telecommunications conglomerate, expresses its vision of future information systems as VIP: *visual, intelligent and personal*. Cognitive science provides the body of knowledge needed to practice the art of human-centered design and is a core discipline required by the teams that are tasked with developing next generation systems. The user interface must be much deeper than the pixels that make up a graphical user interface (GUI). The failure of commercial information systems to deliver human-centered, usable interfaces is well documented (see Zuboff and Norman in the Suggested Readings).

Self-Directed Team Management

Working in multidisciplinary teams requires sharply honed team skills for teams to be effective. The highly specialized backgrounds of individual participants mean that people with differing personalities, perspectives and ways of viewing problems must be integrated into an effective team structure. Real-time simulations and systems based in human cognition simply cannot be designed and constructed without multidisciplinary teams. The ability to manage and participate in diverse work teams is essential, and these skills must be learned.

Object-Oriented Software Engineering

Object orientation provides the framework for managing complexity of next generation systems, but object-oriented software engineering presents the commercial systems developer with a steep learning curve. Habits, ingrained ways of thinking and the mental models we use for problem-solving are very difficult to change. Thus, to transition a working professional to new ways of thinking and doing things is very difficult.

This brief introduction to the disciplines required for developing next generation systems clearly raises a significant question: How do we learn this way of developing systems? Transitions should be carefully planned and executed, not left to chance. Let's examine the core competencies that are needed on an object-oriented systems development team by introducing a curriculum map.

An Object-Oriented Curriculum

If we consider the roles and competencies required on an object-oriented systems development team, we can derive an initial set of learning requirements. Table 1 shows who on the development team needs to know what. Competencies are listed in the leftmost column, and roles requiring the competencies are listed in the column headings.

In addition to the subjects listed in the table, note that highly specialized skill competencies may be needed by individuals participating in a systems development team. Further, individuals may not have the prerequisite background to acquire skills in a particular subject. For example, a systems analyst may require one or more mathematics courses prior to undertaking studies of modeling and simulation. The individual development plans shown at the bottom of the table make the needs for individualized training apparent. No single curriculum can fit all individuals, and specialized training should be available to meet individual needs.

✖ = Core Competency	Manager	Project Lead	System Architect	Developer	Quality Assurance
O-O Fundamentals	✖	✖	✖	✖	✖
O-O Software Engineering	✖	✖	✖	✖	✖
O-O Analysis & Design	Concepts	✖	✖	✖	✖
Introductory Language	Concepts	Optional	✖	✖	Concepts
Advanced Language			Optional	✖	
Tool Sets	As Appropriate	As Appropriate	As Appropriate	As Appropriate	As Appropriate
Software Quality Assurance	Concepts	✖	Concepts	Concepts	✖
Human-Computer Interaction	Concepts	Concepts	✖	✖	Concepts
O-O Database Management		Concepts	✖	✖	
Distributed Computing Technology	Concepts	Concepts	✖	✖	
Real-Time Modeling & Simulation	Concepts	Concepts	✖	✖	Concepts
O-O Project Management	Concepts	✖			✖
Continuing Education	Individual Dev. Plan	Individual Dev. Plan	Individual Dev. Plan	Individual Dev. Plan	Individual Dev. Plan

Table 1
An Example of an Object-Oriented Curriculum

The curriculum outline does not suggest that a person takes a course and, presto, competency is achieved. On the contrary, competencies in the subjects listed in the curriculum can take years to develop.

Mastery Levels

A common mistake made in transitioning an organization to any new technology is to perceive training as a binary proposition: People are either trained or they are not. Experience indicates that this is a flawed assumption.

Meilir Page-Jones, president of Wayland Systems, developed a seven-stage model of what software developers actually go through as they learn and develop skills associated with a new technology.[4] Developing an environment and a process to move people through those seven stages should be high on the CIO's priority list. The following discussion is adapted to Page-Jones' stages:

Stage 1: Innocent — Never heard of the technology.

Most developers have heard of object technology, but their awareness is actually very low. Someone may be considered innocent if he has not learned enough about the technology to be aware of some of the engineering tradeoffs associated with it, some of its costs, some of its benefits, or where and when it might be appropriately applied.

Moving someone from the innocent stage to the next stage is a process of providing gentle introductions to the technology through articles, presentations and seminars. The goal is to inform and educate. Management-level introductory presentations place the more global issues of the technology into perspective.

Stage 2: Aware — Has read something about the technology.

At stage two, the person has become aware of the benefits and costs of the technology, as well as when and where it might be successfully applied. The person can generally describe what is involved with the technology, and at a high level can compare and contrast the technology with older approaches. The person has a talking knowledge of the technology.

A person at this stage has not yet achieved the paradigm shift. His intellectual framework for the technology is still based upon drawing analogies to the old ways of doing things, and the person probably still draws upon erroneous assumptions when thinking or making decisions about the technology.

Moving a person from this stage to the next involves establishing and executing an initial training program of classes, readings, seminars and workshops in the higher level concepts of the technology. With object technology, this training is in the areas of analysis, design and methodologies.

Stage 3: Apprentice — Has studied the technology.

At this stage, the person is well aware of the high level concepts of the technology; however, he may or may not have experienced the paradigm shift. This person cannot effectively apply the technology on his own, but can begin to contribute to the use of the technology.

Moving the person from this stage to the next involves establishing and executing a training program that focuses on the details of the technology. In the case of object technology, it is now appropriate to introduce language and tool training.

At this stage and its transition to the next, hands-on training becomes very important. To this end, an apprentice should be teamed with a mentor, someone who uses the technology naturally and automatically and can explain the internal process involved with the technology. For the apprentice, it is sink or swim at this stage. It is time to throw the apprentice into a development project using the new technology.

The mentor expects that the apprentice will swallow a little water and, at times, gasp for breath. Fortunately, the mentor serves as a lifeguard. The mentor has to closely monitor the apprentice to ascertain progress, capitalize on the lessons that are learned from mistakes, and adjust the detailed goals of the development process.

Stage 4: Practitioner — Ready to use the technology.

At this stage, the person is ready to make engineering decisions on his own. There should be a continuing education program in place to increase his breadth of understanding of the technology and its applications. This is generally a self-managed process.

This stage still needs the presence of a mentor to make assignments and observe results. However, detailed supervision should no longer be required. Mistakes are a significant contributor to the learning process at this level, and the practitioner should be allowed to make them. At this stage, the practitioner is given full responsibility for assignments and is an active participant in project review activities.

Movement to the next stage is a function of time, experience, an increasing knowledge base and specific mentoring.

Stage 5: Journeyman — Uses the technology naturally and automatically.

This is the stage that development staff should achieve by the end of the transitioning process. At this stage, participants are able to apply the technology in normal situations and do not require the presence of a mentor to accomplish quality work.

This stage also requires a self-managed learning program to increase the understanding of the technology. This stage still calls upon the mentor when new or especially complex problems appear.

Movement to the next stage is a function of experience, increasing depth of knowledge, and the evolution of the generic, problem-solving framework. This problem-solving framework is developed through interacting with a Master-level person on new or complex situations. In this stage, the solution process is more important than the solution details.

Stage 6: Master — Has internalized the technology and knows when to break the rules.

This stage is self-explanatory, with continued learning a matter of keeping up with progress being made with the technology.

Every organization needs access to a Master, either on staff or on retainer. The Master can handle new or complex applications of the technology, review Journeyman level work, show alternative or creative solutions to problems, point out subtleties in the engineering decisions, and help keep the organization up to date.

Movement to the next stage is strictly up to the individual. It is based on the individual's thought process and experiences. Moving up to the Expert stage generally requires the individual to be actively engaged in a broad range of applications of the technology in new or unusual situations.

Stage 7: Expert — Writes books, articles, gives lectures and develops ways to extend the technology.

The Expert is at the pinnacle of the technology. He is generally recognized for his contributions to the industry, and is often asked to lecture or give presentations at national meetings for his peers.

In summary, knowledge transfer is the foundation for success in meeting an IS organization's goal of reengineering its software development process. Mentoring, in context of the seven-step process for knowledge transfer, can be an effective approach to building a lasting foundation.

Master-Apprentice Models

Early adopters of object technology deployed traditional classroom training approaches and found these

> *When we are dealing with a paradigm shift for experienced computing professionals, the real world, not the classroom, is the appropriate learning environment.*

methods proved insufficient. Successful organizations now realize that working on real business projects in a master-apprentice relationship accelerates the climb up the learning curve.

We are interested in what the learner can *do* as a measure of what they know. Experience tells us that when we are dealing with a paradigm shift for experienced computing professionals, the real world, not the classroom, is the appropriate learning environment. In the real world, as simply stated by the object training master, Peter Coad, "the example teaches." Successful approaches encapsulate learning with the process of delivery of real projects. Mentoring is the preferred learning method and, as such, IS organizations will need to commit to learning while doing.

Mentoring Responsibilities

"The JOOP Guide to Project Mentoring," published in March 1995, contains a listing of more than 250 providers of project mentoring. Mentoring, or more specifically, O-O mentoring, is all the rage. Fortunately, Ed Swanstrom's article precedes the guide and provides a *caveat emptor* for the buyer of these services. Swanstrom explains, "While it's already gone beyond fashionable to merely mundane to talk about O-O mentoring, the role remains fairly ambiguous. Stripped down, it's 'org-speak' for on-the-job training (OJT)."[5] OJT is not a new teaching paradigm. It is the original teaching paradigm. Thus, those charged with the responsibility of mentoring others require a solid understanding of mentoring. Knowledge Systems Corporation (KSC) is recognized as the company that formalized the apprenticeship and mentoring approach to object-oriented technology transfer. Today, several major companies have adopted and refined the approach, including IBM's Object Technology University, Hewlett-Packard's Professional Services Division and The Technical Resource Connection.

A mentor is an experienced and trusted counselor. In business, a mentor is normally someone who is willing to teach you the ropes of the business — the tricks of the trade. In technology, a mentor is all of the above: a wise counselor and an individual who will teach the tricks of the trade. Using the process of mentoring, an organization can be guided past the traps and pitfalls of object-oriented technology. A qualified mentor will advise, warn and train where necessary to prevent the failures that have plagued other organizations.

Mentoring is the process by which a master object technician provides guidance to an individual object-oriented developer or development team on matters spanning the entire software engineering spectrum. The goal of these activities is to further the team's successful use of object technology. Typical mentoring activities include:

- reinforcement of prior knowledge obtained in classroom training or other learning experiences

- software engineering process guidance

- project planning guidance

- team capability assessments

- project progress reviews

- design and code reviews

- performance and tuning workshops

- configuration management process optimization

- establishing realistic project goals after assessing the learner's needs and capabilities

- providing just-in-time training on project-relevant advanced technology topics (e.g., memory management optimization, design patterns recognition, and real-time event processing) at the time new skills are needed to achieve project deliverables

- creating individual development plans for project members.

The mentoring approach to learning a new technology is generally the most effective in a *one-on-one* environment for systems architects and a *one-to-three* ratio for developers. The process of mentoring developers requires a focus on team learning as well as individual development experiences. Further, mentoring is needed at all levels, including for business executives.

More and more information systems professionals will be asked to add mentoring to their core responsibilities. Mentoring does not mean learning by osmosis. An effective mentor understands the learning process, knows how to identify and document learning requirements and objectives, and knows how to arrange and manage the conditions for learning. The mentor is not just a tutor. In fact, a mentor may not actually do tutoring. Rather, the mentor manages the learning process of the apprentice. The individual development plan provides the mentor with a tool to document goals; learning activities and strategies to reach the objectives; and measures of results. Learning occurs everywhere and at all times. Individual development plans typically include work assignments, training assignments, college courses, conferences, Internet discussion groups, readings, research and other developmental activities deemed appropriate.

In summary, mentoring is a major undertaking and should be approached in a systematic and well-defined way. Mentoring responsibilities should not be taken lightly. In addition to mastering the technology and its application, mentors must master the disciplines of *adult learning* if they are to be effective in transferring knowledge. Adult learning, especially in the context of a paradigm shift, is a challenge in and of itself.

The Problem of Adults Learning New Concepts

Business engineering teams are increasingly turning to object-oriented techniques to model business processes. In the future, the business model and the software model will become fused. Both business and computing professionals must learn to "object think" in order to gain the knowledge and skills needed for business reengineering. However, since object orientation involves a paradigm shift, the principles of adult learning must be carefully applied.

One mainframe programmer who made the transition to objects described the essence of the new way of thinking: "In any kind of procedural language, you are breaking down work flow and coding it. In object-oriented design, you're breaking down events and assigning responsibilities to objects and not really dealing with work flow anymore."[6] Once the new way of thinking is instilled, the syntax, grammar and complexities of object-oriented tools and techniques become manageable to the learner.

Adults have been sufficiently trapped in the boxes of life so that their capacity for learning "for learning's sake" is limited by time and energy constraints of real-life. The adults who run our businesses can be pesky

> *Once the new way of thinking is instilled, the syntax, grammar and complexities of object-oriented tools and techniques become manageable to the learner.*

learners. They demand a lot from learning services and experiences. They expect learning to be:

- available just before the knowledge and skill are needed for the job: just-in-time learning

- hands-on, from the beginning

- preferably skill-building training delivered in the privacy of their own office or workspace (sometimes to overcome any anxiety produced while learning with subordinates)

- on demand, when and where it is needed

- immediately applicable, customized to the immediate need

And, most assuredly, they want a mentor.

When a new concept sinks in, we have reached "aha." We have adapted our inner mental models. But now we have to test our new understanding with application. Our first few attempts at application will produce mistakes. The feedback from those mistakes will in turn continue to reshape our understanding. By the time we reach mastery, we no longer consciously know what we are doing: We just do it.

With this description of learning in mind, it is easy to conclude that to shift to a new paradigm, a person must become two people. One continues to get today's hectic job done. The other learns the new way of doing business. Work teams transitioning to object orientation must continually grapple with these facts. Because reflective time is a scarce resource, work teams must manage it very carefully.

Enterprise Learning Architectures

The Assimilation Process

Corporations require well-thought strategies for transitioning to next generation information systems. These strategies must consider the current business culture, technology culture and current knowledge and skill sets of both business and IS personnel. The transition to objects is not a transition in tools and techniques. It is an evolution into a new way of doing business and a new approach to business problem-solving. Transitions must be incremental and iterative. They must be evolutionary and steeped in today's existing business realities.

Transitioning to the object paradigm is not a computer system "conversion," it is a process of *assimilation*. Furthermore, the process is one of risk and asset management. The massive investments that corporations have in existing information processing assets provide the life blood of current business operations. We are not "converting to a new system," we are designing new types of robust information systems that leverage existing corporate information assets. Preserving and integrating legacy assets into new era applications is not trivial and requires significant experience and expertise (see The Technical Resource Connection's white paper, *Enterprise Computing: The Process*).

Successful technology transfer requires initial help from outside masters who have gone before. Smart business people learn from smart scientists and climb on the

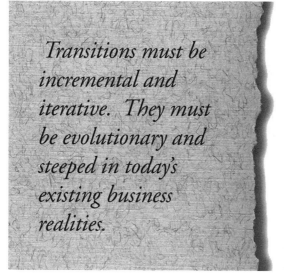

Transitions must be incremental and iterative. They must be evolutionary and steeped in today's existing business realities.

shoulders of others. They will discover that it takes several years to master the technology from scratch and that experienced object-oriented developers are in high demand and hard to find. For these reasons, outsourcing can be an effective business strategy. Providers of object-oriented consulting, training and technical implementation are growing in number and size. Multi-year partnerships are being established between these technology providers and progressive companies determined to deploy the emerging technology for competitive advantage.

A typical arrangement may include the following general steps:

1. The outsourcing firm provides initial education and overall planning assistance.

2. With assistance from the outsourcing firm, the corporation develops a plan of action for a pilot project.

3. The outsourcing firm arranges initial training for the work team, and the pilot project is used in the training so that immediate application of the new skills is assured.

4. The outsourcing firm provides mentoring and coaching throughout development of the pilot project.

5. Pilot projects are expanded in scope, and steps 1-4 repeated. Each iteration reduces the need for outside assistance.

As technology transfer progresses, in-house team members can evolve into consultants to other corporate projects. The goal of successful technology transfer is self-sufficiency in the new paradigm. Self-sufficiency is achieved when the consulting firm is no longer needed and the expertise is entrenched in the business. In other words, the new approaches are mainstream.

Actually, long-term relationships will likely emerge, especially between corporations and business object providers, companies that develop industry-specific class libraries for object-oriented information systems. In the future, corporations will forge long-term relationships that blend the right mix of software acquisition, training, consulting, systems development and technical implementation. Depending upon cost/benefit analyses, any or all of these resources may be insourced or outsourced, or this way today and that way tomorrow.

Although these beginnings are small, they can scale-up in an orderly fashion. Beginning with proof-of-concept projects, a corporation can kick the tires, initiate low-risk demonstration projects, establish a corporate Object Technology Center (OTC) to provide a focal point, and develop learning processes to expand the initial knowledge base. This overall process is shown in Figure 1.

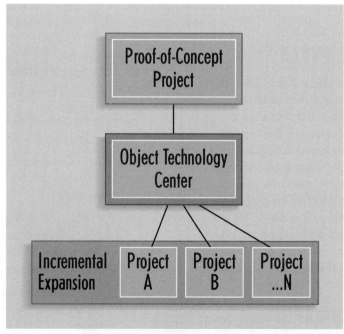

Figure 1
Overall Technology Transfer Process

Since the corporate goal is the insertion of object-oriented technologies into an already complex environment, successful transition strategies must start small, build proof-of-concept prototypes, increment the scope of the problem domain, and iterate. The key to successful transitions is to take small, incremental steps. Each step requires three fundamental learning actions: inform, educate and train. As shown in Figure 2, these three fundamental activities provide a blueprint or architecture for learning that can be applied throughout the process of developing next generation know-how.

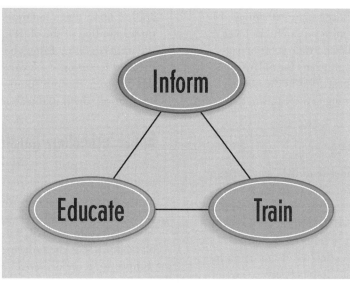

Figure 2
A Learning Architecture

Inform

Object-oriented technology is evolving very rapidly. People working with the technology must keep abreast of both the fast changing technology and the company's plans and projects that involve the technology. Regular briefings, seminars, telecasts, newsletters and other means of company communications can accomplish the following:

- Provide all employees with a working knowledge of technology and how it is being deployed in the business.

- Foster a better understanding of the cross-functional work groups that are developing and supporting the technology infrastructure

and the new object-oriented applications.

- Explain the roles and responsibilities of work groups and their relationships to other work groups.

- Keep all employees informed about changes and new plans for technology resources within the enterprise.

Staying informed involves establishing pipelines to information resources. The professional wishing to keep up will want to subscribe to new publications such as *Object Magazine* and the *Journal of Object-Oriented Programming,* and Internet news groups such as *comp.object.* The number of books being published on the topic is growing as rapidly as the technology is evolving. Corporate and IS libraries can significantly contribute to keeping business and technology professionals informed by acquiring up-to-date books on the emerging technology and business engineering.

Educate

While training is key to acquiring the skills needed, concepts and theory are prerequisite to training. Exploration and discovery are key goals of educating. Learners should be provided with a non-threatening, non-pressured opportunity to learn new concepts. As the goal is to develop "a new way of thinking," educational activities must be *learner-friendly:* fun, interactive, easy, challenging and engaging. Let's develop the big picture before facing the many details and techniques of the technology. Since we are reshaping existing mental models, we must be careful to meet the learners where they are as they participate in educational experiences. Education means formulating concepts and learning first principles in the new paradigm. Conceptual learning is prerequisite to learning new skills.

Train

Being informed helps us understand the "why." Being educated in the basic theories helps us to learn "what." Training provides the "how-to." A complete road map of the training process is developed in the next section of this paper. As we will learn, training should be centered in *doing*. The most effective means of learning a task is to perform that task. To be effective, the performance of the stated task must be based on actual project deliverables.

Once a step has been completed, the scope can be expanded, and the next iteration can proceed with additional information, education, training and experience. The transition requires learning through discovery as there are no cookbook or silver bullet solutions. Learn a little, apply a little; learn a little,

apply a little. Each iteration increases the overall understanding of the object paradigm and the deepening understanding fosters better decision-making for the next iteration. Let's turn our attention to taking the first step in transitioning to next generation computing, the initial technology transfer.

Initial Technology Transfer

Rather than explain a theoretical approach to initial technology transfer, the following discussion is based on the approach that Knowledge Systems Corporation (KSC) has developed and refined over the past six years. The intent is to use KSC's proven approach as exemplary, but not as the only approach. KSC's core competencies are centered on Smalltalk environments, but the learning *process* presented here may be generalized to serve as a model for C++ or other implementation environments.

Figure 3 depicts KSC's process for transitioning organizations and individuals from traditional development environments to object-based projects. This is referred to as KSC's Multi-Step Training Program. The program begins with theory-focused training and hands-on exercises that are presented in a traditional

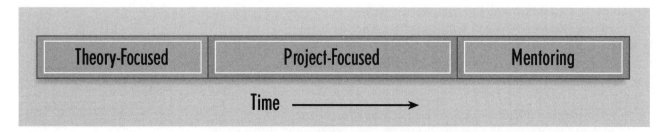

Figure 3
The Multi-Step Process
This approach starts with transferring knowledge about object technology fundamentals, then transitions to the application
of the fundamentals on a client project. Mentoring activities complement the overall strategy.

classroom environment. Development team members are then given an opportunity to apply the theory that they've been taught to a project of their choosing. This project-focused training is centered around the Smalltalk Apprentice Program℠ (STAP℠). Following the STAP are a series of mentoring activities where the development team receives custom, individualized mentoring as necessary to supplement the more formal training activities.

Theory-Focused Training

A wide variety of courses is required to meet the needs of software engineers and managers involved in object-oriented implementation efforts. A subset of the required courses and their recommended completion for different project roles appears in Table 1, An Example of an Object-Oriented Curriculum (page 157).

To optimize their effectiveness, courses must share a common educational philosophy of *learning by doing*. In keeping with this approach, hands-on exercises make up between 50-60 percent of class time. In classes where computers are necessary, each student is given his/her own machine to maximize the opportunity to explore topics independently. Instructors encourage student discovery by giving hints instead of direct answers to questions, thereby furthering the *learning by doing* approach. Pragmatic problem-solving is encouraged by the requirement that instructors have real-world experience in the subject matter they are certified to teach.

Project-Focused Training

Project-focused training takes over where the classroom education ends. Project-focused training goals are to help developers apply the theory learned in the classroom to a project they've been tasked to deliver by their management. These activities help students internalize the previously presented lessons while facilitating significant progress on the organization's development tasks. The core activity in the project-focused model is its Smalltalk Apprentice Program (STAP).

The instructor for a STAP is referred to as the STAP Master. The STAP Master acts both as an instructor and also project leader for the term of the STAP. The STAP model is shown in Figure 4. The STAP is 10 weeks in length with half of that time spent onsite at KSC and the other half working at the client's home office on the project.

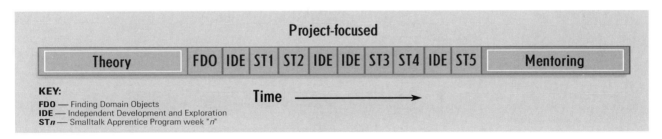

Figure 4
Smalltalk Apprentice Program (STAP)
The STAP provides an intense, project-focused education event to "make real" the O-O training received.

The rationale for the time spent at a remote training facility is twofold. First, it is virtually impossible for any single individual to possess all the technological expertise required by today's typical application development project. The time at KSC allows the STAP Master to draw on additional staff with the expertise required to ensure the success of the STAP students. Second, apprentice programs are designed to be intense, high-productivity learning events. Removing the students from their offices and any associated distractions (e.g., meetings, phone calls, faxes, etc.) allows them to concentrate on the task at hand: object technology transfer and the application of object technology to their project.

The initial activity in the STAP is the *Finding Domain Objects*SM (FDOSM) workshop. The objective of the FDO is to produce an initial domain model for subsequent use in an apprentice program. The resulting model includes domain object definitions, class definitions, class relationships, responsibilities and contracts. The FDO is typically given at the client's

site where one design "master" facilitates the activities of six or more client developers and users.

The FDO is immediately followed by a week of *Independent Development and Exploration* (IDE). IDEs are interspersed throughout the apprentice program. They serve as unsupervised times where client developers work independently of their mentors to extend the results of the supervised sessions (e.g., models, software). This time helps the students gain confidence in their abilities to use the object-oriented techniques and technologies on an independent basis.

Following the IDE week is the STAP itself. The STAP is divided into three segments — each of which is separated by IDE weeks. The initial two-week segment is spent extending and implementing the domain model that was a byproduct of the FDO. After having two weeks to work independently, the students return to begin work on their application models. This development phase includes implementation of the GUI interfaces and any interfaces to

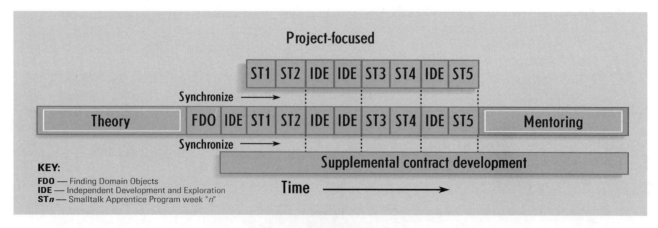

Figure 5
Parallel Smalltalk Apprentice Programs
This STAP variation is useful in large integration efforts.

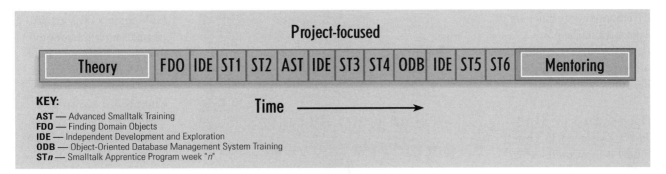

Figure 6
Smalltalk Apprentice Program — Just in Time

external databases. There is an additional IDE week followed by the final week of the STAP. This last week is typically spent on performance tuning, system packaging, and planning for the next iteration in the development lifecycle.

A variation on the STAP that is useful with larger development teams is the Parallel STAP shown in Figure 5. In this model, all members of the development team participate in the same FDO. One additional deliverable from the FDO is a partitioning of the domain model between the project sub-teams that will be working in parallel apprentice programs. STAPs then progress in parallel. Periodically, as the STAPs move forward, the teams are brought back together to share the work they've done independently. This ensures that at the end of the STAP, the individual application components can be smoothly integrated to form the basis of a working system.

Parallel STAP activities can also be supplemented with additional contract development resources if the

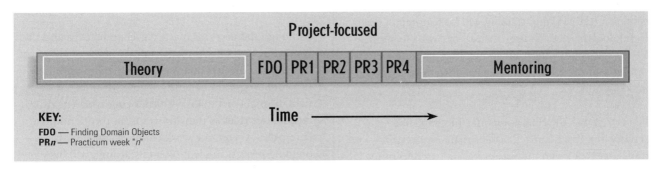

Figure 7
Practicum

development schedules are aggressive to the point that the students would be unlikely to make their deadlines on their own.

Figure 6 shows the STAP *Just in Time* model. This model is most useful when the client's application is reasonably complex and will use sophisticated technologies beyond what are normally available in an off-the-shelf Smalltalk development environment. The basic idea is to defer the classroom education events until the point in the STAP when they are to be used. Then replace the appropriate IDE weeks with the desired classroom training activities.

In Figure 6, it was determined that the target application will need to use some of the techniques taught in an Advanced Smalltalk course. Also, the application will be using an object-oriented database management system (ODBMS) and training will be required in this technology prior to its use. Instead of "front-loading" all the classroom education events, they are interspersed throughout the STAP at times closest to their project introduction.

Figure 7 shows the final apprentice program-like activity, the Practicum. Practicums are for organizations that require an intense, project-focused learning experience but do not have an internal project to drive the experience. Such companies are typically at the

> *To conceive, design and implement a learning organization to meet the enormous, diverse and widespread needs of corporations in the next century, the process of corporate learning must be reengineered.*

exploration and discovery phase regarding migration to next generation technology. Under these circumstances, KSC has developed a number of case studies specific to targeted horizontal and vertical application domains. The client organization simply chooses an application domain that is relevant to its business domain. This application then becomes the target application for the education experience.

Gearing Up for the Long Haul

The introduction of object technology and architectures should not be viewed as a one-time event. The technology and distributed computing architectures will continue to evolve rapidly. As technology becomes more of an enabler for business change, keeping current and properly applying it to business problems will become a critical success factor for business.

Although the need for master-level knowledge and skill is obvious in the technology transfer phase of corporate transformations, the master-apprenticeship approach provides long-term benefits. Those who were apprentices during a technology transfer endeavor will grow into master roles as transitions spread throughout an enterprise. Corporate work teams, charged with ongoing process innovation and learning, will benefit from sustaining this working and learning model over time.

The follow-up to initial technology transfer is developing a visible network of internal masters whose job it is to push the envelope of knowledge, technology and technique. Corporations can establish Object Technology Centers to serve as the focal point. Mentors, provocateurs, top guns and champions will be in continual demand as new projects come on stream. The process of deploying professionals in these or similar roles can be formalized and made a visible part of an Object Technology Center.

As new process engineering projects come on stream, masters are needed to mentor and inject fresh concepts and perspectives. They are essential catalysts needed to stir team chemistry and trigger team actions.

To conceive, design and implement a learning organization to meet the enormous, diverse and widespread needs of corporations in the next century, the process of corporate learning must be reengineered. In his book, *Re-Educating the Corporation*[7] , Dan Tobin provides the rationale, the principles, prerequisites and the foundations for a learning organization. He describes how a corporation can breathe life into a learning organization, how to embrace new ways of learning, and how to create a *virtual training organization.*

In *The Fifth Discipline,* M.I.T.'s Peter Senge asserts that it is possible to create learning organizations. In addition to the cornerstone, *systems thinking,* he describes four other core disciplines required to build such an organization: personal mastery, working with mental models, building shared vision and team learning.[8] These disciplines can be used to build the foundation of the successful corporation of the future. And they are prerequisite to maintaining the know-how needed for next generation computing.

Conclusion

The transition to next generation computing poses a major learning challenge. Corporate training, as usual, is not up to the challenge. Learning next generation computing requires doing — and doing in the real world with real business deliverables. Corporations that want to truly address the paradigm shift will address it and learn it in the real world, not the classroom. To achieve meaningful results, initial transition efforts should be built around a multi-step technology transfer process that centers on live business projects. Companies that *learn how to learn* next generation computing will be the pacesetters in their industries.

References

[1] Fingar, Peter, *The Blueprint for Business Objects,* SIGS Books, New York (1996).

[2] Pinson, Lewis J., "Moving from COBOL to C and C++: OOP's Biggest Challenge," *Journal of Object-Oriented Programming,* p. 54 (October 1994).

[3] Stikeleather, Jim, "Complicated Simplicity," *Computerworld Client/Server Journal,* p. 67 (April 1995).

[4] Page-Jones, Meilir, "The Seven Stages of Expertise in Software Engineering," *American Programmer* (July/August 1990). Page-Jones can be reached at 76334.1247@compuserve.com

[5] Swanstrom, Ed, "Beyond methodology transfer: O-O mentoring meets project management," *Journal of Object-Oriented Programming* (March/April 1995).

[6] "Mainframers Transition," *Computerworld,* p. 103 (March 14, 1994).

[7] Tobin, Daniel R., *Re-educating the Corporation: Foundations for the Learning Organization,* Oliver Wight Publications, Inc. (1993).

[8] Senge, Peter M., *The Fifth Discipline: The Art and Practice of the Learning Organization,* Doubleday/Currency (1990).

Suggested Readings

Barker, Joel Arthur, *Future Edge: Discovering the New Paradigms of Success*, W. Morrow, 240 pp. (1992). Since the pace of change shows no sign of slowing, successful businesses will learn to stay alert to and systematically study paradigm shifts. Barker instructs business to watch for the surprises, not extrapolate the past. The book was reprinted in paperback in 1993 under the title *Paradigms: The Business of Discovering the Future*, Harper Business Edition.

Fingar, Peter, *The Blueprint for Business Objects*, SIGS Books (1996). This book provides an overview of the learning challenges presented by both business engineering and object-oriented technology. Readers are pointed to the key works in both fields, then presented with a model curriculum that corporations can use to design custom training programs. In addition to the model curriculum, the book includes profiles of the companies that have pioneered object-oriented training: IBM's Object Technology University, Hewlett-Packard's Professional Services Division, Iconix, Object International, Knowledge Systems Corporation, and the CARM group. In addition, the book contains an extensive, classified bibliography of business engineering and object-oriented technologies.

Love, Tom, *Object Lessons: Lessons Learned in Object-Oriented Development Projects*, SIGS Books, 256 pp. (1993). Love's highly readable book focuses on building large-scale commercial software projects using objects. The book provides clear insight into the issues and trends as opposed to specific products and services. Love brings more than a decade of experience to this work. The book examines the many questions that technical leaders and managers face as they transition to object technology.

Norman, Donald A., *Design of Everyday Things*, Doubleday (1990); *Things That Make Us Smart*, Addison/Wesley (1993); *Turn Signals are the Facial Expressions of Automobiles*, Addison/Wesley (1992); *User Centered Systems Design*, Lawrence Erlbaum Assoc. (1986). Norman is the founding chair of the Department of Cognitive Science at the University of California. Developers of computer systems are well advised to read Norman's work.

Senge, Peter M., *The Fifth Discipline: The Art and Practice of the Learning Organization*, Doubleday/Currency (1990). Senge's focus on "systems thinking" represents a discipline that is central to business processes. This work has had a major impact on business reengineering.

Tobin, Daniel R., *Re-educating the Corporation: Foundations for the Learning Organization*, Oliver Wight Publications, Inc., 289 pp. (1993). Former education manager at Digital, Dan Tobin brings more than twenty years of training and development experience to the pages of this widely read book. The book provides a complete blueprint and practical tools to create virtual training opportunities and to build a dynamic learning organization.

Zuboff, Shoshanah, *In the Age of the Smart Machine: The Future of Work and Power*, Basic Books, 468 pp. (1988).

Zuboff, Shoshanah, *Psychological and Organizational Implications of Computer-Mediated Work*, Center for Information Systems Research, Alfred P. Sloan School of Management, M.I.T., 26 pp. (1981).

Enterprise Computing: The Process

By Dennis Read
In collaboration with the Object Technology Staff of The Technical Resource Connection

Contents

Abstract

Once a business sets its sights on next generation information systems, the fundamental question that follows is: "How do we get there from here?" This paper provides an overview of the strategic processes needed to adopt, deploy and successfully manage emerging technology. This is a capstone paper providing focus for many other topics in the white paper series. The paper emphasizes a business approach that leverages a corporation's current information assets.

Enterprise Computing: The Process describes the characteristics of successful technology adoption. The success factors discussed in this paper are based on a combination of theory and practical experience. After exploring the success factors, the paper describes a systematic adoption *process* that addresses these factors. The examples reference client/server computing and object-oriented development as illustrations of next generation technologies. However, the principles described here also apply to any major technological change.

Characteristics of Successful Technology Adoption

Does the following scenario sound familiar? *Your business faces mounting pressure to improve. Customer expectations continue to climb, competitors are closing in. So plans are made to respond. These plans call for system capabilities that currently do not exist. You are in some part responsible for creating these capabilities within your organization. The tools at your disposal include current systems, infrastructure, staff and practices. Each of these represents a significant investment and currently provides value. But they are just not up to the task at hand. You know you need more, but more of what? There are numerous advanced technologies and techniques that could help, but which ones? And how do you implement them while leveraging your current investments?*

The path to next generation computing is an obstacle course. Methods, tools, techniques and hype have proliferated over the past few years to the point where it is very difficult for the busy professional to keep up, much less chart a safe course to next generation computing.

In Switzerland, the famous Matterhorn casts a shadow over the town of Zermatt below. The cemetery at the foot of the mountain is a warning to those who would proceed up the steep slopes. Early pioneers who had neither maps nor guides are buried there, along with the primitive tools they thought were up to the task.

Today, Swiss law prohibits the inexperienced from

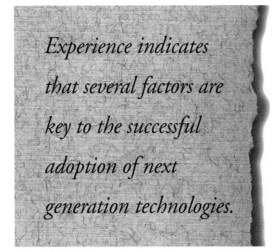

Experience indicates that several factors are key to the successful adoption of next generation technologies.

climbing the steep slopes. Today's business technology professionals tasked with adopting next generation computing should heed the message sent down from the Matterhorn: A guide is needed to survive the journey ahead. Because the trek is through territory unfamiliar to the inexperienced, even years of knowledge and skill in somewhat related domains do not directly apply. Too much is at stake to go it alone without an experienced guide to point out opportunities as well as pitfalls. The guide's map shows many alternative paths, and the guide charts the paths based on current circumstances and the goals of the climber.

Most organizations recognize the need to adopt new technologies to meet their business objectives. However, *change* must be carefully managed, and effective management calls for knowing which facets need to be monitored and controlled. Experience indicates that several factors are key to the successful adoption of next generation technologies:

- preserving and leveraging existing (legacy) systems
- investing in new infrastructure
- transitioning staff to new skills
- emphasizing architecture to facilitate system evolution
- defining and implementing a process to apply the new technology

Legacy Systems Continue to Add Value

Clearly, current information systems do not fully meet the needs of today's rapidly changing and increasingly complex business environment. But they represent a significant investment and still provide value by supporting current business operations. Any new computing environment must leverage this investment in legacy systems. The schedule for their eventual retirement should be based on a balance of business and technical issues.

The following process is based on experience and demonstrates tactics that can be used to leverage existing investments in legacy systems by including them in a new computing environment:

- Identify the logical content of the existing system in terms of the information and functionality it provides.
- Express the system contents as an abstract interface that excludes implementation details.
- Use infrastructure capabilities to publish this interface on an enterprise network.
- Direct new applications to the interface.

Figure 1, *Migrating Legacy Assets to Next Generation Information Systems,* illustrates three stages of the process. Today, systems interact through interface files. Data is exported from one system and imported into another. Before long, these interfaces consume more resources than the systems they interconnect.

In the *near term,* the system's contents are defined as an abstract interface and published on an enterprise network. Clients (users or other systems) gain access to the system's data *and* functionality through this interface. These clients are now insulated from the actual implementation of the system because they see it only as an abstract interface such as "Forecast, Remit, Supply and Receive." Object Request Brokers (ORBs) are an excellent technology for implementing this approach.

In the *long term,* the implementation of the legacy system can be reengineered with whatever technology is appropriate. Since clients see the system as an abstract interface, they are unaffected by this change.

This overall process is known as *wrapping* a legacy system. The near-term benefit is increased access to information and functionality. The long-term benefit is simpler and safer migration to advanced technology.

Wrapping also provides an opportunity to publish a system's true *semantic contents.* Users typically extend a system through usage patterns. For example, multiple billing options may be required for customers of a manufacturing company. Even though the current system does not support this feature, a user may enter information about the same customer several times with various options. When an order is taken, the entry with the desired billing option is selected. As a result of this multiple entry, the total number of customers in the system does not reflect the real customer population. Users may also employ special codes or note field entries to extend a system beyond its original design.

Extended usage patterns are critical to understanding the actual information and functionality supported by existing systems. These extended usage patterns are not seen when studying the technical, data and functional documentation of the system. Exporting the contents of a system through an abstract interface provides an opportunity to include these patterns of usage in the public definition of the system. Filtering mechanisms are inserted to match the usage patterns. In this way, knowledge usually retained by individuals is distributed throughout the organization.

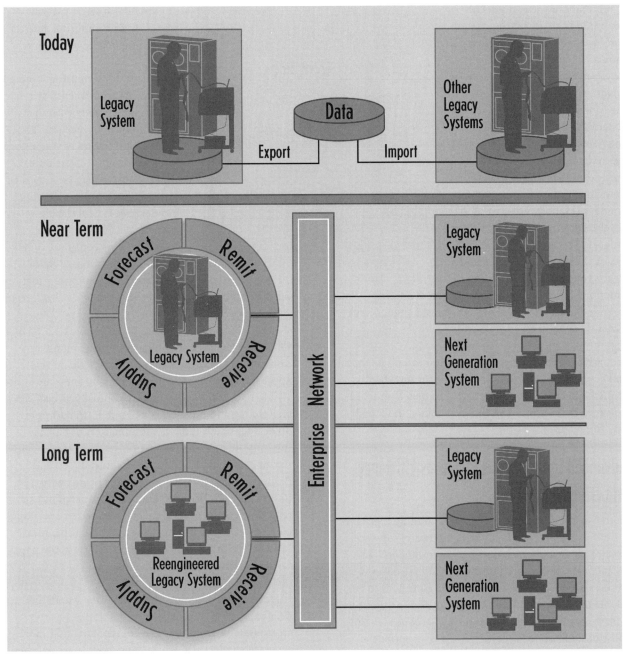

Figure 1
Migrating Legacy Assets to Next Generation Information Systems

A summary of the concepts of wrapping both an existing system and its extended usage patterns is shown in Figure 2, *Wrapping Legacy Systems and Their Extended Usage.* As shown in the figure, the functionality of the legacy system includes Forecast, Order and Cancel. However, as users of the system gained experience, they extended usage of the system to include a special forecast for holidays (Holiday Forecast) and developed procedures to expedite orders (Expedite Order). Regardless of the means used to extend a legacy system, capturing the functionality of both the original system and its extended usage is critical to publishing a system's true semantic contents.

Properly wrapping a legacy system can extend its useful and economic life and minimize disruption when its implementation is reengineered. The benefits include a universal definition, increased availability and a path way for evolution.

Advanced Infrastructure Increases Efficiency and Effectiveness

An infrastructure provides the basic building blocks for system development. It includes hardware, software, development tools and run-time environments. In recent years, there have been significant advances in all of these areas, and the rate of change continues to accelerate. The selection, installation and integration of a new infrastructure has long-term consequences and must be approached accordingly. It is important to select components that are consistent with the needs of the business and that will provide real value. Two areas

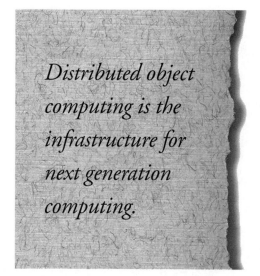

Distributed object computing is the infrastructure for next generation computing.

of particular interest include client/server computing and object-oriented development.

Client/server computing leverages networking investments by providing designers with the ability to locate processing and information resources where they are needed most. Over time, these resources may be moved or scaled in response to changing business needs. Increasing network performance and declining costs continue to make distributed technology more attractive. For more information on this topic, please see our white paper, *Client/Server Architectures.*

Object-oriented development is now being used in mission critical applications. The benefits of this approach are clear. Elements of the business are clearly visible in the software. The conceptual gap between technology and business is narrowed. In addition, objects represent unified combinations of data and function that are independent of their context. This means that they may be used in multiple settings. Achieving the goal of reuse initially begins with program code. With experience, organizations can reap the benefits of reusing analysis models and design patterns. For more information on this topic please see The Technical Resource Connection's white paper, *Getting Started With Object Technology.*

Client/server technology puts resources where they are needed most. Object-oriented development tools create systems from reusable components that more accurately reflect real world concepts. Together, these technologies increase the efficiency and effectiveness of

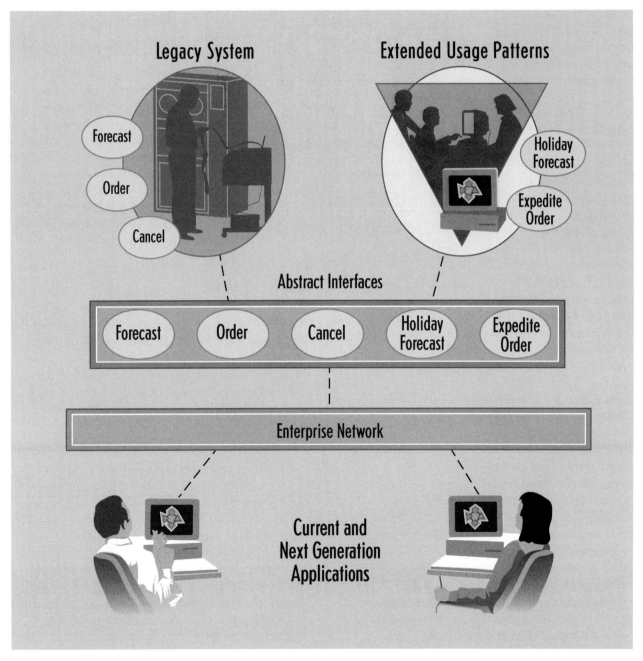

Figure 2
Wrapping Legacy Systems and Their Extended Usage

both developers and end-users. Software that supports their tasks becomes more intuitive and responsive to change.

Distributed object computing blends together the power of client/server computing and object-oriented development by distributing clients and servers (cooperating objects) across a network and allowing the objects to interoperate as a unified whole. This advanced infrastructure can empower businesses to construct new era applications that were once technically impossible. Progressive corporations are embracing this emerging technology for competitive advantage.

Simply stated, many workflow and other new era business applications would not be feasible without a distributed object infrastructure. These applications are highly collaborative and integrate resources from many systems, often within and outside an enterprise. Further, distributed objects can integrate multiple problem-solving paradigms, such as logic-based, procedural and constraint satisfaction. Distributed object computing is *the* infrastructure for next generation computing. But organizations should not be misled. Distributed object computing is as much a *way of thinking* as it is an infrastructure. Without a corresponding paradigm shift, these tools and techniques will not generate the desired results. For more information on this topic please see our white paper, *Distributed Object Computing for Business*.

> *Since the style of thinking that creates a problem can not be used to solve it, new approaches to problem-solving are needed.*

Developers Apply New Skills to New Challenges

Accelerating change in the business environment has placed more and more demands on today's systems development professionals. The adoption of new technologies and techniques places yet more demands on developers as new methods and tools are applied to more complex problems.

The only way to ensure successful adoption of advanced technology is to successfully transition information system developers. Current system development staffs embody significant value and intellectual capital. They understand the current systems and infrastructure. They also possess extensive domain knowledge that takes years to accumulate and that may not exist in written form.

Next generation computing requires developers to:

- adopt new *problem-solving* approaches
- master the use of new *tools*
- understand new *processes*
- work in new *organizations*

Since the style of thinking that creates a problem can not be used to solve it, new approaches to *problem-solving* are needed. Although the term "paradigm shift" has become trite, the cliché does bear the truth that a fundamental shift in thinking is required to apply next generation technologies effectively. Further, the classroom has not proven adequate for learning next generation computing. Learning new ways of thinking and problem-solving is best accomplished in the real world through mentoring and hands-on training. People need time to assimilate new concepts and reinforce them through experience with real business projects.

The ability to change is now more important than the ability to create.

Examples of new *tools* include: design editors that manipulate advanced notations; languages that treat processes, objects and events as first class concepts; middleware that glues together the network; and debuggers that monitor multiple execution threads on distributed processors. Each tool extends a developer's capability, but also requires new skills. In addition, developers need to master integrated project support environments that tie the tools together. For more information on this subject, see The Technical Resource Connection's white paper, *Integrated Project Support Environments.* Time and experience are needed to develop competency and proficiency with these advanced tools and environments.

Enterprise scale projects that apply advanced technologies are often staffed by multiple development teams. These teams may be remotely located and have their work periodically integrated for system level testing. Attempting this scale of development without a well-defined *process* is a sure recipe for failure. Not all developers are accustomed to operating under a well-defined process. Practices like configuration management and quality assurance may be resisted. Education will help developers see the value of a development

process, and training can provide the comfort level needed to be effective in a process-centered environment.

The adoption of advanced technology is more about roles and responsibilities and less about titles and reporting hierarchies. Many of these technologies are better applied under an iterative and incremental process where teams work together to advance the development process. Team-based *organizations* may be new to some developers. Team-building exercises and clear directives can help developers accept change and operate under team-based forms of organization.

Adopting new technologies places extensive demands on developers and their managers. Both are expected to change the way they think and work, as individuals and in groups. Learning should not be viewed as a one-time event. A learning organization is needed to promote continuous learning. The key to a successful transition is setting clear goals and giving developers the time and opportunity to learn from their successes and mistakes. New approaches to problem-solving will not come from sitting in a class or reading a book. For more information on this topic, see our white paper, *Object-Oriented Knowledge Transfer.* A key concept in this paper is the assessment of developers based on seven levels of mastery and subsequent curriculum creation to advance them through these levels.

Architectural Thinking Allows for Change

Advanced technologies increase developer productivity through new tools and techniques. But creating applications is just the beginning. Next generation systems are expected to evolve throughout their lifetime. The ability to *change* is now more important than the ability to create. And the velocity of change continues to increase. These changes may result from new business requirements or the adoption of new technologies. One should not impede the other. Accommodating change requires deliberate planning. Planning for change is one of the goals of software architecture.

The reality is that all systems have an architecture. The real questions are how visible is the architecture and does it provide for business and technical evolution? Software architecture definition has long been an intuitive process with few formal procedures or notations. Today, the increasing rate of business and technological change is forcing developers to seriously examine the architecture of new systems. Formal procedures and notations have emerged that describe

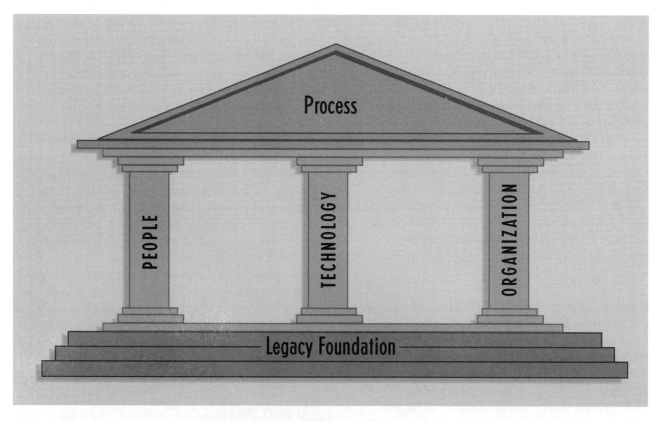

Figure 3
Process: The Capstone of Enterprise Computing

the arrangement and inter-connection of components within a system, the system's architecture. These procedures and notations help us better evaluate a proposed architecture, given the goals of the system. Including architectural planning in the development process helps ensure the longevity of systems being developed.

A Well-Defined Process Ensures Success

Let's assume that all of the bases are covered: Legacy systems have been included in development plans; new infrastructure has been installed and integrated into the development environment; and developers have become members of interdisciplinary work teams. Maybe some training on architectural thinking, planning and notations has also been included. But, what makes it all come together? Those who study physics learned long ago that things do not just "come together." Entropy is the universe's never-ending march toward disorder. Software projects are no exception: They do not just "come together." *Process* brings the ingredients together by interlocking people, technology and organization as a business builds next generation systems on its legacy foundation. These relationships are illustrated in Figure 3, *Process: The Capstone of Enterprise Computing.*

A well-defined process identifies how development work should be done. It also includes measures for determining whether things are going according to plan. A feedback mechanism monitors the current process, determines its effectiveness, and suggests areas for improvement. Continuous process improvement is the key to long-term success.

A Successful Technology Adoption Process

We have outlined the characteristics of successful technology adoption. These factors require careful attention during the transition to new technologies. This section outlines how a qualified guide can assist organizations in transitioning to new technologies by maintaining a focus on the critical success factors. As shown in Figure 4, typical transitions move through three high-level phases:

1. Assessment
2. Planning
3. Execution

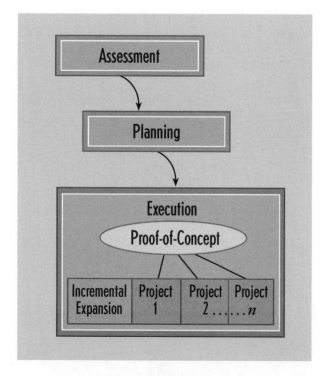

Figure 4
The Three Phases of Technology Transition

Each of these phases is discussed below.

Assessment Defines the Destination

During an assessment, the experienced guide learns about the organization's goals and objectives. The guide documents the current capabilities of the systems, infrastructure and staff. An understanding of the current development process also is acquired. This information is critical to ensure a successful transition and will be used in the planning phase.

Drawing from similar experience, the guide consults with the organization to describe possible alternatives to reaching their goals. Although several paths will be described and reviewed, the actual development plan will reflect the specific needs and preferences of the organization. Regardless of the specific alternatives chosen, certain activities must be present to ensure success. Decisions must take into consideration available resources and sensitivity to risk. There is no "standard" development plan since each business is unique.

Planning Defines the Route

Once the assessment is complete, a plan can be built to realize the organization's goals and objectives. This plan includes activities that address the key elements of success.

Legacy systems are examined, and tasks are created to define their interfaces and integrate them into the enterprise network. An infrastructure sub-plan addresses the selection, installation and integration of any required hardware, software, networking components or development tools. Based on current developer skills, tasks are created for education and training.

Life-cycle tasks are also given adequate time for mentoring activities. Prior to analysis, tasks are created to define an overall system architecture.

Systems created under a well-defined architecture will exhibit the qualities of conceptual integrity. In the short term, this quality helps organize and manage the development process. In the long term, it facilitates business and technical evolution.

The overall shape of the plan is governed by a process framework. This framework identifies essential development life-cycle activities as well as quality management tasks that ensure project success. Quality activities include reviews, inspections and configuration management tasks that protect project deliverables. The framework also includes guidelines for estimation and risk management.

Like software, development plans should be based on an architecture that allows for *change*. During planning, tasks that will be executed in the near term are defined in detail. Long-term tasks are more generally scoped, abstractly defined and roughly estimated at this stage of planning. A mechanism must be provided to replace general or abstract tasks with more detailed versions as the project progresses and more is learned.

A major source of change is the business itself. The detailed initial plans are based on current business goals and objectives. On the other hand, adopting advanced technology is a long-term commitment. It is reasonable to assume that business conditions will change during

Like software, development plans should be based on an architecture that allows for change.

the course of the project. Flexible plans require a component-based framework that permits changes during the project's execution.

Execution

Careful assessment and planning are essential to successful technology adoption. Enlisting an experienced guide will ensure that plans address all of the factors that are required to succeed. However, initial projects introduce change in virtually all facets of development:

- new development paradigm
- new infrastructure and developer skills
- new roles, responsibilities and organization

This much change all at once is a sure formula for high risk.

A Proof-of-Concept Project Manages Risk

Fortunately, risk management can be achieved through a proof-of-concept project that introduces these new facets in a controlled environment. A proof-of-concept project is planned in the same way as any other project. The differences lie in:

- goal selection
- project scope and duration
- development pace

The goal of a proof-of-concept project is to balance risk and validation. The project must demonstrate value to the organization without introducing unnecessary risk.

An organization does not want to bet the business, but the resulting application should not be a toy. Legacy integration projects are good candidates for a proof-of-concept endeavor. Such projects can provide value by delivering seamless access to information that was previously disjointed. This exercises the new infrastructure and provides improved decision-making. Since information remains available in its original form, no new business risk is introduced.

The scope and duration of a proof-of-concept project is usually limited to a maximum of nine months. If results can be produced in six months, so much the better. The short duration and limited scope brings the project to closure so that the effectiveness of the new technology can be assessed. Required adjustments can be made before moving on to additional projects.

The development pace for a proof-of-concept project is generally slowed to allow developers time to learn. Tasks are structured to provide early opportunities for success. It is important that developers build confidence in themselves before moving on to more aggressive schedules. New concepts require hands-on experience and time to be assimilated.

Incremental Delivery Sets A Sustainable Pace

Upon the completion of the proof-of-concept project, any needed adjustment will be made to the development infrastructure and supporting processes. From this point forward, an incremental delivery philosophy should be adopted. Ideally, deliverables should be made every six months, depending on the needs of the organization. The important point is to avoid the multi-year development cycle where products are delivered just after their usefulness has ended.

Frequent deliveries allow the organization to change priorities and direction when appropriate. This arrangement also enhances credibility with customers and builds morale among developers. From a quality perspective, each delivery provides useful feedback for continuous process improvement.

Conclusion

When properly selected and applied, next generation technology can provide significant benefits to an organization. This paper described the *critical success factors* for migrating to next generation technology and outlined an adoption *process* for applying these success factors. The process takes into account the investments in existing systems and provides ways to leverage these valuable assets. The process builds on the foundation of legacy systems, and orchestrates the people, technology and organizations needed to adopt next generation technology.

The magnitude of change is so great that it is forcing organizations to migrate to next generation technology. Although an organization can go it alone, an experienced guide can show the way and allow a company to maintain its business focus during the journey ahead.

Suggested Readings

Ganti, Ph.D., Narsim and William Brayman, *The Transition of Legacy Systems to a Distributed Architecture,* John Wiley and Sons (1995). Both Ganti and Brayman have substantial experience in moving from legacy to architected systems for the Boeing Company. They describe an architecture-based approach to migrating legacy systems, outline a series of steps that can be used to realign information technology with changing business strategies, and offer guidelines on visualizing the transition process.

Mattison, Rob and Michael J. Sipolt, *The Object-Oriented Enterprise: Making Corporate Information Systems Work,* McGraw-Hill, 400 pp. (1994). This book is aimed directly at corporate information systems. Its in-depth coverage of large-scale business information systems makes the book indispensable for business and technology professionals. The book considers immediate and tactical applications of object technology and the use of design methods and CASE tools. More than two and a half years of research went into this book. The results are presented in a thorough discussion of the topic of objectification, the process of migrating to object-oriented corporate information systems. The book covers logical and physical architectures and the development of an object-oriented infrastructure.

Taylor, Ph.D., David, *Object-Oriented Technology: A Manager's Guide,* Addison-Wesley, 146 pp. (1991). This brief and award-winning primer is ideal for the busy manager. It explains the concepts, the business impact, and the advantages and realities of object-oriented technology.

Taylor, Ph.D., David, *Business Engineering with Object Technology,* John Wiley & Sons, 188 pp. (1995). Taylor fuses business and software engineering into a new discipline: convergent engineering. The essence of his method is to express business concepts directly in executable software objects. This work promises to become one of the seminal works in object-oriented business process engineering.

Brodie, Michael L. and Michael Stonebraker, *Migrating Legacy Systems: Gateways, Interfaces & The Incremental Approach,* Morgan Kaufman, 210 pp. (1995). This thorough, well-written book centers on an 11-step migration approach the authors have dubbed the *Chicken Little* approach: step-by-step, controlling risk all the way. The book includes case studies and discussion of available tools.

Understanding
Systems Architecture

A BUSINESS BRIEF

By Victor Chapel, Ronald C. Aronica and Mark Alessi
In collaboration with the Object Technology Staff of The Technical Resource Connection

Contents

Abstract

During the first four decades of business computing, the scope and complexity of most applications were limited to standalone solutions. Limited machine resources further constrained these systems. Architecture was implicit and of little interest to the day-to-day affairs of IS. Today, technological advances and their associated financial improvements make it possible to conceive and to build information systems capable of supporting streamlined business processes that span a major business area or the entire enterprise. Companies are grappling with how to develop next generation information systems—not necessarily because they want to or just because they can, but because the new competitive environment mandates change.

As businesses place more and more demands on their underlying information systems, the complexity of these systems rapidly becomes overwhelming. IS must not only cope with escalating complexity, but must provide leadership for managing business change. Systems architecture is key to the ability of IS to translate increasingly complex business requirements into adaptive information systems just as traditional architecture is key to translating the space requirements of business into effective work environments. Today, systems architecture is a strategic business responsibility of IS regardless of the technologies and platforms used to develop systems. Systems architecture provides the blueprint for mapping technology onto the real-world requirements of business. It produces mental representations that are intelligible to all the information systems participants: business managers, designers and builders.

This business brief presents an analogy between traditional building architecture and systems architecture by showing the steps required to build an office complex and relating the activities of a building architect to those of a systems architect.

Architecture's Role

A bicycle shed is a building, but Lincoln Cathedral is a piece of architecture.

Nicholas Pevsner

There is an urgent need for a comprehensive, rigorously developed computational theory of design that can provide an adequate basis for practical software development work.

William J. Mitchell, *The Logic of Architecture*

Both architects and business managers live in ill-structured, unbounded worlds where analytic rationality is insufficient and optimum solutions are rare. Both have perspectives that are strategic and top-down. Top managers, like chief architects, must architect strategies that will handle the unforseeable, avoid disaster and produce results satisfactory to multiple clients—to boards of directors, customers, employees and the general public. Their common modus operandi *is one of fit, balance and compromise in the overall interest of the system and its purposes.*

Eberhardt Rechtin, *Systems Architecting*

Innovation is power, and information enables innovation. Corporations are struggling with exploding demands for information. Competitive pressures make it necessary to connect islands of information, resources and people into a cohesive whole. New era applications—workflow, collaboration, electronic data interchange, on-line imaging and intelligent documents—can enable business process innovation and alter a company's position in its industry's value chain. The new business objectives demand a fully integrated information framework and infrastructure. Most CEOs and CIOs recognize the business imperative for next generation information systems that can span major business areas or an entire enterprise.

Unfortunately, today's application approaches are simply incapable of handling the requirements of next generation business computing. Organizations built their existing islands of information with incompatible proprietary hardware, software and networks. Today, they cannot integrate these information islands. The same information residing in different systems has different meanings—the context within each system determines the information's meaning. The islands do not scale to handle workloads that span major business areas or the enterprise. The very thought of integrating these disparate systems conjures up a nightmare of complexity.

These legacy information resources, however, contain great business value both in the functions they perform and the business information they contain. As any successful business investor would argue, these are valuable assets, which provide the lifeblood of current business operations. Exciting new technologies seem to offer breakthrough advantages—distributed object computing and fine-grained client/server architectures offer the promise of superior and more cost-effective solutions for tying existing islands of information into a cohesive whole. But the business case dominates the technology case: How do we successfully develop, maintain, enhance and change complex systems given our historically poor track record? It is little wonder the challenge of migrating to next generation information systems is such a difficult business decision.

Many forward-thinking organizations recognize that object technology holds promise for making next generation computing a reality. Object technology and fine-grained client/server architectures can help put our nightmares to rest by helping manage complexity. They allow partitioning both the business and technical domains into their component parts *(decomposition)*, keeping unrelated activities separate *(decoupling)*, and hiding implementation details *(encapsulation)*. Decomposing and decoupling components enhance the potential for reusing these components. Encapsulation simplifies system maintenance and enhancement. Together, they provide the means for developing flexible, adaptable, evolving information systems. Along with making the semantics of the business visible in software, these techniques additionally allow for successfully integrating legacy assets with next generation systems. Indeed, these new technologies are inviting to business, but technology is a double-edged sword.

> *A key aspect of applied first principles is the understanding that business decisions drive most architectural decisions.*

The Need For Systems Architectures

Distributed object computing (the combination of object technology with fine-grained client/server architectures) makes it possible to develop adaptive information systems and to distribute computing power throughout an enterprise network. But these technologies alone will not provide a competitive advantage. Realizing the advantage of next generation business computing requires an overarching structure—an *architecture*—that rationalizes, arranges and connects components to produce the desired functionality both now and in the future. In most businesses, these components include prior, current and emerging generations of technologies and applications. *Without architecture, distributed computing in a heterogeneous environment is certain to result in distributed chaos.* Developing a systems architecture, therefore, is not an option but a necessity for successfully implementing complex, next generation systems. Without architecture, the software crisis—the inability to build enough software, on-time and with sufficient quality—will continue.

Further, systems architecture provides a framework for designing changeable systems even when these systems do not span the entire enterprise. Information systems must be able to respond to changes in the business and in technology. The need for systems to evolve over time and the requirement for ongoing enhancements and maintenance create growing complexity in information systems. A good systems architecture provides a framework for change—and change is one of the few constants in today's business world.

Traditional architecture and systems architecture use similar processes for developing their respective end-products. Traditional architecture results in physical buildings and structures. The architect calls upon architecture's *first principles*[1] and combines them with the experience of doing architecture in the real world. Whom do you want to design *your* new office complex—an architect fresh out of school or one who also has practical architectural experience? The experienced architect works with applied first principles. Applied first principles add practical experience and integrate fit, balance and compromise into the architectural process. In school, architects are first taught lessons and then given tests. *In the real world, architects are given tests first, and then the lessons follow.* One internationally renowned architect told of how he "starved" until he reached age 42; one cannot learn applied first principles overnight.

There is no single, general-purpose architecture that is correct for every situation. There are, rather, different styles—styles that change and come into and go out of favor over time. Architectural style is the way in which something is said, done, expressed or performed. It is a quality of imagination and individuality expressed in one's actions and tastes. Style creates the sense of a unified whole from separately developed—both in time and in space—human artifacts, be they buildings or software. In traditional architecture, we recognize the styles of noted architects and periods—for example, the Frank Lloyd Wright and Baroque styles of architecture.

A systems architecture results in information structures. A good systems architecture is the secret to gaining the competitive advantage through less expensive, faster and better information systems. Systems architectures are the linchpins needed for systems that successfully span an enterprise and embrace change.

Qualified systems architects possess applied first principles including the understanding that most architectural decisions are driven by business decisions, particularly business investment decisions. The cost of developing a systems architecture is a relatively small fraction of the total enterprise information systems cost. It does, however, provide the necessary structure and rationale for making the investment decisions.

Systems architectures have their own styles just as do building architectures. Aesthetic demands and technological improvements influence systems architectural style. Layering, isolating volatility, establishing protocols, and technological improvements, such as distributed object technology, strongly influence today's architectural styles.

Placing a system within a context and using it within that context are what makes architecture important. The enterprise that successfully designs complex systems appreciates the need to match process and style with the organization. What if we simply ignore architecture and continue to build more information systems as we have done in the past? The Winchester House, near San Francisco, is an example of constructing a building without an architecture. The similarities between the Winchester House (see inset) and many of today's information systems are all too obvious.

The enterprise that recognizes the importance of

> A popular tourist attraction in the San Francisco Bay area, the Winchester House, is a result of nonstop construction spanning a 38-year period and which consumed vast resources. Supposedly haunted by ghosts of those poor souls killed by rifles made by her husband, Mrs. Winchester turned to her spiritual advisors who told her that she would live as long as she continued to build her house. Today, people tour the mansion that has, as its highlights, a chimney that does not quite reach the roof, doors and windows shut off by walls, a greater number of hallways than rooms and stairways that lead to ceilings.

---

[1] First principles are axioms, laws or abstractions that represent the highest possible degree of generalization.

systems architecture needs to ask several fundamental business questions: What business problem does architecture solve? What is the value added by having a systems architecture? What are appropriate architecture investment levels? What are the tangible results, i.e., deliverables of a systems architecture?

The Essence of Systems Architecture

All systems have an underlying architecture or logical scheme for defining their interfaces and arranging their components. Today, most systems architectures are *implicit,* but next generation business systems require that systems architectures be made *explicit.*

Nature is an example of what happens without an explicit architecture. Replication with random variation in a selective environment is the process that determines which species survive. Through natural selection, some variations prove valuable and survive; others do not and die out. Millions of years go into selecting the valuable variations. The result has the appearance—but only the appearance—of an architecture, a seamless whole to which each component effectively and efficiently contributes. Information systems do not have this amount of time to evolve and to rely on natural selection. Having a logical construct, a blueprint—an *architecture*—removes the randomness from the process. An architecture allows us to avoid spending time and effort developing systems only to find out later that they are not valuable and are dead-ends.

Business organizations also have an underlying architecture.

> *Systems architecture goes beyond any individual technology and provides the foundation for integrating disparate resources into enterprise solutions.*

For example, an organization's chief financial architect is its CFO. Rather than designing buildings, CFOs develop architectures generally using work breakdown structures. Arranging and connecting the concepts and semantics of corporate tax accounting, investment portfolio management, cost accounting and bookkeeping help ensure the financial organization's effectiveness and efficiency. The successful CFO is a successful architect who synthesizes the right components to build solid financial structures for serving the corporation.

The architectural framework needed for information systems probably will not come from within the IS community. *Architecture* is an emotionally charged word within this community: We have vested job interests in network architectures, client/server architectures, software architectures and the like. Yet traditional architecture, with 2,000 years of evolution, provides a relevant model. IS can adopt the ideas contained within traditional architecture and apply its definitions, notions and first principles to systems architecture. Increasing numbers of forward-thinking systems architects have, on their personal bookshelves, classic architecture books by recognized authorities such as U.C. Berkeley's Christopher Alexander and Harvard's William Mitchell.

With *Next Generation Architectures,* we can meet the challenge of enterprise computing by integrating current and emerging technologies. Systems architecture goes beyond any individual technology by providing the foundation for integrating disparate resources into solutions with an enterprise reach. Architecture addresses the selection, connection and arrangement of components to produce a desired result—a result that is much greater than the sum of its parts. Today's new and existing components—hardware, software, networks and applications—are disparate, scattered and isolated. Tying them together can appear to be overwhelmingly complex, but an explicit systems architecture can provide the framework for helping to manage this complexity.

How does a systems architect create a successful architecture? To answer that question, this business brief presents the analogy of developing an architecture for an office complex and relates the steps a building architect follows to those a systems architect follows.

Architectural Analogy

Developing an architecture for an office complex provides an easy-to-follow analogy for the process of creating a systems architecture. We turn to the imaginary Tennis Research Corporation, Inc. (TRCINC) to provide us with the analogy.

A couple of Harvard drop-outs who had a better idea for tennis racquets began TRCINC. After gaining initial market acceptance, TRCINC became wildly successful. Over a very short period, the company experienced rapid growth and diversified, grabbing the attention of Wall Street. Today, the company has headquarters located next to a cow pasture in Florida and has departments scattered throughout the United States: Advertising in New York City, Procurement in San Francisco, Manufacturing in Detroit and Distribution in Atlanta.

Halfway into its fifth year of operation, its CEO, Matt Allbright, noticed the first negative blip on the screen — productivity had begun to fall as a result of its scattered operations. Looking out at the cow pasture, he envisioned a new office complex that would integrate TRCINC's disparate resources into a consolidated, lean mean productivity machine capable of sustaining leadership in TRCINC's fast-paced industry.

TRCINC called upon a renowned architect to design and to build a new office complex. To meet the overall requirements of the corporation, Matt asked that the new office complex use the existing office buildings where possible and support the company's expected growth.

We will follow the process the architect used for designing and building the new office complex.

Today

Tomorrow

The Architectural Process

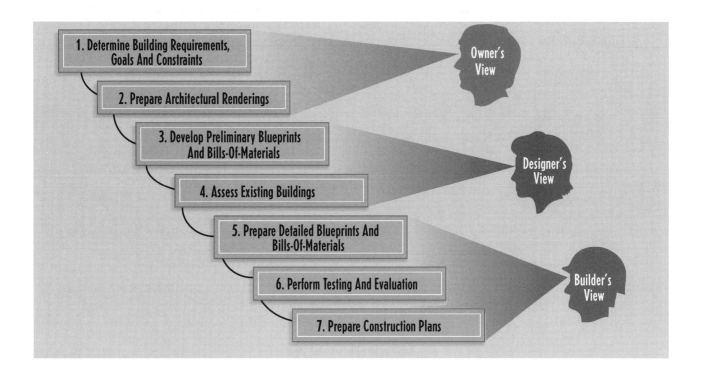

1. Determine Building Requirements, Goals And Constraints

2. Prepare Architectural Renderings

3. Develop Preliminary Blueprints And Bills-Of-Materials

4. Assess Existing Buildings

5. Prepare Detailed Blueprints And Bills-Of-Materials

6. Perform Testing And Evaluation

7. Prepare Construction Plans

Owner's View

Designer's View

Builder's View

TRCINC's architect is going to construct the new office complex by completing a three-phase architectural plan. Each phase describes the same entity, the office complex, but views the entity from the perspective of the process' different participants—owner, designer and builder. Many of these ideas were first formulated in 1987 by IBM's John Zachman (see Suggested Readings).

1. Owner's View. The first phase develops an understanding of TRCINC's requirements and produces conceptual renderings of the office complex. The representation is from the owner's perspective. Renderings show an office complex that captures all of TRCINC's perceived requirements. The equivalent systems architectural component is a business model that describes the architecture from the view of the business, not from the view of IS.

2. Designer's View. The second phase produces the designer's view (preliminary blueprints and bills-of-materials) and assesses existing resources. The view translates TRCINC's requirements and perceptions into a design for the office complex. It is the architect's representation of the complex and provides a specification of the materials used. It is the basis for developing the builder's view during the next phase.

3. Builder's View. The third phase develops blueprints, bills-of-materials and construction plans. These

DEVELOPING AN OFFICE COMPLEX ARCHITECTURE	DEVELOPING A SYSTEMS ARCHITECTURE
I. Develop Owner's Renderings 　1. Determine building requirements, goals and constraints 　2. Prepare architectural renderings	**I. Develop Business Architecture** 　1. Determine business requirements, goals and constraints 　2. Prepare proposed business architecture
II. Develop Design Plans 　1. Develop preliminary blueprints and bills-of-materials 　2. Assess existing buildings and other resources	**II. Develop Information Systems Model** 　1. Determine system architecture description and proposed functional components 　2. Prepare information systems model, which includes assessing legacy systems, technical infrastructure and implementation options
III. Develop Builder and Shop Plans 　1. Prepare detailed blueprints and bills-of-materials 　2. Perform testing and evaluation 　3. Prepare construction plans	**III. Develop Technical and Implementation Architectures** 　1. Specify process framework and detailed component list 　2. Do proof-of-concept project 　3. Prepare implementation plan

Table 1
Architecture Phases and Steps

are the detailed plans for building the office complex. They reflect applying the realities of existing resources and constraints to the conceptual renderings. They are the detailed blueprints—site, electrical, plumbing, masonry, etc.—of the entire complex. The building contractor and sub-contractors will use them for constructing the complex.

Table 1, "Architecture Phases and Steps," shows the three phases and the seven steps that implement them. In this and the following Tables, the left columns describe traditional architecture activities, and the right columns describe equivalent systems architecture activities.

1. Determine Building Requirements, Goals and Constraints

The first step is the most difficult. Uncovering the new office complex's true requirements is perhaps the most challenging task faced by the architect. TRCINC has general, high-level notions of its requirements. The architect must apply analytical methods and rely on his experience to flesh out the true requirements. The architect must incorporate the overall requirements into TRCINC's specific goals and constraints. What is the purpose of the new office complex? What is the required functionality? What are its limiting factors and constraints?

OFFICE COMPLEX REQUIREMENTS

Provide adequate space for employees to conduct business.
Provide meeting rooms for employees and guests.
Reduce costs of operating multiple locations.
Use existing Florida property.

INFORMATION SYSTEMS REQUIREMENTS

Provide enterprise-wide information access.
Allow for developing reliable systems in a timely manner.
Electronically interact with customers and suppliers.
Leverage legacy system investments.

OFFICE COMPLEX GOALS

Improve efficiency and workflow by grouping staff by work unit.
Allow for normal business operations when building new office complex.
Control heating and air conditioning costs.
Use existing wiring for voice and data.

INFORMATION SYSTEM GOALS

Reduce application development time by 50 percent.
Reduce processing, retrieval and storage time by 30 percent.
Reduce the time for doing research and development.
Implement reengineered processes.

OFFICE COMPLEX CONSTRAINTS

Must house 500 employees.
Zoning limits building to fifteen stories.
Lot size is five acres.
Must meet building and environmental codes and regulations.
Working with fixed budget.
Competitors have on-site demonstration facilities; we need them, too.

INFORMATION SYSTEMS CONSTRAINTS

Must support 500 users.
Users are at ten facilities throughout the United States.
Data Center is in New York.
Must meet government regulations and reporting requirements.
Working with fixed budget.
Competitors have Internet access for customers; we need it, too.

Table 2
Business Requirements, Goals and Constraints

Goals reflect activities that will improve TRCINC's bottom line. Requirements differ from goals in that an architecture either meets or does not meet a requirement. The architect and owner, on the other hand, use a scale to measure goals. It is possible to completely achieve, to partially achieve, or not to achieve a goal. Goals can conflict with one another. The architect, along with TRCINC's management, determines which goals to satisfy and to what extent to satisfy them.

Constraints are factors unaffected by architectural changes. Constraints differ from requirements and goals in that they involve factors from the larger world outside the office complex's design space, such as building codes and site layout. Constraints identified during this phase directly relate to the business; they are not resource or technology constraints. Later phases will identify resource and technology constraints.

Some things that first appear to be constraints may not, in reality, be constraints; they may be opportunities. For example, the possibility that customers refuse to change tennis racquets more frequently than once every three years is a concern to TRCINC. This, if true, will limit TRCINC's growth and its need for additional manufacturing facilities. What at first appears to be a constraint may actually be an opportunity for developing new and improved marketing strategies. It may be possible, for example, to convince players that they

> *An architecture incorporates three representations, each from a different perspective — the owner's, the designer's and the builder's.*

need different racquets for playing under different conditions.

The architect studies the requirements, goals and constraints. The first architectural deliverable is an initial representation (Zachman refers to this as a *bubble chart*) that depicts, in gross terms, the shape, size, spatial relationships and essential purpose of the office complex. Requirements, goals and constraints define the *ballpark* within which further design work takes place. Interaction and conversation between the architect and Matt Allbright must convince Mr. Allbright that the architect fully understands the intent of the new office complex. From this definition of the project's scope and objectives, the architect and TRCINC have a common ground from which the architect can move forward.

2. Prepare Architectural Renderings

During this step, the architect develops and presents one or more possible sketches, scale models and renderings of the new office complex. The architect repeats this process until the client, TRCINC, and he agree upon the broad outlines for the design. Renderings are a representation of TRCINC's view of the complex. When developing the renderings, the architect takes into account all the business requirements, goals and constraints. This helps ensure the design accommodates the needed functionality.

The architect must present possible solutions with sufficient clarity so the client can envision the proposed solution. As happens in so many arenas, *the client will know the solution when he sees it.*

The architect adds his training, experience, style and æsthetic senses to the client's requirements, goals and constraints. Equally important, the architect brings unarticulated assumptions to the process.

Consider the variety of structures people throughout the world use for offices. Imagine describing such a structure simply in terms of its requirements, goals and constraints. The person describing the structure may have a good—but unarticulated—idea of what its appearance "should be." The architect gives these assumptions substance and helps develop the same mental images with architectural renderings. The same problem occurs when developing information systems. The user, the client, has unarticulated ideas of what the system "should be." It is the business model that helps ensure both the systems architect and user have the same understanding and vision of the new system.

Architectural renderings, conceptual drawings and scale models help bring a meeting of the minds on a form that will accommodate the function. They help the client to envision how the office complex may look after initial construction and, perhaps years later, after completing an entire master plan.

ARCHITECTURAL RENDERING	CONCEPTUAL SYSTEMS ARCHITECTURE & BUSINESS MODEL
Shows the office complex as it exists within its environment. Contains floor plans with major features, workspaces and facilities. Includes representations showing the complex's artistic motif.	Bounds the system within the real world. Presents a high-level, business-oriented systems representation. Presents conceptual user interfaces.

Table 3
Architectural Rendering

3. Develop Preliminary Blueprints and Bills-Of-Materials

The representation shifts to the designer's view during this step. The architect combines the requirements, goals, constraints and renderings to create the designer's preliminary representation of the office complex. This representation may include specifications for site-work, heating and air conditioning, electrical and masonry. These plans will serve as the basis for communicating and negotiating with the builders.

The architect develops the preliminary bills-of-materials by studying the requirements, goals and constraints in light of the current blueprints.

The architect generates several ideas for plans and materials. After synthesizing the promising ideas, he subjects them to rigorous analysis before selecting the best ones. Applied first principles are essential to the process. The architect subjects the components, requirements and constraints to financial analysis. He weighs and re-weighs them by using a combination of *art, science* and *finance* to arrive at the optimum architectural and functional solutions that exhibit the maximum return-on-business-investment. This return-on-investment is the return from investing in an architecture.

PRELIMINARY BLUEPRINTS	ARRANGEMENTS AND CONNECTIONS
Floor plans that facilitate communication among business units, privacy when necessary and material and information flow.	Translates business domain into information system domain. Specifies the best arrangement for information, software and technical components.

PRELIMINARY BILLS-OF-MATERIALS	COMPONENTS LIST
Best materials for the office complex based on the properties of the materials and on cost/benefit analysis.	Best system components for architecture based on the attributes of the components and on cost/benefit analysis.

Table 4
Preliminary Blueprints and Bills-Of-Materials

4. Assess Existing Buildings

Before preparing the detailed design plans, the architect assesses the existing buildings and facilities and presents TRCINC with options for integrating the existing structures into the new office complex. If existing structures provide value, the architect integrates them into the plan. If they are impractical, he eliminates them from further consideration. As an example, TRCINC recently remodeled and renovated two of its headquarters' buildings. Can TRCINC leverage these assets by including them in the new office complex?

Notice that the architect did not start by analyzing the existing buildings. He started by determining requirements, goals and constraints. This distinction is vitally important. He wanted to be unbiased while studying the requirements, goals and constraints. Now, however, is the time to conduct an in-depth assessment, which allows basing recommendations on the *business case* for

incorporating existing assets as opposed to basing them on preconceived notions either in favor of or against the existing buildings.

After reviewing and analyzing the existing headquarters buildings, the architect presents TRCINC with the opportunities for integrating, eliminating or salvaging some of these structures. At this stage, Matt Allbright has sufficient information with which to make sound business decisions about the existing assets.

Before moving forward, TRCINC and the architect must agree on the best way to achieve the proposed model. With the target design in view, both parties should be able to agree on the best course of action.

Including existing buildings in the new office complex represents one of the few times that a business can

EXISTING BUILDINGS ASSESSMENT	LEGACY SYSTEMS ASSESSMENT
Inspect existing buildings and furnishings.	Conduct legacy systems architectural assessment.
Determine state of existing headquarters buildings.	Determine state of current systems architecture.
Determine which existing furnishings to use in new office complex.	Evaluate other resources (hardware, software and telecommunications) available for building new systems.
Balance architectural and financial requirements for integrating existing facilities.	Determine which legacy assets to incorporate into new systems architecture.
	Balance architectural and financial requirements for integrating legacy systems and other resources.

Table 5
Existing Buildings Assessment

actually *increase its rate-of-return* on its existing assets. For example, the new office complex may increase the value of the existing buildings. It may be tempting to always include existing assets, but sound business decision-making requires rigorous analysis of existing (legacy) assets that considers the near- and long-term requirements of the office complex.

The same integration issues face the systems architect. Corporations have significant investments in legacy system assets. Systems architects and users must make rational decisions about which legacy systems to include in new systems architectures and the best methods for integrating them. A first principle of finance is "sunk costs don't count" when making new or additional investment decisions. The same applies when reviewing legacy systems. They only have value in terms of their future contributions, not in terms of their past costs.

5. Prepare Detailed Blueprints and Bills-Of-Materials

This step produces TRCINC's bottom line needs of what it must spend to construct the new office complex. The architect moves the project from a design perspective to a construction perspective. He identifies the final resources for constructing the complex by subtracting existing resources from the preliminary bills-of-materials. The representations produced during this phase are for the builders and subcontractors.

It is during this step that the architect makes *buy-or-build decisions*. Others may have elegant solutions to some of the problems that exist within the architecture under design. The architect must evaluate the benefits of using these solutions versus developing a new solution. If the architect finds that an existing solution is proper, the client, TRCINC, saves the cost of researching and developing a new solution.

The client, whether a building client or a systems client, should expect changes and should be ready to accommodate them. A communication system architecture may substitute fiber optic cable for copper wiring. A legacy system originally designed to use a relational database can be part of a new systems architecture by encapsulating the database and presenting an object-oriented interface to new system components. The relational database can coexist with object databases, which can result in substantial speed and cost savings.

DETAILED BLUEPRINTS	TECHNOLOGY ARCHITECTURE
Compares initial blueprints with existing buildings and determines which requirements are not being met by existing buildings.	Compares initial blueprints with infrastructure inventory and determines what requirements are not being met by legacy systems.
Provides site plans.	Uses standard, off-the-shelf components whenever possible.
Provides detailed floor plans showing all components.	Describes detailed technical architecture, classes and objects, and object interactions.
Provides phased plan for building new office complex.	Provides phased implementation plan.
Shows how to incorporate existing components into new buildings.	Shows how to incorporate legacy assets into the new system.

Table 6
Detailed Blueprints

6. Perform Testing and Evaluation

The architect has documented all relevant data; client and architect have agreed upon the blueprints; the architect has assessed the existing structures and specified the bills-of-materials. The architect is now ready to synthesize all this information into a proof-of-concept model. Good architects always test their designs before beginning real construction. They want to know that the buildings will stand up to both earthquakes and hurricanes. Testing should use the best and most current methods available. This can include: building scale models; using computer simulations; and prototyping portions of the buildings. Historians tell us that even the ancient Egyptians built scale models of the pyramids and stress tested them before construction.

Airplanes, for example, go through a final testing and wind tunnel evaluation before being put into production. The airplane manufacturer conducts extensive computer simulations even before the wind tunnel tests. The building construction industry performs similar testing and evaluations. A successful simulation proves the concepts to all interested parties. These tests are critical to proper *risk management,* which, in turn, is critical to sound business management.

FINAL TESTING AND EVALUATION	PROOF-OF-CONCEPT PROJECT
Develop scale models. Perform computer simulations. Build (prototype) portions of the buildings. Test critical components.	Stress test critical infrastructure components. Prototype key portions of the system. Simulate software, hardware, telecommunications interactions and processing loads. Prototype user interfaces.

Table 7
Perform Architecture Testing

7. Prepare Construction Plans

Now that the architect has proven designs, it is time to plan and to schedule the actual construction. The architecture allows for decomposing and decoupling individual components, for developing them in parallel and, most important, for producing an integrated whole—whether it is a building or a system.

Change management allows the project supervisors to coordinate changes with all affected activities. Quality assurance ensures that the actual office complex matches the complex represented by the blueprints. *Quality assurance* provides measures of progress at regular intervals. It provides the management controls that help ensure the project stays on schedule and follows the blueprints, while at the same time allowing

for unforeseen change. An essential measure of an architecture's quality is its ability to accommodate change.

The design is complete. But the world is constantly changing, so the final product will probably not exactly match the original plan. This should not be a source of alarm. Many buildings undergo change as conditions during construction change. *Change* is a critically important concept of good architecture. Quality and the ability to gracefully handle change are two characteristics essential to good architecture, good business and good technology.

CONSTRUCTION PLAN	IMPLEMENTATION PLAN
Contains detailed assembly and fabrication drawings.	Specifies detailed program module descriptions.
Provides numerical control tool specifications (if required).	Specifies physical database structures and optimization methods.
Specifies metrics for quality assurance.	Specifies detailed network architecture.
Specifies change management process.	Defines metrics for measuring quality.
	Specifies change management process.

Table 8
Construction Plan

Conclusion

Investments, whether in new buildings or new information technology, must meet strict return-on-investment criteria: risk management, ability to support change, and cost/benefit ratios. Individual investments are simple and straightforward. Large investment portfolios are complex, requiring analytical methods and techniques to ensure optimal return on the portfolio's overall investment, and to balance its assets.

Architecture is a discipline that addresses complexity by arranging and connecting individual components in a way that globally optimizes the results. Whether developing an architecture for a building or an information system, the architect must carry out the steps in the process in the correct sequence and in adequate detail. Without following these steps, design decisions will not correspond to the available information, and this information will not support the decisions.

The seven steps of the architectural process provide a framework for information gathering, analysis and business decision-making. The example of developing an architecture for an office complex produces a set of architectural representations. The client, the architect and the builder require unique representations that meet their individual conceptual and semantic needs. All three are observing the same entity, but they need representations unique to their perspectives. The representations are not a matter of adding more detail at each step in the process. Rather, the representations differ in their very nature—they differ in their content and semantics. They serve the unique perspectives of each participant.

Systems architecture is the secret to gaining a business advantage from next generation technology. Systems architecture provides the organizing principles needed to manage overwhelming complexity inherent in next generation information systems. Systems architecture provides the blueprint for mapping technology onto the real-world requirements of business. Business and technology professionals responsible for charting the future of their organizations should build that future on a solid systems architecture.

Suggested Readings

Many people are researching the impact emerging technologies has on systems architecture. This is a list of references of current research and a few of the pivotal works that can significantly influence those who develop information systems architecture.

Rechtin, Eberhardt, *Systems Architecting: Creating and Building Complex Systems,* Prentice-Hall (1991).

Shaw, M. and D. Garlan, *Software Architecture: Perspectives on an Emerging Discipline,* Prentice Hall (forthcoming).

Software Engineering Institute at Carnegie Mellon University. Technical Reports are available through Research Access, Inc., 800 Vinial Street, Pittsburgh, PA 15212, USA, (800) 685-6510. SEI is on the Web at http://www.sei.cmu.edu/.

Spewak, Steven H., *Enterprise Architecture Planning,* Wiley (1992).

Zachman, John A., "A Framework for Information Systems Architecture," *IBM Systems Journal,* Vol. 26, No. 3 (1987), pp. 276–292. Available from IBM T. J. Watson Research Center, PO Box 218, Yorktown Heights, NY 10598, (914) 945-3836. This paper is the result of an effort to improve IBM's Business Systems Planning (BSP) and Information Planning Strategy (ISP). Many consider the Zachman Framework to be a *de facto* architectural standard for commercial information systems. Although Zachman developed his framework before the object paradigm, it provides useful background information for systems architects.

The following are classic architecture books that contain important insights for systems architects.

Alexander, Christopher, *Notes on the Synthesis of Form,* Harvard University Press (1964).

Alexander, Christopher, *The Timeless Way of Building,* Oxford University Press (1979).

Alexander, Christopher, S. Ishikawa and M. Silverstein, *A Pattern Language,* Oxford University Press (1977).

Mitchell, William J., *The Logic of Architecture: Design, Computation, and Cognition,* MIT Press (1990).

Object-Oriented Business Engineering

By Robert Shelton of Open Engineering, Inc.
In collaboration with the Object Technology Staff of The Technical Resource Connection

Open Engineering, Inc., is a San Francisco-based firm recognized for its pioneering work in object technology and business engineering.

The Technical Resource Connection gratefully acknowledges the firm's contributions to *Next Generation Computing*.

Contents

Abstract

Business objects provide a powerful mechanism for dynamic business modeling and reengineering. Business objects can be used for packaging shared business policy, process, data and definitions. They help to manage the architectural complexity of distributed object and three-tier client/server computing.

Business objects allow sharing of process, policy and data, so a business is no longer limited to sharing data only. Applying objects to understand and reengineer business processes can provide a breakthrough for companies that want to succeed in the complex and ongoing endeavor of business engineering. Object-oriented business engineering can fuse business process engineering with the underlying information systems. This paper explains the fundamental concepts and outlines the role of business objects in designing and implementing innovative business processes.

Just as many companies have adopted object-oriented analysis and design techniques without using object technology for implementation, it is reasonable to adopt object-oriented business engineering even if the information systems organization is not ready to adopt object technology for implementation. The benefits of completeness, clarity, traceability and shared understanding of the enterprise is justification enough without requiring the additional benefits of object-oriented technology.

Rethinking Business Process Reengineering

Current management wisdom is to reinvent your company or die! Decades-old business practices, structures and assumptions are invalid in today's high-tech business environment. Yet businesses continue to follow archaic practices because no one has asked the most basic question: *"Why?"* Business process reengineering (BPR) is about finding fundamentally better ways to serve customers and dispensing with unproductive activities that do not add value.

It was the hierarchy, not the process or flow of work, that structured the organization, the systems and our thinking.

In the past, we could only think of organizations in hierarchical terms. We would decompose business functions into tasks and tasks into subtasks. We would look at the world in terms of work output that went into the in-baskets of the next workers as input for their processes, whose output... We would build information systems based on this task-based hierarchy because the objective of those information systems was to automate the routine tasks within the hierarchy. It was the hierarchy, not the process or flow of work, that structured the organization, the systems and our thinking.

The historical approach to information systems has consistently produced applications with some very undesirable characteristics such as redundant data and procedures, rules that are difficult to change, and fragmented business processes. These same problematic processes are at the center of the vast majority of business process reengineering efforts.

Values, Organization and Process Determine Outcomes

Business process reengineering challenges the values, organization and processes we use to deliver our results. BPR is about ground-up rethinking, searching out best-of-breed solutions, and improving on those solutions instead of inventing from scratch a company's unique "way of doing things."

Each application system became an island unto itself. The term for this type of construction is "stove pipes." Each application was built to serve the needs of a specific part of the hierarchy. We created application systems that did not efficiently integrate with other systems in a manner that supported the flow of work or process. Manual re-entry of the output of one system into the next system was commonplace. Any connections between these systems were more like back-end pipes, shuttling output from one system to the input of the next — fragile substitutes for manual data entry. As a result, businesses cannot answer such basic questions as "Which customers are buying what product?" or "Which products are making money in what markets?"

Today's information systems do not provide integrated, cross-structural data flow because they are products of decompositional thinking. Practices such as Hierarchical Input Process Output (HIPO), Structured Analysis and Design, and Information Engineering institutionalized decompositional thinking. These practices have served us adequately in the past; however, they are now obsolete.

Today, businesses that want to grow and profit are demanding systems that integrate information, present the big picture and break down the traditional stove-pipes. Businesses are moving toward mass customization, flexible manufacturing and rapid process change in highly competitive markets. The new focus is on the series of necessary and sufficient processes that transform raw materials and resources into finished goods or services, and deliver them to customers. Businesses are thinking in a different paradigm, and they need their information system organizations to do the same.

Why Business Process Reengineering Should be Reinvented

Business process reengineering is about finding new processes, yet the traditional tools used to represent the new business processes are based on the decomposition of *process* hierarchies and input-output *processing*. Distinctions are needed between *process* and *processing*, and between *decomposition* and *composition*. We need to ask new questions. What roles and actions are required to compose the best — the most *effective* — process to fulfill customer orders? What must be known about the results of these actions and the relationships between the roles to operate the process?

Alvin Toffler observes in his book *The Third Wave*, "Industrial civilization placed an extremely heavy emphasis on our ability to dismantle problems into

their components; it rewarded us less often for the ability to put the pieces back together again."[2] Hammer and Champy address the same theme: "For two hundred years people have founded and built companies around Adam Smith's brilliant discovery that industrial work should be broken down into its simplest and most basic *tasks*. In the post-industrial business age we are now entering, corporations will be founded and built around the idea of reunifying those tasks into coherent business *processes*."[3]

We will follow this advice and explore a business process reengineering approach that is based on seeing the integrated big-picture. This approach is called object-oriented business engineering. Object-oriented business engineering applies object-oriented technology to business engineering. It is the design of information systems and business applications using business objects.

Object Orientation and Business Objects

Business objects allow reengineering teams to represent business concepts directly in software. To understand business objects, we must first understand what is intended by the term *object*. The white paper, *Getting Started With Object Technology*, provides a clear definition of objects and describes the application of object orientation to business. Objects are not just software building blocks. Objects can take the form of design abstractions, analysis abstractions or a natural-language description. Regardless of the use of object orientation, *objects are packages of data, procedures and constraints around a domain-meaningful concept. Business objects, therefore, are packages of data, procedures and constraints designed around a business domain.*

By suppressing non-relevant properties, an object can be used to hide complexity and to clearly communicate the central defining concept it represents. Furthermore, an object can present different facets of its interface in different situations, making available only those properties relevant to the situation in which it is participating. This characteristic makes objects excellent units of modularity for business analysis, systems design and program construction. An external business view can be used to define the object instead of a programming-limited view.

Business objects, then, can be an alternative to viewing the business world in computer programming terms.

> *An object can present different facets of its interface in different situations, making available only those properties relevant to the situation in which it is participating.*

Business objects allow us to see both the business and its underlying information systems in business terms.

Kinds of Objects

Let's define and work with three major categories of objects as shown in Figure 1: *business, technology* and *application*. These three major categories of objects reflect the areas of responsibility for information systems organizations. Each category serves a specific purpose, and is not interchangeable with the others. An object lives in one and only one category. Different issues must be addressed in identifying and developing objects in each category. Thus, a different process must be in place for each category. The power of this approach is that the information systems organization can be reengineered to practice just-in-time delivery of objects that are required for specific business or application requirements. The traditional application development paradigm can be replaced with flexible software manufacturing.

Business objects represent people, places, things, concepts and events that make up our every day business environment. Examples include vehicles, products, bills, employees, customers and temporal events, such as a quarterly earnings period or annual tax cycle. They package business procedures, policy and controls around business data. Business objects serve as a storage place for business policy and data. This creates a semantic life preserver that holds together in a

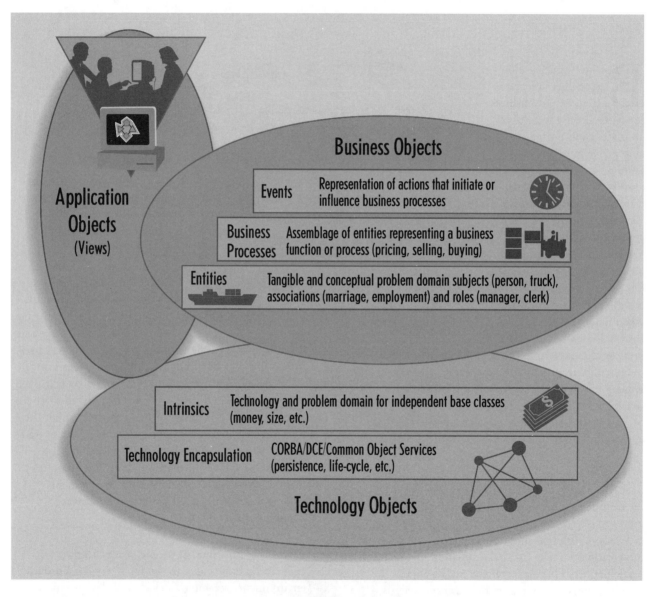

Figure 1
Business, Technology and Application Objects

coherent unit the right business policy with the right data and ensures that data is used only in a manner consistent with business intent. This is called *semantic normalization* — putting the right data with the right procedures in the right place. Common examples include purchase order, customer, product, invoice, payment, stock swap, flight segment and vehicle. A person is an entity represented by a business object and may play several roles, including employee, customer or stockholder. Business events are special types of business objects. They cause other business objects to appear, to disappear or to associate with other business objects. They are the medium of exchange in the value chain of business processes.

The Business Object Management Special Interest Group (BOMSIG) provides a useful definition of a business object: "A business object is a representation of a thing active in the business domain, including at least its business name and definition, attributes, behavior, relationships and constraints. A business object may represent, for example, a person, place or concept. The representation may be in a natural language, a modeling language or a programming language."[4]

Technology objects represent a programming or technology concept, and are the building blocks of applications and implemented business objects (someone has to design and program business objects if they are to be implemented). Examples of technology objects include graphical user interface components, object request broker services, databases, base data structure classes, and application frameworks. Shown in Figure 1, the Intrinsics Layer supplies a higher level of business intrinsics such as a "money object," which includes formatting, decimal arithmetic and currency conversion. These objects should be off-the-shelf technical assets that are selected by the information systems designer and developer both in program development and maintenance. Technology objects provide common functionality such as presentation (graphical user interface and data

exchange), event notification, persistence, platform independence, process engines (inference engines, neural nets and statistical packages) and communication (object request brokers or distributed computing environments). Technology objects should be selected for conformance to central industry standards, such as the Object Management Group's CORBA[5], so that third-party products can be integrated intelligently.

Application objects are custom-built to solve business problems just as applications are built today. These objects focus on a specific work task or problem, though they may be useful in other situations if well designed. They are assemblies of business objects and technology objects glued together with program code. Application objects are software packages that present information, produce reports and manage interaction with human users or external information systems. Using client/server terms, application objects can be viewed as clients of business and technology objects. Examples include Order Entry, Quarterly Report and New Account Setup applications. Traditional applications are standalone solutions to business problems. In contrast to traditional applications, application objects provide a "view" layer supplying the human interface to the underlying business model. This layer is intelligent and recognizes both the context and content of the information being exchanged with the external world.

Why do we focus on these three categories? Each represents a separate and independent source of change. Business processes and components change in structure, constraints and composition in response to changes in the business environment. Technology infrastructure changes as new products and product classes are introduced. Well-designed technology objects can provide an insulating layer between the business and application objects, and the underlying implementation environment. Applications change as business professionals seek to manage their businesses in better ways that do not necessarily result in a change to the under-

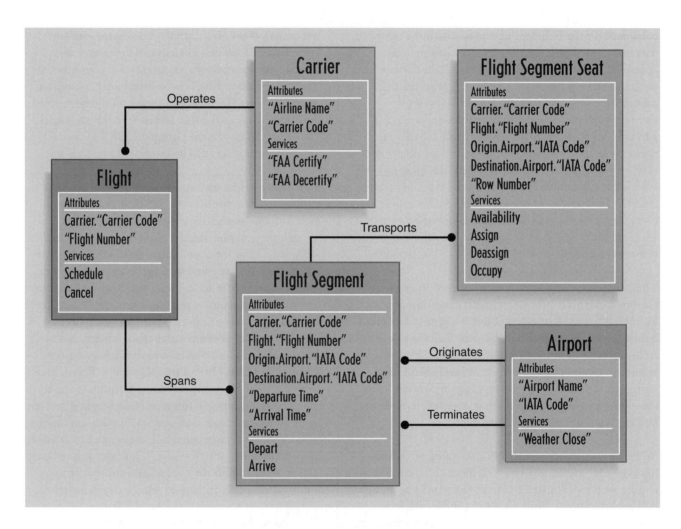

Figure 2
Typical Business Entity Objects

lying business structure. In fact, application objects are representations of data and process for some specific purpose. Business objects are independent of specific applications. They provide services that directly reflect how the business works. Application objects add services that control how the data or processes are presented, and how they can be manipulated by the end-user.

Business Objects: A Closer Look

Partitioning business objects along semantic boundaries helps implement practical solutions to business modeling, business process reengineering and business systems development. Business objects can be divided into layers that assist in directing behavior of the layers below any given object: *entities, business processes and events* (refer to the business objects component of Figure 1). This fine-grained approach is key to managing complexity. Each layer suppresses the details and complexities of the layer below it. With the layered approach to work breakdown, developers can focus on the business domain (the entity layer and above) and will rarely need to venture into the technology domain. The design of the business model is not constrained by the limitations or considerations of the technology model.

Entity objects are what usually come to mind in a discussion of business objects. They represent people, places and things, in much the same manner as a data entity. Key differences between a data entity (typically used in traditional entity-relationship diagrams) and a business entity object include:

- The business entity object packages procedure and rules that are specific to the concept being represented, whereas the data entity packages only data.

- The business entity object can engage in a far richer set of structural relationships than are available to the data entity. A business entity object represents a tangible business noun such as employee, customer and shareholder, and it can also represent an intangible concept such as *employment*. Business entity objects then are packages of data or facts about the business noun. Figure 2 shows a typical airline flight information system's business entity objects.

Some practitioners use the term *data objects*. This term should be used carefully as it is often misused to imply data-only "objects." Data-only objects are objects with no behavior that we traditionally call an entity. The distinction between entities and objects should not be blurred. A traditional *entity* has only data and relationships and may have data integrity constraints. An *object* has behavior, data, relationships and business rules, as well as integrity constraints. Objects generally contain other objects as attributes, not just "data."

The business entity object stores, takes action upon and animates the data the business stores and uses. The business entity object's services act upon the data, query the data and invoke actions in the context of a business process. In many cases, a principle reason for implementing business entity objects is to manage and to use business data. Yet thinking about data from an object perspective returns us to the idea of "animating" the data. The object is not static data; it is capable of activity. If we anthropromorphize an object, we could say that it "behaves" in a particular way and is an "actor" capable of playing a role in a business process.

Business process objects bring together business entities to define a business process. They represent business processes where the process is characterized by the interaction of a set of entity objects. A business entity object is data with behavior, while a business process

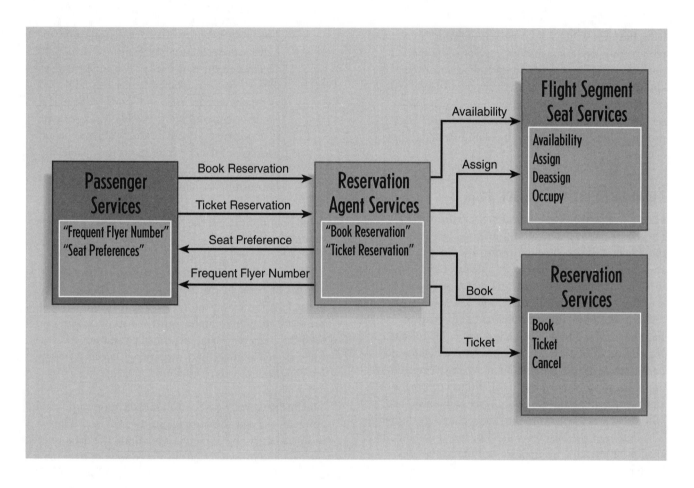

Figure 3
Interactions Between Business Entity Objects

object is behavior with data. Business processes encapsulated in business process objects interact in a predictable, repeatable manner to produce a recognized business result. Business entity objects are the actors or role-players that carry out the business process. Each interaction between a pair of business entity objects represents one work step in the business process. Figure 3 shows entity objects interacting to accomplish a very common business process — reserving and ticketing a flight on an airline. The business entity objects package the policy and controls that determine how the process is carried out, and the business process object packages the "how" into an object or set of objects.

Business event objects are representations of actions that initiate or influence business processes. Business event objects essentially replace the "traditional transaction" by allowing users to define business events that may influence previously defined business processes; event examples include when a competitor changes his price, a new employee is hired or an inventory item drops below a preset limit. Such business events tend to generate many transactions that must be applied to many traditional legacy systems. In traditional systems, several transactions must be cascaded to satisfy the requirements of a single business event. In next generation systems, business processes will subscribe to events of interest, replacing traditional transaction models.

Many business event objects represent boundaries in time, while others recognize that some significant action has taken place. Events can cause the creation of entities, assign roles, modify attributes, and cause entities to enter into associations. Business event objects seem similar to business entity objects in that they are a repository for business information and rules about the event; however, they primarily serve as actors to initiate business activity.

Businesses retain data about events, expend much effort trying to trigger events, and measure performance before and after events. A business event object has a name, definition, procedures and constraints. Business event objects, however, occupy an important place in a business object model. They are found at the initiation and termination of interactions between business process objects.

For more information on events, please see "What Are Events and Messages?" in the white paper, *Asynchronous Message Communication Between Distributed Business Objects.*

Business Modeling with Business Objects

In previous approaches to business modeling and systems design, business models were static blueprints of data and function. Static models are primarily useful for defining corporatewide data and designing shared databases. In contrast, business objects provide the ability to create business models that are active representations of the business world. The components of a business object model are defined using predefined business concepts that focus on the entire business instead of on separate data and program modules. This is where business objects enter the picture.

Business objects can be used to integrate and to migrate legacy systems and data structures because next generation applications built with business objects need not deal with the implementation of the business objects.

— what we know about it, what it does in the business context, the rules that constrain its behavior, and the interactions and relationships that it forms with other business objects.

Business objects can be used to integrate and to migrate legacy systems and data structures because next generation applications built with business objects need not deal with the implementation of the business objects. Business objects when combined with technology objects shield the developer from the complexities of the legacy systems. Integration with legacy systems frequently requires direct interaction with the legacy

Let's use a *customer* as an example. In an information engineering model, a developer includes a corporate data entity for *customer*. On a separate hierarchical functional decomposition model, the developer finds the business functions that use *customer* data. One model provides the "data picture," and the other model provides an abstract and arbitrary decomposition of which functions comprise the business. Nowhere is a complete picture of the *customer* developed. In addition, multiple-role entities, such as an employee who is also a customer, cannot be represented through separate decomposition of customer and employee data and processes. A business object model, on the other hand, represents all aspects of the business concept *customer*

systems' implementations. Tight coupling is undesirable because if the legacy implementation changes, clients are impacted. Migration strategies based on objects provide several benefits, including a clear separation of implementation issues and a buffer against change through consistent, meaningful interfaces.

Traditional information engineering models cannot approach business modeling in small segments or steps because their representation of business components are split across separate modeling paradigms — network data models and hierarchical function models. Business objects are active players, so the business model is closer to a *simulation* than a blueprint of the business.

Because object models can be built and modified incrementally, this business simulation can be constructed incrementally. Furthermore, because object models represent complete components working together in a context, that context with its business objects can be simulated in software. This business simulation finally connects high-level business models with implemented business systems, and provides development traceability between the model and the system.

Business objects neatly mesh with both data and process views of business, an important factor for anyone planning to make real-world use of business process reengineering. A business process is a sequence of steps that delivers a primary, value-added business result. The most important processes lead directly to the delivery of a result to the customer. From an object perspective, a business process is a finite set of business objects that interact in a predictable, repeatable manner to produce a recognized business result that can be named and clearly identified. The business objects are the actors or role-players that carry out the steps toward that result. Each interaction between a pair of business entity objects is one work-step in the process represented by the business process object.

Thinking About Business Processes With Business Objects

Consider an approach to business process reengineering that focuses on *actors* (often called *roles*), their interactions (these may be labeled tasks, activities, actions or responsibilities) and their context. Instead of decomposing business processes into their sub-processes, consider *composing* business processes from collections of interacting actors. This approach places the focus on the *business process*. Furthermore, this approach breaks away from a stove-pipe answer to the question: Given this new business process, who performs which activi-

ties, how do they do them, and how will the information systems support the process? In short, this approach avoids building new stovepipes that would constrict our new business processes.

Business entity objects package business procedures, policy and the controls around data, and represent a person, place, thing, event or concept. A business process object is a set of business entity objects that interact in a predictable, repeatable manner, responding to business events to produce a recognized business result. Business event objects are the triggers in this interaction; they are the business' way of tracking and scheduling its life.

Business entity objects are the actors or role-players that carry out the business process. They package the policy and controls that determine how to carry out the process. They do this in such a way that their interactions mirror activities in the business. If a customer and a sales representative negotiate a sale, business objects representing the customer and the sales representative can be designed to support the essential elements of that business event. If the result of the sale is removal of product from inventory and the initiation of manufacturing to fill the order balance, business objects that represent inventory, product, various manufacturing roles and machines, shipper, package, and invoice become involved. The idea is straightforward: Business objects can be used to model what is happening in the real world. The business object model becomes a working analogy of the business, the players, the processes and the events. The resulting model is a mirror reflecting the organization, resources and information systems.

Business reengineering then becomes an exercise in fresh thinking applied to an actor-based business model. The business process can be changed by disconnecting requests from one object and reconnecting them to another to form a more efficient process, creating "missing" objects and removing unproductive or non-value-adding objects and interactions. The business can be evaluated by testing process flow against business rules and constraints, and by assessing the time/cost performance of new processes against existing ones. Further, the proposed new business process can be communicated to others in the business by explaining which actors and actions are needed to conduct the process. The business value is clear: Object-oriented business engineering creates efficient business processes that can be continuously improved and that can add profit to the bottom line of any business.

Implementing Business Processes with Business Objects

Business objects simplify control and simulation of business procedure change, database redesign for management or remodeling, physical data distribution, and synchronization of distributed or multi-database transactions. How do business objects affect this change? In each case, encapsulation (packaging) is the key. Many of the business changes we make to our systems are contained within the business objects themselves, such as the changes to data structures and formats, data location, business rules and integrity constraints. Similarly, much of the technical complexity of multi-database transactions, replication, or redundancy created by departmental applications can be hidden behind business and technology objects.

Business objects simplify the implementation of three-tier client/server systems by providing the middle "business logic" tier that includes both rules and processes. Business rules and processes become visible and maintainable in a single entity — the business object. Instead of having business logic imbedded in either the presentation layer or the back end as required by popular two-tier tools, business objects encapsulate the business logic. This provides an important advantage over conventional approaches; business objects mirror the

Object-oriented business engineering provides corporations with a framework, methods and tools for not only rethinking business process reengineering but for acting on the approach.

business and can provide enterprise-wide applications.

Business objects make a significant contribution to the integration and migration of legacy systems. Business objects can wrap around existing databases, transactions and application screens to conceal the underlying legacy implementation. New applications can be built on correct data and process models represented by the business objects. Migration can occur without changing new client applications because the legacy systems are hidden behind the business objects. Business objects will not, however, inherently correct problems in the legacy systems, and integration requires a substantial knowledge of these systems, their definitions and interactions.

Object-oriented business engineering provides corporations with a framework, methods and tools for not only rethinking business process reengineering but for acting on the approach. Process innovation is not solving a one-shot problem. As long as businesses are facing change, continuous process improvement will be essential to success. Companies that recognize these competitive realities recognize the need for adopting industrial-strength methods and enabling tools — the kind of methods and tools provided by object-oriented business engineering.

The Object-Oriented Business Engineering Approach

Object-oriented business engineering is a framework and discipline for business modeling and reengineering, business object design, client/server application development and architecting enterprise-wide infrastructures. A thorough treatment of object-oriented business engineering concepts appears in *Understanding Business Objects* (see Suggested Readings).

One of the driving forces behind an object-oriented approach to business engineering is that information systems can and should be assembled from components. Thus object-oriented business engineering is made up of a set of processes, and each process is tuned to provide a particular type of component. This makes component assembly possible. Components can be bought, built or specialized. This is the essence of reuse. To describe object-oriented business engineering in non-computer terms, it is a *manufacturing process for business and systems components* — a way to achieve flexible manufacturing of business and systems components.

Object-oriented business engineering builds on the separation of business objects into three categories: entity, event and process. The process of delivering systems to support the business, especially a business that has undergone business process reengineering, by its nature, must address the business, the information technology that supports the business, and the applications that provide specific information and process-related services to the business. Object-oriented business engineering is characterized by developing application-independent business object models and integrating these models in software components. The role of application development then shifts to customizing the resulting components for a particular task. Fundamental differences exist between analysis and design methods and object-oriented business engineering. Object-oriented business engineering:

- creates and maintains a link from strategy to software, so the software components reflect the strategy

- has multiple processes, so business and technology are actually considered and developed separately from applications. Software is then delivered for each process, and software business objects can be shared by multiple applications and can operate on multiple technology platforms.

Object-oriented business engineering applies basic patterns derived from architectural engineering to the structure of data processing and business engineering. For background, we highly recommend reading Sowa and Zachman[6] and Alexander[7]. The concepts behind object-oriented business engineering emerged from the determination that business process, event and entity objects are required to describe a business. Furthermore, the organization structure and distribution characteristics of an enterprise must be mapped against the business model to fully describe the enterprise.

The object-oriented business engineering framework for business modeling in Figure 4 consists of three sets of core models: business, organization and distribution. The three core models must bridge the gap from strategic thinking about the business to the actual implementation of software components that represent the business. Thus, object-oriented business engineering is based on the "Concept to Code" idea that business representations can be transformed into systems models that run and track changes in the business.

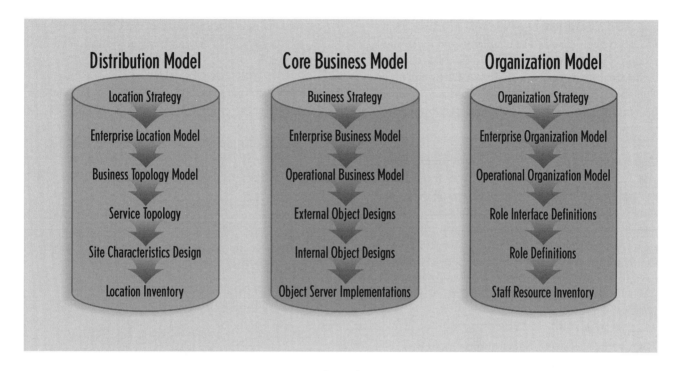

Figure 4
The Object-Oriented Business Engineering Framework

The object-oriented business engineering framework provides a structure that guides all activities from business modeling and business process reengineering through the design and implementation of business components upon which applications are developed. Each level in the framework is constant across the three models. The contents of each level are specialized to the context of the model. Dividing the models into levels does not imply or require a "waterfall" approach to the resulting process. Object-oriented business engineering advocates an *iterative process* applied to each model, and accomplishes this by scoping tasks within each level of the model.

The *Strategy* level represents the goals, objectives, visions and strategies of the business. It represents what the business seeks to achieve with technology, and how applications can leverage key business processes. In parallel with the Core Business Model, the Distribution and Organization Models also begin with a strategy level.

The *Enterprise* level represents best-of-class, generic business solutions for each model. In this context, Enterprise means *generic*, but not necessarily abstract or "high level." The Enterprise Business Model, for example, contains best-of-class business components, processes, relationship types and role structures, process-tuned organization templates, and logistic models. At the Enterprise level, best-of-class can be defined within a specific industry, or across industries. The object orientation of business engineering allows the reuse of previously defined business concepts and structures.

Object-oriented business engineering presumes that an organization will import best-of-class solutions for re-use and specialization, instead of inventing everything from scratch. Many consulting and business professionals have come to realize that business concepts and structures are about 80 percent common across industries, and up to 95 percent common between businesses in a given industry. Recently, object standards organizations have developed such enterprise-level or generic models[8].

The *Operational* level helps customize the chosen Enterprise Model to meet the needs and strategy of a particular organization. Because it is company-specific, an Operational Model defines the "unique 5 percent;" that is, the Operational Model defines those parts of the business organization that are different from the generic organization to create a unique competitive advantage. In very complex organizations (generally conglomerates or government agencies such as the U.S. Department of Defense), more than one Operational Model exists. Multiple models are necessary since the different parts of an organization can be radically different.

The *External* level of the Core Business Model contributes to the design of the external interface or protocol of each component, and contributes to the class hierarchy that supports specialization of business objects to the needs of particular technologies or applications. As with the subsequent levels, external models are environment-specific and reflect such

technology interface standards as the Object Management Group's CORBA[9] or a particular implementation language.

The *Internal* level of the Core Business Model provides for design of the internal structure and workings of each object. The Internal level of the Business Model, for example, supports design diagrams and tasks for:

- object data and method structures
- storage keying and indexing
- data and process distribution mapping
- data and process mapping to legacy data structures and on-line transactions
- mapping of business rules and integrity constraints onto attributes and methods.

The *Implementation* level, called "Object Server Implementations" in the Core Business Model, is the level of generated or written code based on the designs... that were based on the operational model... that were based on the enterprise business model... that were based on strategy. This results in design traceability from beginning-to-end in object-oriented business engineering.

In order to represent the Core Business Model, object-oriented business engineering uses four integrated diagrams as shown in Figure 5: Business Process Diagram, Object Behavior Diagram, Object Relationship Diagram and the Object State Diagram.

The Business Process Diagram models high-level business processes, usually between two and five levels deep. This diagram provides scope (in business process terms) for pairs of Object Behavior Diagram-Object Relationship Diagrams that represent the structure of the business process itself. Object-oriented business

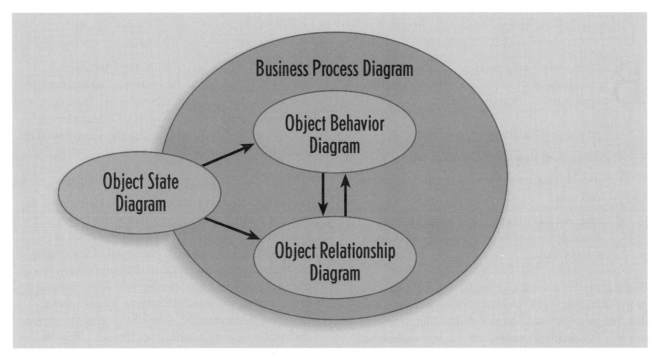

Figure 5
Object-Oriented Business Engineering

engineering emphasizes using existing, industry standard constructs where possible. As a result, existing process diagrams can often be "imported" into object-oriented business engineering to define high-level processes. Object-oriented business engineering provides:

- a way to transform processes into less abstract representations of the business by using objects and interactions

- a method for translating these representations into systems.

The Business Impact

Business objects are powerful. They package many parts of a business and its processes into sharable units. Business objects:

- provide definitions of key concepts

- encapsulate data about those concepts

- provide processes that work on those concepts and data

- integrate business rules and integrity constraints that govern process, data and concept membership.

Business objects provide one logical source for data and procedures about each essential business concept. The data and procedures can be modeled and implemented in a way that guarantees consistency across applications, departments, the enterprise and even multiple enterprises.

These business objects and their inclusion in processes provide business systems a way to mirror the business by allowing the new business systems to be built in terms of these objects and their interactions. This implies a substantial change in the traditional approach to business analysis and systems development because business objects are independent of applications in both conception and implementation. Object-oriented business engineering is about building a working model of the business and its processes in terms of business objects, then building systems to operate that model.

Experience gained from applying object-oriented business engineering reveals that business objects truly mirror the business instead of the computer system. The strength of business objects extends beyond business process reengineering: Designers can use business objects to "draw" models of the business during BPR endeavors, then transform these models into designs for implementable objects. Developers can implement these business objects on mainframes as mid-tier servers, or as load modules in a distributed or traditional computing environment.

Business objects are not magic, and major work is required to conceive, design and implement them. A growing body of industry experience shows that a business object approach to business process reengineering can make the challenges of reinventing the business more manageable. Business reengineering does not result in a final product; business processes must be designed for continuous change in an ever-changing business world. Business objects can provide the vehicle for synchronizing continuous improvement in both business processes and their underlying information systems. Progressive companies that recognize the business advantage of robust and adaptive business processes have already taken steps to fuse business process reengineering and object technology. Companies that wish to maintain leadership in their industry should place the fusion of business and technology high on their lists of priorities.

References

[1] Object-Oriented Business Engineering and OOBE are registered trademarks of Open Engineering, Inc.

[2] Toffler, Alvin, *The Third Wave*, William Morrow (1980).

[3] Hammer and Champy, *Reengineering the Corporation, A Manifesto for Business Revolution*, HarperBusiness (1993).

[4] "Minutes of the Berlin Meeting," Business Object Management Special Interest Group, Object Management Group, Document No. 94.5.1 (April 1994).

[5] "The Common Object Request Broker: Architecture and Specification," Object Management Group, Document No. 91.12.1 (1992).

[6] Sowa and Zachman, "Extending and Formalizing the Framework for Information Systems Architecture," IBM Systems Journal, Vol. 31, No. 3 (1992).

[7] Alexander, Christopher, "Notes on the Synthesis of Form," Harvard Press (1964).

[8] Shelton, Robert, "Distributed Enterprise," Patricia Seybold Group, *Distributed Computing Monitor* (October 1993).

[9] "Common Object Request Broker Architecture and Specification," Vol. 1.1, Object Management Group, Document No. 91.12.1 (1992).

Suggested Readings

Davenport, Thomas, *Process Innovation: Reengineering Work Through Information Technology,* Ernst & Young, Harvard Business School Press (1993). Davenport shows how to implement the reengineering process by fusing information technology with new ways of managing people. He provides an in-depth study of the strategic and operational dimensions, and a step-by-step guide to reengineering.

Ganti, Narsim, Ph.D. and William Brayman, *The Transition of Legacy Systems to a Distributed Architecture,* John Wiley and Sons (1995). Both Ganti and Brayman have substantial experience in moving from legacy to architected systems for the Boeing Company. They describe an architecture-based approach to migrating legacy systems, outline a series of steps that can be used to realign information technology with changing business strategies, and provide guidelines for visualizing the transition process.

Hammer, Michael and J. Champy, *Reengineering the Corporation: A Manifesto for Business Revolution,* Harper Business (1993, 1994 updated paperback edition). Hammer is a father of the reengineering movement, and this is the opening volley of the reengineering phenomena. The book's thesis is that American corporations must undertake nothing less than a radical reinvention of how they do their work. Whether one agrees with the approach or not, this work is widely known and referenced in business discussions.

Kilov, Haim and J. Ross, *Information Modeling: An Object-Oriented Approach,* Prentice Hall, 320 pp. (1994). By using an object-oriented approach, Kilov and Ross seek to make systems analysis as disciplined as programming. They show how the systems analyst can use concepts programmers use, such as abstraction, precise understanding of behavior and reuse. The concepts are applicable to many methods.

Shelton, Robert, *Understanding Business Objects,* Addison-Wesley (1996). Shelton covers the basics of business entity, event and process objects, and explains the process of business modeling with these tools and the basic set of OOBE diagrams. The OOBE framework and the technical architecture required to implement business objects is discussed in more detail than in this paper. Also, Shelton covers Business Object Management — an approach he has developed to manage large-scale reuse and the reengineering of IS.

Sims, Oliver, *Business Objects: Delivering Cooperative Objects for Client/Server,* McGraw-Hill (1994). Sims' approach is the application of business-sized objects to the user interface, where cooperative business objects correspond to an on-screen object needed by the user. The book also explains the need for middleware between applications and the operating system.

Tkach, Daniel and Richard Puttick, *Object Technology in Applications Development,* Benjamin/Cummings, 225 pp. (1994). The authors, both with IBM's International Support Center, focus on technology transfer. The book provides a high level road map of object-oriented application development, describes the role of CASE tools and the use of frameworks for reuse, and describes how legacy code can be reused in object-oriented environments.

Spurr, Kathy, Paul Layzell, Leslie Jennison and Neil Richards, *Business Objects: Software Solutions* and *Software Assistance for Business Re-Engineering,* John Wiley & Sons (1994). These books, based on the work of the British Computer Society CASE Group, answer questions about reengineering methods and tools.

Epilog as Prolog

By Jim Stikeleather
In collaboration with the Object Technology Staff of The Technical Resource Connection

Contents

Abstract

The papers in this anthology presented the basics and the current state-of-the-practice in business technology. We will now look at some possible futures that will result from where we are today and the directions we choose to follow. Pondering the future can minimize the surprises it brings.

We learned about numerous tactics within a strategic context. A common thread throughout all the papers is the subordination of technology to business decisions when addressing distributed objects and other emerging technologies. We do not aspire to speed up what we are currently doing; we want, rather, to put computers to completely new uses. We no longer look to automation for cost containment derived from economies-of-scale and a defensive strategy. The emerging technologies provide us with an offensive business weapon that we can use, not just to save money but more important, to make money. The papers emphasize that an enterprise can buy products, but it cannot buy a plan. Simply buying object technology will accomplish nothing and can waste valuable business resources.

Going beyond the information and lessons contained within the individual papers, we now focus on the future state of the world beyond objects — the world of *ubiquitous* computing. We also will briefly explore the essential foundations needed for future information systems: *engineering discipline, systems architecture* and *technical skills*.

Future Business and Technology

Most science fiction films and books make an implicit assumption about how computers of the future operate. The essential concept is *ubiquitous** computing, where all the information (data, process and control) needed to perform a function moves seamlessly from computer to computer. Rich and pervasive information resources change the user's perception — the computer, *per se*, disappears. Even a cursory review of the literature can identify the precursors of ubiquitous computing — products like Sun's *Java*™, General Magic's *Magic Cap*™, and the new developments and standards that are defining the World Wide Web. Sun's battle cry sums up the future of computing: *The network is the computer*™.

In the same way that the computer itself heralded the end of the industrial age and the start of the information age, new developments in network-centric computing herald a new age of knowledge rather than of information. Not only can future technology distribute information, it can distribute an enterprise's knowledge base by interconnecting people and their intelligence. We are not speaking of artificial intelligence technology as we know it today; we are speaking of amplifying the knowledge contained in individuals' heads and in business rules stored in computer systems, and of making it available to anyone or any system anywhere, at any time. In his book, *The Digital Economy*, Don Tapscott explores the promise and peril of the phenomena of networked intelligence.[1] This capability truly empowers individuals — whether on the shop floor or in a customer's office — to make optimal business decisions on-the-spot, wherever and whenever required. It is this magnitude of empowerment that is required for true business innovation.

Information Appliances?

What really happens if the network becomes the computer?

IBM commits to the network-centric computing paradigm, buys Lotus Notes™, opens the Object Technology University, announces its "inter-personal computer" (IPC) and licenses Java.

Apple Computer hires the renowned cognitive scientist, Donald Norman. Ease-of-use is the key to ubiquitous computing, and Norman will redefine the meaning of "user-friendly."

Steven Jobs unveils Next Computer's *WebObjects*™ by personally demonstrating the technology to a packed house at Object World '95 in San Francisco.

The front page headline of the Dec. 11, 1995, *Computerworld* reads, "Capitulation! Microsoft to license Java; Internet standards war avoided." Is Redmond going to play by the rules?

Internet discussion groups begin to argue the future of the PC itself. Why bother with hardware, wires and continual software upgrades when you can simply buy a *HotJava*™ appliance and let the network handle the grief?

What happens when an enterprise codifies, digitizes and makes available its rules, policies, techniques, workflows and business processes, to its entire

* Existing or being everywhere at the same time: constantly encountered. — *American Heritage Dictionary*

workforce as well as its customers and suppliers? Something very new starts to happen: Enterprises begin to change the fundamental way they conduct business.

People used to say that any product can be good, fast or cheap, but only two of the three. Japanese competitors taught American manufacturers new lessons in the 1970s and '80s. Corporations such as Sony demonstrated that a single company could successfully pursue all three paths and thereby own a market.

Japanese manufacturers are not content to be just good, fast and cheap. They are already putting the next generation of manufacturing in place. It is not *mass production*; it is *mass customization*. For example, consumers can walk into a next generation bicycle shop where vision systems collect the individual's body metrics (weight, build and proportion); expert systems query the individual about their style of riding; CAD (computer assisted design) systems work within the individual's budget and personal preferences (i.e., color, weight and style); and within days, a totally custom-built bicycle — a product with a market of *one* — is delivered. This situation exemplifies how far manufacturing has come. The potential for ubiquitous computing in this environment is evident. With it, a consumer in the United States can have a local system collect his metrics to create a digital mannequin; have another determine his preferences; and have yet a third in Japan design the bicycle and transmit CAM (computer assisted manufacturing) software to the fabricator

The ultimate goal of distributed computing is to provide the ability to bring together software components that have absolutely no knowledge, implicit or explicit, of each other and to create functional services from them.

nearest the consumer to build the bike.

A ubiquitous computing environment changes the face of business computing. The entire point of automating human activity changes. Instead of using technology to automate a clerical task, we can now harness ubiquitous computing resources to mediate our business collaborations, to reposition traditional business alliances by integrating our information systems, and to drive core business processes, workflows and corporate knowledge bases.

In the past, the goal of automation was cost savings through economies of scale — a defensive business strategy. In the future, automation will increasingly center on the goals of making money and of winning in very competitive, even hostile, business environments. Next generation uses of computers will focus on revenue and profit by giving enterprises offensive business weapons to command leadership within their industries. This is a far different world than is the one that uses automation defensively to squeeze costs. Next generation businesses place higher value on efficacy than on efficiency. They intend to use advanced technology as a strategic business weapon, not as a back office accounting machine. Again, we see ubiquitous computing as a business, not a technological, issue.

The ultimate goal of distributed computing is to provide the ability to bring together software components that have absolutely no knowledge, implicit or explicit, of each other and to create functional services from them. Ubiquitous computing requires a truly distributed design, not a centralized design with tentacles. Ubiquitous computing and distributed design have the following qualities:

- They distribute software as well as data, processing cycles and control.

- They are naturally asynchronous — they use a loosely connected design model.

- They design engines-of-creation separate from engines-of-consumption. Objects register and publish their services, other objects register and subscribe to these services.

- Applications are often document-centric and bring the impact of component software architectures to individual desktops.

- The spectrum of connectivity ranges from *indifferent* to *exceptionally allied*, which enables all manner of connectivity for the extended enterprise.

- They are event-driven and mirror the way business occurs naturally — responding to and initiating events.

- Ubiquitous computing returns to the economic model where costs of incremental change or usage are commensurate with benefits.

We are moving toward a business environment that requires "outsiders" to have direct and unplanned access to an enterprise's information systems. Science fiction

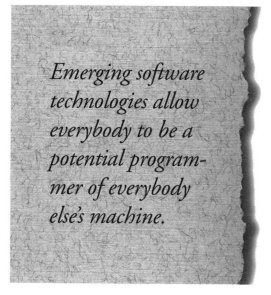

Emerging software technologies allow everybody to be a potential programmer of everybody else's machine.

writers, futurists and now computer vendors talk about "software agents" that wander networks finding information and performing services for their originators. Products like General Magic's *Magic Cap*, Sun's *Java* and *HotJava*, and Borland's *Latte* will characterize future computing. These products and tools allow others, including those unknown to the enterprise, to write software that will run on the enterprise's computers.

With emerging software technology such as Microsoft's IP², which stands for *Intentional Programming*, billions of dollars of hard-working, proven legacy code has the potential of being incorporated into software component repositories — intention repositories. The "intention" defines the semantics, look and behavior of both legacy and object-oriented abstractions.

These emerging software technologies allow everybody to be a potential programmer of everybody else's machine. A person in these advanced software environments can build software agents much more readily than by asking a professional programmer or analyst to determine application requirements and then to create a solution. Work shifts to the beneficiary, the person who has a vested interest in doing it right. Although some of the required technologies are still in the laboratory, their commercial availability will help solve the problem of too few programmers to build all the applications of the future. Meanwhile, the rise of mobile computing means that, at any moment, we cannot sufficiently plan to be able to ensure every person working remotely in a virtual corporation has precisely what he needs to do his job. He may need *ad hoc*, throw-away applications capable of handling the requirements of an individual business deal put together in a Manhattan pub during rush hour — such applications may live for a minute or for years.

The new role of IS becomes one of ensuring information integrity and making the business model readily available. Interpolation and presentation become the issues of the user, where they belong. In an age characterized by extended and virtual enterprises, enterprises need self-organizing systems that can adapt to and be integrated with other information systems as these enterprises dynamically forge new alliances and partnerships. Software agents are central to providing this capability.

Software agents become solutions to rapid and adaptive software development especially within disparate computing environments. Software agents handle the interoperability issues, because they do not have to care about operating systems, database schemas and programming languages. The behavior of software agents is conversational — like that between two people who negotiate to get what they need from each other. Magic Cap, software agents, Intentional Programming and Java are signposts pointing to a future of ubiquitous computing.

If enterprises do not apply these tools of the future within the context of a solid foundation of a true engineering discipline, architectural frameworks and corresponding technical skills, they will provide no value. Progressive companies are preparing for the future by building the foundation today.

Establishing a True Engineering Discipline

Engineering implies a collection of proven principles and generally accepted heuristics that can be used to design and construct man-made artifacts. From the beginning of software development, computer scientists such as Constantine, Dijkstra and Weinberg have pointed the way for transforming software development into software engineering. Instead of pursuing these paths, IS has pursued a path of expediency, dictated by the day-to-day realities of business. This is underscored in the story of the Winchester house in the white paper, *Understanding Systems Architecture.*

New business realities demand sophisticated integrated systems that exceed the capabilities of our current software development processes, techniques and everyday heuristics. Fortunately, the technologies and processes discussed in these white papers are enablers and facilitators of a true engineering discipline for software development.

A quick perusal of trade publications shows legions of vendors offering tools promising software *reuse* — with its better quality results, reduced development times and lower costs. These claims conjure up memories of past claims and remind us of a working definition of insanity: repeatedly performing the same actions while expecting different results. How many tools have IS organizations bought over the years, yet quality, speed and cost-effectiveness still elude us? Buying a tool is like taking sugar-coated cough drops for that nagging cough, when a lifestyle change — quitting smoking — is the real answer.

The lifestyle change — the real answer — for IS is *process.* The quality experts (Deming, Juran, Crosby and others) have said repeatedly that quality, productivity and reduced cycle times are a function of process.

What Are the Results of Years of Tooling?

Tom DeMarco (1984) reported that 15 percent of software projects with more than 100,000 lines-of-code failed to deliver anything useful.

In 1989, Capers Jones reported that for software projects with more than 64,000 lines-of-code, 25 percent failed to deliver anything, 60 percent were significantly over-budget and behind schedule, and only 1 percent finished on-time, on-budget and met user requirements.

The IEEE estimates there are 10 billion lines-of-existing-code in the United States that cost $70 billion/year to maintain. Currently, 31 percent of new projects are canceled before completion at an estimated cost of $81 billion/year. Additionally, 53 percent of completed projects are 190 percent over-budget at an additional cost of $59 billion.

A 1991 study by the Software Engineering Institute showed 86 percent of organizations in the industry at the lowest possible level of maturity in software development.

Likewise, software reuse is achievable only if there is a software development process that enables and encourages reuse.

Numerous "standards" exist for software development processes. For commercial purposes, the standards

Software Engineering Standards

- The Software Engineering Institute at Carnegie Mellon University's five-level Capability Maturity Model (CMM) for software development

- The International Organization for Standardization in Geneva's ISO 9000 series (ISO 9001, 9002, 9003 and 9004)

- The IEEE Standard for Developing Software Life Cycle Process (IEEE Std 1074-1991)

- The ACM's Coordinated Software Development Model (Kraut and Streeter, *Communications of the ACM*, March 1995)

- ANSI 016, the working number of the planned ANSI standard that will adapt ISO/IEC 12207, "Information Technology: Software Life Cycle Processes," for U.S. software

- Assorted military standards for process (for example, MIL-STD-498).

developed by the SEI and the ISO are the most pertinent. They are mature and undergo formal assessment and certification processes. More and more software development contracts are referencing both standards, and they are often required for organizations wanting to do business in some countries.

ISO 9000 is derived from the manufacturing world and years of applying TQM techniques. It relies on specific deliverables and demonstrable control mechanisms. It is principally a deductive process. The SEI Capability Maturity Model (CMM) grew out of the study of successful organizations and is primarily an inductive process that distilled general principles of success. An SEI assessment, while looking for tangible process documentation, focuses on results and the application of principles, such as collecting metrics and analyzing them. Work is currently under way to merge the ISO and the SEI standards or, at least, to allow cross-certification equivalence between them.

While the standards are broad and increasingly deep models, they are really sets of assertions as to what constitutes good software development practice. Process alone is not enough. People and their interactions contribute mightily to any endeavor. Process may even get in the way of true excellence. Process is, however, definable, repeatable, quantifiable and, therefore, manageable. It is a starting point on the road to quality software. The risk is of placing too great a focus on process to the exclusion of other factors like people, training, tooling, resource constraints, culture and business requirements.

Invest $1: Get $5 Back

Watts Humphrey has statistics showing that SEI Level 2 companies produce 250 defects per thousand lines-of-code (KLOC), but by Level 2.5, this drops to 85 defects per KLOC.

The U.S. Navy and Air Force have released information to the SEI that contractors working at Level 1 will be, on average, 75 percent over initial schedule; contractors at Level 2 will tend to be on-schedule; and contractors at Level 3 will tend to be under-schedule.

In a survey posted on the ISO's WEB page of certified companies, 89 percent noted "greater operational efficiency" and 48 percent stated they were "more profitable after certification."

*Herbsleb (*Benefits of CMM-based Software Process, *CMU/SEI-94-TR-13, Software Engineering Institute, Carnegie Mellon University, Pittsburgh, Pennsylvania, March 1994) documented the benefits of process for the SEI. These included a 9-67 percent programmer productivity improvement (35 percent median); a 15-23 percent reduction in development time (19 percent median); a 10-94 percent reduction in defects (39 percent median); and, perhaps most important, a $4-$8.80 return on every dollar invested in process improvement ($5 median).*

The Foundations of Systems Architecture

After 20 years of mixed success in building and delivering distributed, client/server and object systems, a critical factor has surfaced as first in importance to ensure success: a complete, consistent and well-understood architecture — an underlying structure with a rationale. In his book, *Object-Oriented Analysis and Design*, object pioneer Grady Booch explains, "We have observed two traits common to virtually all of the successful object-oriented systems we have encountered, and noticeably absent from the ones that we count as failures: the existence of a strong architectural vision and the application of a well-managed iterative and incremental development cycle." [3]

Larry Constantine goes straight to the point for commercial IS: "Architecture, whether in the organization of the internal functionality or in the structure of the user interface, is often among the first victims felled by today's time-boxed software projects, short release cycles, and rapid application development. There seems to be no time to think through the consequences of architectural decisions. Often there is barely time to think. Full Stop." [4] An obvious conclusion is that the lack of systems architectures may be the root cause of the software crisis we live with today.

So, what is an architecture? If there was a survey of systems professionals asking for a definition of architecture, the results would be as varied as the number of people asked. Architecture has so many meanings within IS because it has different definitions depending on the context. Many describe architectures in terms of the hardware, software, tools and coding standards they use for implementation. This is like a building architect describing architecture by describing the building's rivets, beams and building codes — an obviously unsatisfying description.

Many describe architecture in terms of methodology or process, which as Jim Coplien explains, "There have been many attempts to introduce formalism in architecture and design, but it is more often in the dictionary sense of formal as "methodical" (having form or rote) rather than "conventional" (following rules or axioms)" [5] — another ultimately unsatisfactory (and rarely followed) description.

What IS developers need are abstractions, semantics and specifications for the patterns of information content and context, cognitive completeness, decision-making and delegation — applied explicitly or implicitly in software or buildings or any other "successful system." This body of knowledge needs translation into a framework for thinking and reasoning about the engineering trade-offs and their consequences during the design process.

To avoid the formalism trap referred to by Coplien, any architectural framework or process must be intuitive. It must, however, be both synthesis-based for generating ideas — intuitive, judgmental and inductive (artistic); and analysis-based for eliminating ideas — factual, logical and deductive (scientific). As Gerald Weinberg points out in *Rethinking Systems Analysis & Design*, the architect must "strike a balance between variation and selection and design for understanding," [6] which means the architecture must be both intuitive and reasonable — that is, people can reason about it. Lastly, it must be in such a semantic — and perhaps someday syntactical — form that its methods, axioms, heuristics, specifications, processes and experiences can be communicated among and between generations of architects and developers.

The Dimensions of Architecture

There are four dimensions of architecture that are useful in building information systems: *state, time, space* and *composition*. An architecture developed within these four dimensions is the product of context: the requirements, goals and constraints of the problem space being architected.

State is the static representation of the systems architecture. State is the structure, the sum of components and their interrelationships, of the system at any moment in time. In application architectures of the past, state referred to the data content of the system. This was an adequate definition for the transactional, historical record-keeping and reporting systems but is incomplete for the dynamic, real-time simulations that we are being asked to build today. State represents the *thing* aspects of the environment. From the structural perspective, it provides the heuristics for representing information from data-based components and the possible interrelationships among the components.

Time represents the dynamic nature of an architecture and is the *process* element of an architecture. It represents the transformations from one state to another and the dependencies and integrity of these transformations. Traditional data-driven design processes are giving way to object-oriented approaches, which combine data and process. As object-oriented development activities begin to push the envelopes of concurrency and reuse, the temporal aspects of systems become increasingly important and require formalization. Equally critical, the *content* of data changes over time as it did in traditional systems, but the *context* or structure of the system changes as well and the architecture must account for it.

Space represents the physical and logical topologies within which the static or *thing* components and the temporal or process components operate. Adding to the development of information systems is the complexity of distribution caused by the rise of distributed object technologies and client/server computing, which is driven by businesses changing to geographically dispersed operations. Much of the late 1980s and early 1990s standards work addressed the space problem with techniques such as naming and directory services standards. Along with the networking and performance issues that must be addressed by an architecture's space dimension, the logical affinity of the information components may dictate the proximity of information components in design as well as in implementation space.

Composition represents the synthesis of state, time and space. Neither the static view nor the dynamic view can fully represent the entire system. The architecture must give full consideration to additional information — how to compose the static elements, how to assemble the dynamic elements with the static elements and how to sequence them, to serialize them and to make them parallel. Composition defines how to bring components into being, to eliminate them from existence and to distribute them throughout the execution space. It is the composition domain that allows the static and dynamic components of the architecture to be decomposed into human manageable artifacts, which are later assembled or composed into systems.

Architecture and Its Process

Looking beyond information systems *per se*, an architectural framework should be robust enough to span the realms of business process reengineering (BPR) as well as the enterprise's software development process (SDP), not just its technologies and applications. An architectural framework of this scope can allow synthesizing business processes and their underlying information systems — a goal that we have failed to reach since computers were first introduced to business.

Whether the context is a building or an information system, there is a natural sequence of steps that makes up the process of developing an architecture. The white paper, *Understanding Systems Architecture*, provides a summary of these steps. As a result of the step-wise approach, each cognitive layer builds upon others to achieve the final result. For example, floor plans are useless without a representation of the plumbing, electrical and hvac components. The internal structure of each cognitive component is not visible to other components, only the component's interface is revealed. The floor plan shows only where electrical, plumbing and hvac services are available, not how they are being supplied.

An architectural framework for building information systems operates across at least three domains: the real world, the business model, and the machine model. The left side of Figure 1 shows these domains. A critical goal of an enterprise systems architecture is to divorce those who work using the paradigm (framework for thinking) of the machine model from having to know the internals of the business model and vice versa.

Cognitive psychologists know that it is difficult — often impossible — to hold more than one paradigm and more than seven to nine concepts in mind at one time. The purpose of a systems architecture's semantic layers or boundaries is to allow useful work to take place while limiting the number of concepts to the capabilities of human cognition. The semantic boundaries of a systems architecture provide interfaces between the machine model (very technical, procedural and construction-based) and the business model (non-technical, declarative and assembly-oriented). People working above this boundary think using the paradigm of the business model; those below use the machine model. Therefore, when working on a problem within one layer, only one paradigm is in play at a time.

Systems architecture is a set of heuristics applied to a set of *requirements* (features desired), *goals* (qualities of performance) and *constraints* (fiscal, technical, temporal or human limitations) for breaking a problem space into cognitively useful, semantically complete and consistent chunks for human creation, manipulation, utilization and assimilation. Abstractions are used to create components that represent information and its transformations; interfaces, connections and bindings among components; and the topology within which components exist, independent of their implementations.

When applied to the machine model, the definition of a systems architecture expands to include the process of translation, representation and implementation on computer systems. These include the hardware, software and network representations characteristic of the traditional view of systems architecture.

The goals of an architectural framework are to manage complexity, to minimize the impact of change, to incorporate and to leverage existing components and, most important, to allow an overall perspective of the systems to be developed and maintained. If accomplished, good architecture accelerates the systems development process, reduces systems costs and improves systems quality.

By mapping the components of systems architecture to the architectural domains, the composite presented in Figure 1 reveals the relationship of sub-architectures (information, technical and application) and work-breakdown (from business process reengineering to the software development process) to the domains.

An *information architecture* describes the content, behavior and interaction of business objects. It models the information and activities of the enterprise and provides the organizing abstractions in the business domain for solving business problems. The information architecture defines the building blocks for application development and provides a framework for the business information components. More generally, its primary role is to provide an environment and overall structure to support modeling the information and activities of the enterprise. The information architecture provides the business model and, in the

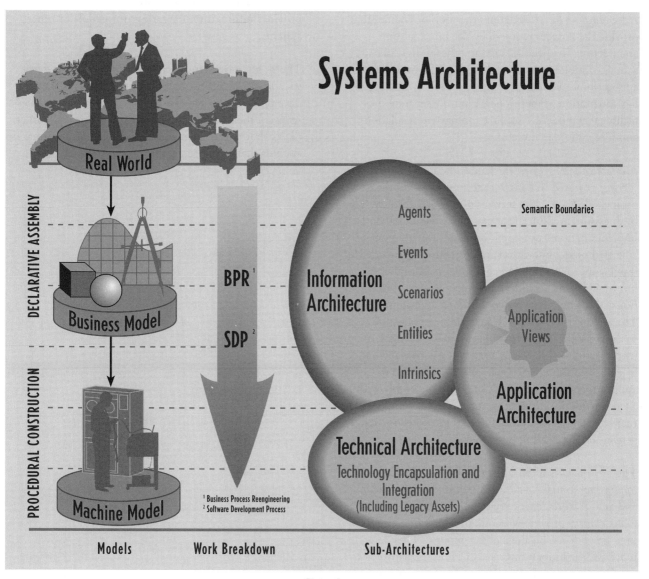

Figure 1
Systems Architecture

world of objects, the business object model. Additional discussion of the components of an information architecture appears in the white paper, *Distributed Object Computing for Business.*

A *technical architecture* defines the tools or engines that provide the services required by the information architecture. It specifies, among other things, the actual technologies and products used to implement applications. Moreover, it provides the key to technology integration. Practitioners typically separate the technical architecture into technology encapsulation and integration architectures.

An *application architecture* defines the fundamental services required to construct solutions within the business domain. The services provide an abstract business-oriented interface that hides the underlying implementation from application software developers. The goal of an application architecture is to provide the framework for assembling components from the information and technical architectures into applications — a whole new way of building applications. The architectural approach to building applications is so different that the term application architecture is used carefully — the term application carries mental baggage from the traditional, procedural world of application development. Component assembly within a framework of information and technical components that have been logically architected is the key to next generation application development.

The term *view* is often substituted for the word *application* to make a clear distinction between older and architecture-centric styles of application development. Views provide windows that look into and interact with the business object model. They often represent the human interface but must be capable of rendering information for foreign software agents, EDI transactions, and other non-human entities and

systems. Views are objects that "observe" some aspect of one or more components in the information architecture — business scenarios or individual subjects and associations. Views themselves can be considered as representing yet another architectural component that provides information renderings for people or other systems.

The single most significant contributor to long-term success in implementing object technology is the early development of a systems architecture. As companies redesign themselves to compete in the coming marketplace, they will implement their designs on information systems that have been architected for the 21st century.

The Changing Nature of IS Skills

In much the same way that plug-board program-mers had difficulty with stored program computers and procedural programmers had difficulty with 4GLs and SQL, many of today's programmers will have difficulty making the transition to the new style information systems.

Today's commercial IS professionals are experiencing the maturity of their chosen disciplines. In other fields, such as engineering and medicine, engineers and doctors (once a role of the local barber) also experi-enced upheaval as their disciplines matured. Today's

skill set for IS professionals is a combination of analyst, designer and programmer with little formal training or knowledge about the first principles of general systems theory and engineering disciplines. The focus is on the machine model with too little concern for the overall business model. The primary drivers for IS organiza-tions are their customers' immediate support, enhance-ment and repair needs.

Even though engineers, doctors and lawyers are driven by their customers, they are equally driven by their evolving disciplines — continuous certification require-

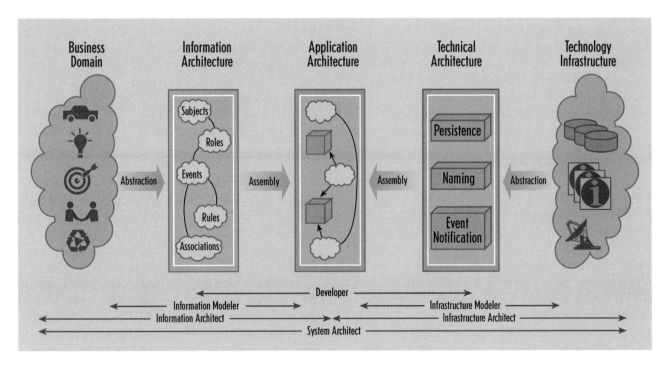

Figure 2
New Roles for Architecture-centric Software Development

ments make the need to keep current a reality, and testing for certification sparks their interest in continuous learning. Like it or not, we can expect to see a growing interest in IS skills-certification for both software development organizations and individuals.

How is the IS workforce changing? If we revisit the activities related to an architectural approach to information systems (see the top portion of Figure 2), we can identify the kinds of tasks, methods, tools and skills needed to do the work associated with each activity. Intellectual resources are packaged into roles for handling the work responsibilities (see the bottom portion of Figure 2). What roles make up an architecture-centric information systems development team?

Systems Architects (a.k.a. project leaders, enterprise architects and enterprise modelers) ensure the successful application of technology to the enterprise. They map the technology to business problems and opportunities of the enterprise. They coordinate the activities of the information and technical architects and develop the enterprise's application architecture. The systems architect integrates the information and technical architectures into business solutions. They provide overall management control to the development process by balancing business needs with technical realities.

Information Architects (a.k.a. project leaders, enterprise modelers, chief business object modelers and business object designers) organize requirements into independent domains. For each domain, they oversee modeling activities that define key abstract business services. Although the models are devoid of implementation details, they capture quality-of-service objectives for use by infrastructure architects.

Infrastructure Architects (a.k.a. project leaders, technical architects and chief technology modelers) define abstract technical services common to all applications. For any given application, they evaluate, select and install components (whether through acquisition or construction) that conform to the service specification and meet the application's quality-of-service objectives. They develop and maintain the enterprise's technical architecture.

Information and *Infrastructure Modelers* are less broad in scope and experience than architects. They work under the guidance of information and infrastructure architects and focus in-depth on the modeling aspects of architecture.

Object Developers (a.k.a. programmers, object builders and application developers) implement objects using procedural construction and component assembly. Today, object developers still require technical knowledge of inheritance (is it an object or an intrinsic?); network address spaces (is it local or remote?); memory management (pass by reference or pass by value?); reference mechanisms (shallow or deep copy?); and remote procedure calls. The actual building of objects in either the business object model or the technical infrastructure requires mastery of object-oriented programming languages like C++ or Smalltalk, and developers achieve many of the tasks using procedural construction.

After the inital building of information and technical objects, *application developers* focus on business needs and through declarative assembly, create or "snap together" applications. This programming paradigm is different from that of procedural construction. Most companies, therefore, split the roles of object builders and application developers. Rather than mastering programming languages, application developers work in environments presaged by products such as VisualAge, OpenStep and VisualWorks. In these environments developers are the ultimate beneficiaries of reuse. As architecture-centric environments evolve, business professionals (end-users) will take responsibility for much of the analysis role and go straight to plug-and-play business solutions — but only after they are empowered with a solid business object model.

The natural evolution that we have seen in all professions is to focus on domains of knowledge and to specialize in them. In some ways this is an example of de-skilling because it reduces the scopes of individual jobs; in other ways, it expands skills because it significantly increases the depth of each job. Instead of people moving back and forth between modeling, analysis, design and code — and mastering none — the focus shifts to doing just one of these activities correctly and with quality and discipline.

The architectural approach to information systems has an impact on creativity. Today, IS creativity often centers on inventing or revolutionizing some algorithm (creativity in the machine model) and is often achieved by the "art of hacking." In the future, creativity will be measured by solutions to business problems, not computer algorithms.

The end result is a new skills mix where more disciplined IS practitioners support larger and more sophisticated systems. This is a natural evolution of a creative process that migrates from one of individual craftsmanship to one of reproducible manufacturing. Manufacturing initially failed because of the lack of "architecture," but evolution — accelerated by Deming's influence on the Japanese — corrected that failure with empowered teams and continuous quality improvement; IS will do the same.

The changing nature of IS work applies not only to software development jobs. Architecture, process and technology will all team to change the landscape of the work of people within operations and support. Technology-makers are using the distributed object paradigm to embed intelligence into hardware, software and networking equipment, such as Microsoft's software registration utility in Windows 95, Sun's *Solstice*, HP's

Openview and new contenders, such as Tivoli's management environment. Software using the distributed object paradigm can observe and monitor itself and can request preventive action — Compaq's new desktop computers and systems do this now.

What happens to today's systems programmers and database administrators in tomorrow's information infrastructure? Will *Mach, Spring, Plan 9, Cairo* and IBM's *micro kernel*, change support requirements? Who will custodian object repositories and event dictionaries? IS will need a new mix of technically adept practitioners (professional engineers) who work with the keepers of the process and with integrated, consistent tools to automatically anticipate, report and fix problems. Distributed object computing also makes redundancy, fail-safe and other fault-tolerant processing techniques "natural" as opposed to current "unnatural" efforts required to use these features.

In addition, the demand for business support professionals knowledgeable in the business domain will accelerate. These are less technical and more business-savvy professionals who specialize in sales, marketing, accounting or other domain-specific fields.

Whatever the precise outcomes, business and technology professionals should buckle their seat belts for the career ride ahead. The future is likely to hold different, more exciting and ultimately more fulfilling jobs for those who prepare themselves. For those who do not, maybe the epilog of this book is not a prolog for the future, but a career epitaph. As Chris Stone said in the Foreword, "these are the same people that will end up looking for work in three to five years."

References

[1] Tapscott, Don, *The Digital Economy: Promise and Peril in the Age of Networked Intelligence*, McGraw-Hill (1996).

[2] "Programming Transformation in the Works," *Computerworld*, p. 96 (Oct. 2, 1995).

[3] Booch, Grady, *Object-Oriented Analysis and Design: With Applications*, Benjamin/Cummings (1994).

[4] Constantine, Larry, "Peopleware" (re: Architecture), *Software Development*, pp. 87-88 (January 1996).

[5] Coplien, Jim, *C++ Report*, SIGS Publications (July-August 1995).

[6] Weinberg, Gerald, *Rethinking Systems Analysis & Design*, Dorset House (1988).

Suggested Readings

Next Generation Business

Davidow, William H. and Michael S. Malone, *The Virtual Corporation: Structuring and Revitalizing the Corporation for the 21st Century*, Harper Collins (1992).

Goldman, S. L., R. N. Nagel and K. Preiss, *Agile Competitors and Virtual Organizations: Strategies for Enriching the Customer*, Van Nostrand (1994).

Hamel, Gary, and C. K. Prahalad, *Competing for the Future: Breakthrough Strategies for Seizing Control of Your Industry and Creating the Markets of Tomorrow*, Harvard Business School Press (1994).

Kelly, Kevin, *Out of Control: The Rise of Neo-biological Civilization*, Addison-Wesley (1994).

Martin, James, *The Great Transition: Using the Seven Disciplines of Enterprise Engineering to Align People, Technology and Strategy*, AMACOM (1995).

McKenney, James L., *Waves of Change: Business Evolution Through Information Technology*, Harvard Business School Press (1995).

Moody, Patricia E., *Breakthrough Partnering: Creating a Collective Enterprise Advantage*, Organizational Dynamics, Inc., 256 pp. (1993).

Naisbitt, John, *Global Paradox: The Bigger the World Economy, the More Powerful Its Smallest Players*, William Morrow (1994).

Peters, Tom, *Liberation Management: Necessary Disorganization for the Nanosecond Nineties*, Macmillan (1992).

Sakaiya, Taichi, *The Knowledge-Value Revolution*, or *A History of the Future*, Kodabsha International (1991).

Tapscott, Don and Art Caston, *Paradigm Shift: The New Promise of Information Technology*, McGraw-Hill (1993).

Tappscott, Don, *The Digital Economy: Promise and Peril in the Age of Networked Intelligence*, McGraw-Hill (1996).

Quality Software Engineering

Devlin, Keith, *Logic and Information*, Cambridge University Press (1991).

Humphrey, Watts, *Managing the Software Process*, Addison-Wesley (1989).

Humphrey, Watts, *A Discipline for Software Engineering*, Addison-Wesley (1995).

Holdsworth, Jacqueline, *Software Process Design: Out of the Tar Pit*, McGraw-Hill (1994).

Keyes, Jessica, *Software Engineering Productivity Handbook*, McGraw Hill (1993).

Jones, Caper, *Assessment and Control of Software Risks*, Prentice Hall (1994).

Jones, Caper, *Applied Software Measurement: Assuring Productivity and Quality*, McGraw Hill (1991).

Weinberg, Gerald, *Quality Software Management, Vol. 1, Systems Thinking,* Dorset House (1991).

Weinberg, Gerald, *Quality Software Management, Vol. 2, First Order Measurement,* Dorset House (1993).

Systems Architecture

Mowbray, Ph.D., Thomas J. and Ron Zahavi, *The Essential CORBA: System Integration Using Distributed Objects,* John Wiley & Sons (1995).

Rechtin, Eberhardt, *Systems Architecting: Creating and Building Complex Systems,* Prentice-Hall (1991).

Shaw, M. and D. Garlan, *Software Architecture: Perspectives on an Emerging Discipline,* Prentice Hall (forthcoming).

Spewak, Steven H., *Enterprise Architecture Planning,* Wiley (1992).

Zachman, John A., "A Framework for Information Systems Architecture," IBM Systems Journal, Vol. 26, No. 3, pp. 276-292 (1987). Available from IBM, T. J. Watson Research Center, PO Box 218, Yorktown Heights, New York 10598, (914) 945-3836.

Witt, Baker and Merrritt, *Software Architecture and Design: Principles, Models and Methods,* Van Nostrand (1994).

Classic Architecture with Insights for Systems Architects

Alexander, Christopher, *Notes on the Synthesis of Form,* Harvard University Press (1964).

Alexander, Christopher, *The Timeless Way of Building,* Oxford University Press (1979).

Alexander, Christopher, S. Ishikawa and M. Silverstein, *A Pattern Language,* Oxford University Press (1977).

Mitchell, William J., *The Logic of Architecture: Design, Computation and Cognition,* MIT Press (1990).

A Glossary of Object-Oriented Terminology for Business

Compiled by Mike Aube and Leslie Newberry
In collaboration with the Object Technology Staff of The Technical Resource Connection

The Object Management Group, Inc., (OMG), is a non-profit consortium dedicated to the creation of standards for object-oriented computing environments of the future.

The Technical Resource Connection gratefully acknowledges OMG's contributions to this chapter of *Next Generation Computing*.

Term	Definition
4GL	An acronym meaning *Fourth Generation Language.* A 4GL is typically non-procedural and designed so that end users can specify what they want without having to know how computer processing is to be accomplished.
Abstract Class	A specialized class used solely for subtyping. It defines a common set of behaviors to be inherited by its subtypes. It has no instances. (Synonymous with Virtual Class in C++)
Abstract Data Type (ADT)	A data type defined to model the data characteristics of real-world objects. An ADT provides a public interface via its permitted operations, but the internal representation and implementation of this interface are private.
Abstraction	The act of concentrating the essential or general qualities of an object or objects. The resulting concept embodies the "essence" of the objects under consideration.
Accessibility	The ability or permission to invoke a service provided by a particular object. Object-oriented programming languages implement both public and private methods of accessibility. (Synonymous with Visibility)
Accessor	A method or member function that provides a public interface to allow the "setting" or "getting" of an object's private instance variables or data members.
Activation	Copying the persistent form of methods and stored data into an executable address space to allow execution of the methods on the stored data. [OMG]

Term	Definition
Actor	An external agent that interacts with an application or system. This is also a model for concurrent programming.
Agent	An entity that performs operations on behalf of other objects, systems and agents.
Analysis	The process of developing a specification of what a system does and how it interacts with its environment.
Application	A program or a set of programs that provides functionality to the end user.
Application Facilities	Common facilities that are useful within a specific application domain. [OMG]
Application Objects	Applications and their components that are managed within an object-oriented system. Example operations on such objects are "Open," "Install," "Move" and "Remove." [OMG]
Application Program Interface (API)	The programming interface used to access and control a library or program.
Architecture	A high-level description of the organization of functional responsibilities within a system. Many different levels of architectures are involved in developing software systems, from physical hardware architecture through the logical architecture of an application framework.
Assertion	An expression that evaluates to either true or false. Generally used to protect the integrity of a system or component.

Term	*Definition*
Assignment	The activity of copying the values of one object into another object. The details of such an assignment vary according to the implementation language used.
Association	Meaningful links between objects. A person associated with a company creates the concept of employment.
Asynchronous Message Communication	Asynchronous message communication provides the capability for objects to send messages, even without the existence of the receiving object at the instant the message is sent. The receiving object can retrieve messages at its convenience. There is no blocking or synchronization required between objects. Asynchronous message communication is a foundation for constructing concurrent computing environments.
Asynchronous Request	A request in which the client object does not pause or wait for delivery of the request to the recipient; nor does it wait for the results. [OMG]
Atomicity	The property that ensures an operation either changes the state associated with all participating objects consistent with the request, or changes none at all. If a set of operations is atomic, then multiple requests for those operations are serializable. [OMG]
Attribute	An identifiable association between an object and a value. An attribute A is made visible to clients as a pair of operations: get_A and set_A. Read only attributes only generate a get operation. [OMG] A characteristic or property of an object. Usually implemented as a simple data member or as an association with another object or group of objects.

Term	*Definition*
Audience	The kind of consumer (caller) of an interface. An interface might be intended for use by the ultimate user of the service (functional interface), by a system management function within the system (system management interface) or by other participating services in order to construct the service from disparate objects (construction interface). [OMG]
Base Class	A class that has one or more derived classes that inherit its attributes and methods. (Synonymous with Superclass)
Bearer	The kind of object that presents an interface. An object might be fundamentally characterized by the fact that it has a given interface (a specific object bears an interface), or an object can have an interface that is ancillary to its primary purpose in order to provide certain other capabilities (a generic object bears the interface). [OMG]
Behavior	The behavior of a request is the observable effects of performing the requested service (including its results). [OMG]
Behavior Consistency	Ensures that the behavior of an object maintains its state consistency. [OMG]
Binding	The selection of the method to perform a requested service and of the data to be accessed by that method. (See also Dynamic Binding and Static Binding) [OMG]
Block	A class primarily consisting of a compound statement made up of a series of operations and control structures. Block objects are used in control structures, usually as arguments for repeated or conditional execution. Instances of this class essentially allow language constructs and operations to be bundled into an object.

Term	Definition
Browser	A software facility used to view and modify classes, attributes and methods.
Built-In Type	An abstract data type that is provided as a part of the language. Also provided are the operators used to manipulate instances of built-in types.
Class	An implementation that can be instantiated to create multiple objects with the same behavior. An object is an instance of a class. Types classify objects according to a common interface; classes classify objects according to a common implementation. [OMG]
Class Attribute	A characteristic or property that is the same for all instances of a class. This information is usually stored in the class type definition.
Class Hierarchy	Embodies the inheritance relationships between classes.
Class Inheritance	The construction of a class by incremental modification of other classes. [OMG]
Class Member	A method or an attribute of a class.
Class Method	A class method defines the behavior of the class. Such a method performs tasks that cannot or should not be done at the instance level, such as providing access to class attributes or tracking class usage metrics.
Class Object	An object that serves as a class. A class object serves as a factory. (See Factory) [OMG]

Term	*Definition*
Classification	The act of determining which class or type applies to a specific object.
Client	An object that requests a service from a server object in a client/server relationship. The code or process that invokes an operation on an object. [OMG]
Client/server	A relationship between a client that requests services and servers that provide services. This relationship is paralleled in an O-O environment by message senders and receivers.
Cognition	The act or process of knowing; perception. O-O technology is intricately tied to how people think, act and interact while accomplishing work.
Collaboration	Two or more objects that participate in a client/server relationship in order to provide a service.
Common Facilities	Provides facilities useful in many application domains and which are made available through Object Management Architectures (OMA)-compliant class interfaces. (See also Application Facilities) [OMG]
Common Object Request Broker Architecture (CORBA, CORBA 2)	A specification for objects to locate and activate one another through an object request broker. CORBA 2 extends the specification to facilitate object request brokers from different vendors to interoperate.

Term	Definition
Component	A conceptual notion. A component is an object that is considered to be part of some containing object. [OMG] Classes, systems or subsystems that can be designed as reusable pieces. These pieces can then be assembled to create various new applications.
Composition	The creation of an object that is an aggregation of one or more objects.
Compound Object	A conceptual notion. A compound object is an object that is viewed as standing for a set of related objects. [OMG]
Computed Characteristic	An attribute derived from the values of other attributes.
Computer Aided Software Engineering (CASE)	A collection of software tools that support and automate the process of analyzing, designing and coding software systems.
Concrete Class	A class or type that can have instances. (Contrast with Abstract Class).
Configuration Management (CM)	The discipline of identifying a system and its component parts at discrete points in time. Monitoring throughout versions and revisions enables CM to systematically control changes to maintain integrity and traceability of the system throughout a product's lifecycle. This includes hardware, environment, code, documents and objects.

Term	*Definition*
Conformance	A relation defined over types such that type x conforms to type y if any value that satisfies type x also satisfies type y. [OMG]
Constraint	A relational or behavioral restriction or limit. Usually regarded as a property that must always hold true.
Construction Interfaces	Interfaces that define the operations used to communicate between the core of an Object Service and related objects that must participate in providing the service. They are typically defined by the service, and inherited and implemented by participants in the service. Objects that participate in a service must support these interfaces. An Object Service Definition. [OMG]
Constructor	A method that is called when a new instance is created. Constructor methods are used to initialize the new instance.
Container Class	A class designed to hold and manipulate a collection of objects.
Context-Independent Operation	An operation in which all requests that identify the operation have the same behavior. (In contrast, the effect of a context-dependent operation might depend upon the identity or location of the client object issuing the request.) [OMG]
Contract	Defines the services provided by a server, along with the pre-conditions and post-conditions that apply to the use of those services.

Term	*Definition*
Coupling	A dependency between two or more classes, usually resulting from collaboration between the classes to provide a service. Loose coupling is based on generic behavior and allows many different classes to be coupled in the same way. Tight coupling is based on more specific implementation details of the participating classes and is not as flexible as loose coupling.
Data Member	The named variables defined and used to hold the values of the attribute of a class. (Synonymous with Attribute)
Data Model	A collection of entities, operators and consistency rules. [OMG]
Data Type	A categorization of values, operations and arguments, typically covering both behavior and representation (e.g., the traditional non-OO programming language notion of type). [OMG]
Declassification	The act of removing an object from a specific set of objects of a given type.
Deferred Synchronous Request	A request where the client does not wait for completion of the request, but does intend to accept results later. Contrast with synchronous request and one-way request. [OMG]
Delegation	The ability of a method to issue a request in such a way that self-reference in the method performing the request returns the same object(s) as self-reference in the method issuing the request. (See Self-Reference) [OMG] The ability of an object to issue a request to another object in response to a request. The first object therefore delegates the responsibility to the second object.

Term	Definition
Derivation	The act of subclassing an existing class to define a new subclass. (See Inheritance)
Derived Class	The class created through inheritance. A derived class inherits the methods and attributes of its superclass(es) and usually adds its own to distinguish its capabilities or services.
Design	A process that uses the products of analysis to produce a specification for implementing a system.
Design Pattern	(See Pattern)
Destructor	A method involved whenever an object is ready to be destroyed. It is usually implemented to revise the actions that were performed during initialization, such as recovery of allocated resources.
Distributed Object Computing (DOC)	A computing paradigm that distributes cooperating objects across a heterogenous network and allows the objects to interoperate as a unified whole.
Domain	A formal boundary that defines a particular subject or area of interest.
Domain Expert	A person who has special skill or knowledge of a particular domain.
Dynamic Binding	Binding that is performed after a request is issued. (See Binding) [OMG]

Term	Definition
Dynamic Classification	Classification of an object at runtime. This implies that an object's classification can change over time.
Dynamic Invocation	Constructing and issuing a request whose signature is not known until runtime. [OMG]
Dynamic Link Library (DLL)	A dynamically loaded run-time library.
Dynamic Object-Based Application	The end-user functionality provided by one or more programs consisting of interoperating objects. [OMG]
Embedding	Creating an object out of a non-object entity by wrapping it in an appropriate shell. [OMG]
Encapsulation	The technique used to hide the implementation details of an object. The services provided by an object are defined and accessible as stated in the object contract. (Often used interchangeably with Information Hiding)
Enterprise Modeling	A technique for modeling an entire business enterprise from the business manager's point of view. An enterprise model is composed of the objects, events and business rules that describe the enterprise. Separate but related business systems can be built from this model to enhance the efficiency and consistency of the operation of the enterprise.
Event	A significant change in the environment or the state of an object that is of interest to another object or system.
Exchange Format	The form of a description used to import and export objects. [OMG]

Term	*Definition*
Expectation Management	The process of guiding the user's expectations regarding the functionality and characteristics of any proposed system or technology.
Expert System	A rule-based program that implements the domain knowledge of a human domain expert. It is usually able to "reason" through new problems by applying its rules.
Export	To transmit the description of an object to an external entity. [OMG]
Extension of a Type	The sets of values that satisfy the type. [OMG]
Externalized Object Reference	An object reference expressed as an ORB-specific string. Suitable for storage in files or other external media. [OMG]
Factoring	The process of extracting the common properties or behavior from a group of objects so that the common elements can be propagated to a common subclass. Factoring eliminates duplication.
Factory	A concept that provides a service for creating new objects. [OMG]
Fault-Tolerance	The characteristic of a system that allows it to handle the loss of a particular component without interrupting normal operations.
Formal Parameter	A named local object used as an argument to an operation. The value of the object (actual parameter) is assigned by the client who runs the method.

Term	Definition
Framework	A set of collaborating abstract and concrete classes that may be used as a template to solve a specific domain problem.
Functional Decomposition	The process of refining a problem solution by repeatedly decomposing a problem into smaller and smaller steps. The resulting steps are then programmed as separate modules.
Functional Interface	Interfaces that define the operations invoked by users of an object service. The audience for these interfaces is the service consumer, the user of the service. These interfaces present the functionality (the useful operations) of the service. An Object Service Definition. [OMG]
Fusion	A second generation object-oriented development method that provides a systematic approach to O-O software development. It integrates and extends other methods: OMT/ Rumbaugh, Booch, CRC and Formal Methods.
Garbage Collection	The recovery of memory occupied by unreferenced objects, usually implemented by the language or environment.
Generalization	The inverse of the specialization relation. [OMG]
Generic Object	An object (relative to some given Object Service) whose primary purpose for existence is unrelated to the Object Service whose interface it carries. The notion is that the Object Service is provided by having (in principle) any type of object inherit that object service interface and provide an implementation of that interface. An Object Service Domain. [OMG]

Term	Definition
Generic Operation	The concept that an operation is generic if it can be bound to more than one method. [OMG]
Graphical User Interface (GUI)	Any interface that communicates with the user, primarily through graphical icons.
Handle	A value that identifies an object. [OMG]
Heuristic	A rule of thumb or guideline used in situations where no hard and fast rules apply. An empirical rule, or educated guess based upon past experiences.
Implementation	A definition that provides the information needed to create an object and allow the object to participate in providing an appropriate set of services. An implementation typically includes a description of the data structure used to represent the core state associated with an object, as well as definitions of the methods that access that data structure. It will also typically include information about the intended interface of the object. [OMG]
Implementation Definition Language	A notation for describing implementations. The implementation definition language is currently beyond the scope of the ORB standard. It may contain vendor-specific and adapter-specific notations. [OMG]
Implementation Inheritance	The construction of an implementation by incremental modification of other implementations. The ORB does not provide implementation inheritance. Implementation inheritance may be provided by higher level tools. [OMG]

Term	Definition
Implementation Object	An object that serves as an implementation definition. Implementation objects reside in an implementation repository. [OMG]
Implementation Repository	A storage place for object implementation information. [OMG]
Import	Creating an object based on a description of an object transmitted from an external entity. [OMG]
In-Line Method	A mechanism that allows the compiler to replace calls to the method with an expansion of the method code.
Incomplete Partition	A partition composed of some, but not all, of its partitioned subtypes.
Information Hiding	(See Encapsulation)
Inheritance	The construction of a definition by incremental modification of other definitions. (See also Implementation Inheritance) [OMG]
Initialization	Setting the initial attribute values of a new object.
Instance	An object created by instantiating a class. An object is an instance of a class. [OMG]
Instance Variable	A variable that contains a value specific to an object instance.

Term	Definition
Instantiation	Object creation. [OMG]
Integrated Project Support Environment (IPSE)	An environment that specifies the processes for systematically managing development projects to minimize costs, increase productivity, and build quality software products.
Interface	A description of a set of possible uses of an object. Specifically, an interface describes a set of potential requests in which an object can meaningfully participate. (See also Object Interface, Principal Interface and Type Interface) [OMG]
Interface Definition Language (IDL™)	When used in conjunction with an ORB, IDL™ statements describe the properties and operations of an object.
Interface Inheritance	The construction of an interface by incremental modification of other interfaces. The IDL™ provides interface inheritance. [OMG]
Interface Type	A type that is satisfied by any object (literally, by any value that identifies an object) that satisfies a particular interface. (See also Object Type) [OMG]
Interoperability	The ability for two or more ORBs to cooperate to deliver requests to the proper object. Interoperating ORBs appear to a client to be a single ORB. [OMG]
Invariant Relation	A relation that cannot be changed so long as it has instances.

Term	Definition
ISO 9000 Certification/Standards	The International Organization for Standardization (ISO) issues the ISO-9000 guidelines for the selection and use of the series of standards on quality systems.
Language Binding or Mapping	The means and conventions by which a programmer writing in a specific programming language accesses ORB capabilities. [OMG]
Legacy System	A previously existing system or application.
Leveling	The process of grouping information or concepts at various levels of increasing detail. The top-most level is general in nature and each successive level adds more detail until all aspects of the given subject matter have been explained in detail.
Life-Cycle Service	The Object Life-Cycle Service provides operations for managing object creation, deletion, copying and equivalence. An Object Service Definition. [OMG]
Link	Relation between two objects (a concept). [OMG]
Literal	A value that identifies an entity that is not an object. (See also Object Name) [OMG]
Managed Object	Clients of System Management services, including the installation and activation service and the operational control service (dynamic behavior). These clients may be application objects, common facilities objects, or other object services. The term is used for compatibility with system management standards (the X/Open GDMO specification and ISO/IEC 10164 System Management Function, Parts 1 to 4). An Object Service Definition. [OMG]

Term	Definition
Mapping	A rule or process, the O-O equivalent of a mathematical function. Given an object of one set, a mapping applies its associative rules to return another set of objects.
Member Function	(See Method)
Message	The mechanism by which objects communicate. A message is sent by a client object to request the service provided by the server object.
Meta-Model	A model that defines other models.
Meta-Type	A type whose instances are also types. [OMG]
Meta-Object	An object that represents a type, operation, class, method or object model entity that describes objects. [OMG]
Method	Code that can be executed to perform a requested service. Methods associated with an object are structured into one or more programs. [OMG]
Method Resolution	The selection of the method to perform a requested operation. [OMG]
Method (Systems Development)	A cohesive set of rules, methods and principles used to guide the modeling and development of software systems.
Multiple Classification	Ability of an object to belong to more than one type.

Term	Definition
Multiple Inheritance	The construction of a definition by incremental modification of more than one other definition. [OMG]
Object	A combination of a state and a set of methods that explicitly embodies an abstraction characterized by the behavior or relevant requests. An object is an instance of a class. An object models a real world entity and is implemented as a computational entity that encapsulates state and operations (internally implemented as data and methods) and responds to requests for services. [OMG] An object is a self-contained software package consisting of its own private information (data), its own private procedures (private methods), which manipulate the object's private data, and a public interface (public methods) for communicating with other objects.
Object Adapter	The ORB component that provides object reference, activation and state-related services to an object implementation. There may be different adapters provided for different implementations. [OMG]
Object Creation	An event that causes an object to exist that is distinct from any other object. [OMG]
Object Data Base Management System (ODBMS)	These systems provide for long-term, reliable storage, retrieval and management of objects.
Object Destruction	An event that causes an object to cease to exist and its associated resources to become available for reuse. [OMG]
Object Identity	(See Handle)

Term	Definition
Object Interface	A description of a set of possible uses of an object. Specifically, an interface describes a set of potential requests in which an object can meaningfully participate as a parameter. It is the union of the object's type interfaces. [OMG]
Object Library/Repository	A central repository established expressly to support the identification and reuse of software components, especially classes and other software components.
Object Management Group	A non-profit industry group dedicated to promoting object-oriented technology and the standardization of that technology. [OMG]
Object Modeling Technique (OMT)	An object-oriented systems development life cycle developed by General Electric.
Object Name	A value that identifies an object. (See Handle) [OMG]
Object Reference	A value that precisely identifies an object. Object references are never reused to identify another object. [OMG]
Object Request Broker (ORB)	Provides the means by which objects make and receive requests and responses. [OMG] The middleware of distributed object computing that provides a means for objects to locate and activate other objects on a network, regardless of the processor or programming language used to develop and implement those objects.
Object Services	The basic functions provided for object lifecycle management and storage such as creation, deletion, activation, passivation, identification and location. [OMG]

Term	Definition
Object State	The current information about an object that determines its behavior.
Object Type	A type the extension of which is a set of objects (literally, a set of values that identify objects). In other words, an object type is satisfied only by (values that identify) objects. (See also Interface Type) [OMG]
Object Wrapper	The result of encapsulating a set of services provided by a non O-O application or program interface in order to treat the encapsulated application or interface as an object.
Object-Based	A programming language or tool that supports the object concept of encapsulation, but not inheritance or polymorphism.
Object-Based Architecture for Integration (OBAI)	An architecture developed to facilitate legacy application migration to open systems, client/server and object-based computing. The primary function of OBAI is to allow new systems to be developed without having to abandon existing information systems and to allow the new systems to take advantage of the knowledge, information and data contained in the old systems.
Object-Oriented	Any language, tool or method that focuses on modeling real world systems using the three pillars of objects: encapsulation, inheritance and polymorphism.
Object-Oriented Analysis	The process of specifying what a system does by identifying domain objects and defining the behavior and relationships of those objects.

Term	Definition
Object-Oriented Business Engineering (OOBE)	A framework and discipline used to effectively model business processes. It involves identifying business objects, processes, structures, rules, policies, organizational structure and authority, location and logistics, technology and applications. Its goal is to produce precise descriptive models of business objects that can be converted into reusable and easily modifiable software components.
Object-Oriented Design	The process of developing an implementation specification that incorporates the use of classes and objects. It encourages modeling the real world environment in terms of its entities and their interactions.
Object-Oriented Programming Language (OOPL)	A programming language that supports the concepts of encapsulation, inheritance and polymorphism.
One-Way Request	A request in which the client does not wait for completion of the request, nor does it intend to accept results. Contrast with deferred synchronous request and synchronous request. [OMG]
Operation	A service that can be requested. An operation has an associated signature, which may restrict which actual parameters are possible in a meaningful request. [OMG]
Operation Name	A name used in a request to identify an operation. [OMG]
ORB Core	The ORB component that moves a request from a client to the appropriate adapter for the target object. [OMG]

Term	Definition
Overloaded Operation	Multiple methods of the same name, each having a unique signature. This allows the methods of the same name to be invoked with various argument types.
Paradigm	A broad framework for thinking about and perceiving reality. A theoretical, philosophical model composed of identifiable theories, laws and generalizations used in defining and solving problems.
Parallel Processing	The simultaneous execution or computation of two or more programs or operations.
Parameter Passing Mode	Describes the direction of information flow for an operation parameter. The parameter passing modes are IN, OUT and INOUT. [OMG]
Parameterized Class	A class that allows users to declare member functions and data members of "Some Type," which can be used as a template for declaring specialized subclasses that supply the "Missing" types.
Participate	An object participates in a request when one or more actual parameters of the request identifies the object. [OMG]
Partition	Decomposing a type into its disjoint subtypes.
Pattern	A pattern describes a problem, a solution to a problem, and when to apply the solution. Patterns may be categorized as design patterns, business process patterns and analysis patterns.

Term	*Definition*
Persistent Object	An object that can survive the process or thread that created it. A persistent object exists until it is explicitly deleted. [OMG]
Pointer	A variable that can hold a memory address of an object.
Polymorphic Operation	The same operation implemented differently by two or more types.
Polymorphism	The concept that two or more types of objects can respond to the same request in different ways.
Post-Condition	A constraint that must hold true after the completion of an operation.
Pre-Condition	A constraint that must hold true before an operation is requested.
Principal Interface	The interface that describes all requests in which an object is meaningful. [OMG]
Private	A scoping mechanism used to restrict access to class members so that other objects cannot see them.
Property	A conceptual notion. An attribute, the value of which can be changed. [OMG]
Protected	A scoping mechanism used to restrict access to class members.

Term	Definition
Protection	The ability to restrict the clients for which a requested service will be performed. [OMG]
Public	A scoping mechanism used to make member access available to other objects.
Query	An activity that involves selecting objects from implicitly or explicitly identified collections based on a specific predicate. [OMG]
Rapid Prototyping	The iterative process of quickly developing a prototype of an application, usually with the aid of specific GUI-building tools. This process is used to help uncover unknown details of the system under consideration, and to build the system in small increments.
Referential Integrity	The property that ensures that a handle which exists in the state associated with another object reliably identifies a single object. [OMG]
Relation	An object type that associates two or more object types. A relation is how associations are formed between two or more objects.
Repository	Usually a central location used to store and organize software components and related definitions, rules, etc. (See Object Library/Repository)
Request	An event consisting of an operation and zero or more actual parameters. A client issues a request to cause a service to be performed. Also associated with a request are the results that can be returned to the client. A message can be used to implement (carry) a request and/ or a result. [OMG]

Term	Definition
Requirements	A document describing what a software system does from a user's point of view. This document is input into the object-oriented analysis process, where it will be transformed into a much more precise description.
Responsibility	A service or group of services provided by an object; a responsibility embodies one or more of the purposes of an object.
Result	The information returned to the client, which can include values as well as status information, indicating that exceptional conditions were raised in attempting to perform the requested service. [OMG]
Reuse	Reuse is the process of locating, understanding and incorporating existing knowledge, design and components into a new system. Reuse should occur at all levels of system development: analysis, design, implementation, testing, documentation and user training.
Role	A sequence of activities performed by an agent.
Rule	Rules exist in two types: constraints and generic functions.
Scalability	The ability of a system to grow without sacrificing performance.
Schema	A formal presentation with a defined set of symbols and rules that govern the formation of a representation using the symbols. There are many different kinds of schema, including object, event and activity schemas.

Term	Definition
Security Domain	A subset of computational resources used to define a security policy. [OMG]
Self-Reference	The ability for a method to identify the target object for which it was invoked. This notion is referred to by the key words "self" in Smalltalk and "this" in C++. [OMG]
Semantics	The meaning — the essence — of the definition.
Server Object	An object providing response to a request for a service. A given object might be a client for some requests and a server for other requests. (See also Client Object) [OMG]
Service	A computation that can be performed in response to a request. [OMG]
Signature	Defines the parameters of a given operation including their number order, data types and passing mode; the results, if any; and the possible outcomes (normal vs. exceptional) that might occur. [OMG]
Single Inheritance	The construction of a definition by incremental modification of one definition. (See also Multiple Inheritance) [OMG]
Skeleton	The object-interface-specific ORB component that assists an object adapter in passing requests to particular methods. [OMG]

Term	Definition
Software Engineering Institute (SEI)	The SEI is located at Carnegie Mellon University. Originally a U.S. Air Force project, the SEI objective was to provide guidance to the military services when selecting capable software contractors. The resulting method for evaluating the strengths and weaknesses of contractors proved valuable for assessing other software organizations. Since the late 1980s, SEI has been addressing the maturity of software within commercially developed applications.
Specialization	A class x is a specialization of a class y if x is defined to directly or indirectly inherit from y. [OMG]
Specific Object	An object (relative to a given Object Service) whose purpose for existence is to provide a part of the Object Service whose interface it carries. The concept is that a limited number of implementations (and potentially a limited number of instances) of these objects exist in the system, commonly as "servers." An Object Service Definition. [OMG]
State	The information about the history of previous requests needed to determine the behavior of future requests. [OMG]
State Consistency	Ensures that the state associated with an object conforms to the data model. [OMG]
State Integrity	Requires that the state associated with an object is not corrupted by external events. [OMG]
State-Modifying Request	A request that by performing the service alters the results of future requests. [OMG]

Term	Definition
Static Binding	Binding that is performed prior to the actual issuing of a request. (See also Binding)
Static Member Function	In C++, a function declared part of a class declaration. These functions can be invoked independent of any instances of the class. [OMG]
Static Invocation	Constructing a request at compile time.
Strong Typing	A language characteristic that requires an explicit type declaration for every value or expression. Strong typing makes static binding feasible. [OMG]
Stub	A local procedure corresponding to a single operation that invokes that operation when called. [OMG]
Subclass	(See Subtype)
Subtype	A specialized or specific object type.
Superclass	A class that provides its methods and attributes to another class derived from it via inheritance.
Synchronous Request	A request in which the client object pauses to wait for completion of the request. [OMG]
System Object Model/ Distributed System Object Model (SOM/DSOM)	SDM is a class library, and DSOM is an ORB. Both provided by IBM.

Term	*Definition*
Target Object	An object that receives a request. (Synonymous with Server Object)
Transient Object	An object whose existence is limited by the lifetime of the process or thread that created it. [OMG]
Trigger Rule	A cause-and-effect relationship. When a certain event type occurs, a specific operation will be performed.
Type	A predicate (Boolean function) defined over values that can be used in a signature to restrict a possible parameter or characterize a possible result. Types classify objects according to a common interface; classes classify objects according to a common implementation. [OMG]
Type Interface	Defines the requests in which instances of this type can meaningfully participate as a parameter. Example: If given document type and product type in which the interface to document type comprises "edit" and "print," and the interface to product type comprises "set price" and "check inventory," then the object interface of a particular document that is also a product comprises all four requests. [OMG]
Use Case/Scenario	A description of the sequence of actions that occurs when a user participates in a dialogue with a system. It describes the behavior that is invoked by a system function.
Value-Dependent Operation	An operation in which the behavior of the corresponding request depends upon which names are used to identify object parameters (if an object can have multiple names). [OMG]

Term	*Definition*
Virtual Class	(See Abstract Class)
Virtual Member Function	A member function that can be overridden by derived classes in order to implement a general behavior in a specific manner. Dynamic binding is used at run time to determine which of these functions to actually invoke.
Visibility	(See Accessibility)
Weak Typing	A language characteristic that does not require an explicit type declaration for each value or expression. Weak typing makes dynamic binding feasible.
Workflow	The structured flow of information through the well-defined steps of a business process where tasks are performed on elements of the information. Typical workflows have both sequential and concurrent tasks.

Index

General Index

People Index

Your Guide to the Next Step in Business Technology

The Blueprint for Business Objects

PETER FINGAR
THE BLUEPRINT FOR BUSINESS OBJECTS
MANAGING OBJECT TECHNOLOGY SERIES

Peter Fingar
Foreword by Rob Mattison

*"**F**ull of information, both general and specific. Peter Fingar's new book is a tremendous resource for anyone involved in object orientation and in other modern ways of melding information technology with business. My copy spends more time on my desk than on my shelf. Better not start OO without it!"*
— *Meilir Page-Jones, methodologist and popular author*

Driven by rapidly developing technology and the globalization of markets and competition, companies are using information technology to make radical changes in the way they organize work and conduct business. As companies redesign themselves, you'll need additional knowledge and skills to master business reengineering and the advanced information systems that make reengineering possible.

The Blueprint for Business Objects provides a clear and concise guide to making informed decisions about emerging object technology and to mastering the skills you need to make effective use of the technology in business.

Based on the workplace experiences of several major corporations, **The Blueprint for Business Objects** presents a framework designed for business and information systems professionals. It provides the reader with a roadmap, starting at the level of initial concepts and moving up to the mastery level. It also includes information on how to select and find further learning resources.

February 1996/300 pages/softcover/ISBN 1-884842-20-8/Order # 2208/$39

Contents:

- The New Business Know-How

- A Curriculum Model for Object-Oriented Information System Development

- A Plan of Action for Learning

- Profiles of the Object Training Masters

- *Appendix A*: The Essential Object Oriented Library for Business and Other Learning Resources

- *Appendix B*: A Guide to Useable Interface Design for Object-Oriented Systems

- *Appendix C*: Classified Bibliography

ORDER FORM

❏ **YES!** Please send me _____ copies of **The Blueprint for Business Objects** at $39 each.

Subtotal: _____
Shipping: _____ * see below
Total: _____

❏ Enclosed is my check (payable to SIGS Books).

Please charge my
❏ Amex ❏ Visa ❏ Mastercard

Card # _____

Exp. _____

Signature_____

*Please add $5 shipping and handling in U.S. ($10 shipping in Canada, $15 everywhere else). NY State residents add appropriate sales tax. Prices subject to change without notice.

SIGS Guarantee: If you are not 100% satisfied with your SIGS book, return it within 15 days for a full refund (less S+H).

Name _____

Address _____

_____

City/State/Zip_____

Phone (in case we have trouble with your order)

_____

Return this form to:
SIGS Books
71 West 23rd Street, New York, NY 10010

For faster service, call **SIGS BOOKS**

1-800-871-SIGS

Fax: 1-212-242-7574 • http://www.sigs.com